Narrative, Affect and Victorian Sensation

Nineteenth-Century and Neo-Victorian Cultures
Series editors: Ruth Heholt and Joanne Ella Parsons

Editorial Board
Rosario Arias, University of Malaga, Spain
Katherine Bowers, University of British Columbia, Canada
Jessica Cox, Brunel University, UK
Laura Eastlake, Edge Hill University, UK
Kate Hext, University of Exeter, UK
Elizabeth Ho, University of Hong Kong, Hong Kong
Tara MacDonald, University of Idaho, USA
Charlotte Mathieson, University of Surrey, UK
Royce Mahawatte, Central Saint Martins, University of the Arts London, UK
John Miller, University of Sheffield, UK
Grace Moore, University of Otago, New Zealand
Antonija Primorac, University of Rijeka, Croatia

Recent books in the series
Domestic Architecture, Literature and the Sexual Imaginary in Europe, 1850–1930
Aina Marti

Assessing Intelligence: The Bildungsroman and the Politics of Human Potential in England, 1860–1910
Sara Lyons

The Idler's Club: Humour and Mass Readership from Jerome K. Jerome to P. G. Wodehouse
Laura Fiss

Michael Field's Revisionary Poetics
Jill Ehnenn

Forthcoming
Lost and Revenant Children 1850–1940
Tatiana Kontou

Olive Schreiner and the Politics of Print Culture, 1883–1920
Clare Gill

Literary Illusions: Performance Magic and Victorian Literature
Christopher Pittard

Pastoral in Early-Victorian Fiction: Environment and Modernity
Mark Frost

Spectral Embodiments of Child Death in the Long Nineteenth Century
Jen Baker

Women's Activism in the Transatlantic Consumers' Leagues, 1885–1920
Flore Janssen

Life Writing and the Nineteenth-Century Market
Sean Grass

British Writers, Popular Literature and New Media Innovation, 1820–45
Alexis Easley

Oscar Wilde's Aesthetic Plagiarisms
Sandra Leonard

The Provincial Fiction of Mitford, Gaskell and Eliot
Kevin A. Morrison

Reading Victorian Sculpture
Angela Dunstan

Mind and Embodiment in Late Victorian Literature
Marion Thain and Atti Viragh

Drunkenness in Eighteenth and Nineteenth-Century Irish Literature
Lucy Cogan

Philanthropy in Children's Periodicals, 1840–1930: The Charitable Child
Kristine Moruzi

Violence and the Brontës: Language, Reception, Afterlives
Sophie Franklin

The British Public and the British Museum: Shaping and Sharing Knowledge in the Nineteenth Century
Jordan Kistler

Narrative, Affect and Victorian Sensation
Wilful Bodies

Tara MacDonald

EDINBURGH
University Press

Edinburgh University Press is one of the leading university presses in the UK. We publish academic books and journals in our selected subject areas across the humanities and social sciences, combining cutting-edge scholarship with high editorial and production values to produce academic works of lasting importance. For more information visit our website: edinburghuniversitypress.com

© Tara MacDonald 2023, 2025

Edinburgh University Press Ltd
13 Infirmary Street,
Edinburgh, EH1 1LT

First published in hardback by Edinburgh University Press 2023

Typeset in 11/13pt Sabon
by Cheshire Typesetting Ltd, Cuddington, Cheshire

A CIP record for this book is available from the British Library

ISBN 978 1 3995 2219 9 (hardback)
ISBN 978 1 3995 2220 5 (paperback)
ISBN 978 1 3995 2221 2 (webready PDF)
ISBN 978 1 3995 2222 9 (epub)

The right of Tara MacDonald to be identified as the author of this work has been asserted in accordance with the Copyright, Designs and Patents Act 1988, and the Copyright and Related Rights Regulations 2003 (SI No. 2498).

Contents

Acknowledgements	vi
Series Preface	viii
Preface: Centring Sensationalism	ix
Introduction: Hyperrealism and Victorian Affects	1
1. Immersive Reading and Sensational Emplotment	40
2. Morbidity and Sensational Authorship	71
3. Privacy and 'Public Feeling' in *Salem Chapel* and *Armadale*	96
4. Crowds and Bodily Sympathy in Wood and Clive	131
5. Collins, Hardy and Reade's Sympathetic Doubles	156
Coda: The Affective Pleasures of Reading and Not Reading	189
Works Cited	194
Index	208

Acknowledgements

I am happy to have the space to thank the many people who have supported this project over the years. My early ideas were developed during a Social Sciences and Humanities Research Council of Canada Postdoctoral Fellowship (2008–10) studying Amelia Edwards's sensation novels. I am grateful to SSHRC for providing me with two years of funding and time, and to Jill Matus for supervising this work. The project in its current form truly took shape, however, during my time in London (2009–10), Amsterdam (2010–15) and Moscow, Idaho (2015–today). At the University of Idaho, I benefited from two grants that supported my work: a Summer Research Grant in 2016 and a Seed Grant in 2017–18.

I was lucky that my arrival in London in September 2009 coincided with the first conference of the Victorian Popular Fiction Association. I felt instantly welcomed by this wonderful group, and the advice that I received at VPFA conferences and study days over the past decade has shaped this book in significant ways. Feedback from audiences at ISSN, INCS, NAVSA and VISAWUS conferences was also indispensable. Thank you to the many friends and colleagues who read and commented on book chapters, including my research assistants, Katie Krahn and Shannon Roman. Anne-Marie Beller deserves a special mention for being such a generous friend and collaborator. Our work on *Rediscovering Victorian Women Sensation Writers: Beyond Braddon* was inspiring in all the best ways. My colleagues at the University of Amsterdam helped me to further develop my ideas and survive my early years as an academic. I will forever be grateful that I was there at the same time as Kristine Johanson and Jane Lewty. At the University of Idaho, I got lucky again: thank you to my current and former colleagues, especially Erin James, Jennifer Ladino, Jodie Nicotra and Alexandra Teague, dream team of kind, generous and brilliant friends. A special thanks to Erin for discussing so much of the book with me and offering incisive advice. Lindsay Holmgren has been there through all of it, pushing my own thinking further and cheering me on. Finally, when I felt stuck in summer 2020, a virtual writing retreat with Dagni Bredesen, Louise Penner, Tabitha Sparks and Jessica Valdez helped me to reorient the project and to remember why I love this field so much.

Everyone at Edinburgh University Press has been encouraging and efficient, from commissioning editors Michelle Houston and Emily Sharp to senior assistant editor Susannah Butler. A special thank you to Ruth Heholt and Joanne Ella Parsons, editors of the Nineteenth-Century and Neo-Victorian Cultures series, for their support of this project. Thanks, too, to my anonymous readers for their thoughtful suggestions, which certainly improved the book.

Final thanks go to my family for their constant support, good humour and love. I am grateful to my parents, Roderick and Valerie MacDonald, and my brother, Brad MacDonald. And to my husband, Chad Burt: I dedicate this book about deep feelings to you.

Material from Chapter 4 appeared in *Critical Survey* (2011). Some passages from my chapter in *A Feel for the Text: Affect Theory and Literary Critical Practice* appear in the Introduction and Chapter 5, and some of my early ideas for the project were sketched out in 'Sensation Fiction, Gender and Identity' in *The Cambridge Companion to Sensation Fiction* (2013). I am grateful for the opportunity to reprint material here.

Series Preface

Nineteenth-Century and Neo-Victorian Cultures
Series Editors: Ruth Heholt and Joanne Ella Parsons

This interdisciplinary series provides space for full and detailed scholarly discussions on nineteenth-century and Neo-Victorian cultures. Drawing on radical and cutting-edge research, volumes explore and challenge existing discourses, as well as providing an engaging reassessment of the time period. The series encourages debates about decolonising nineteenth-century cultures, histories and scholarship, as well as raising questions about diversities. Encompassing art, literature, history, performance, theatre studies, film and TV studies, medical and the wider humanities, *Nineteenth Century and Neo-Victorian Cultures* is dedicated to publishing pioneering research that focuses on the Victorian era in its broadest and most diverse sense.

Preface: Centring Sensationalism

This project on Victorian sensation fiction and historical affects began when I discovered the sensation novels of Amelia Edwards over a decade ago. Edwards was well known to Victorian scholars as a travel writer and Egyptologist but not as a sensation author. When I read Edwards's popular *Barbara's History* (1864), I found it playful regarding its own generic classification. Barbara reads constantly and details her affective and melodramatic reactions to the narratives that she encounters. Yet the novel is also attentive to the pitfalls of using romantic novels as a guide for life and implies that Barbara feels too much, too deeply. When she attends the opera for the first time, she writes that the experience 'carried me out of myself. I could not believe that all was not real' (219). And she overreacts when she believes that her husband is hiding a secret mistress à la *Jane Eyre* (1847); she runs away and has a child on the continent, only to have her stern aunt chide her for being so 'dramatic' (448). When I first encountered this novel, I puzzled over how to categorise it, as it revels in the plotlines and affective language typical of sensationalism but is also critical of the genre and the reading practices associated with it.

Initially, I classified Edwards as an ambivalent sensationalist, placing her alongside Margaret Oliphant, a critic of the genre who wrote a sensation novel, *Salem Chapel* (1863), or Ellen Wood, whose Christian moralising worked to temper her sensationalism. Yet even 'classic' sensation authors like Mary Elizabeth Braddon and Wilkie Collins are generically playful, indulging in sensational plots and melodramatic language, only to question and critique such devices. Rather than see Edwards as anomalous, I came to see her work as characteristic of novels called sensational. It is this combination of detailed affective descriptions *and* self-reflexive commentary on reading, feeling and realistic representation that defines sensationalism. In Mary Elizabeth Braddon's *Lady Audley's Secret* (1862), amateur detective Robert Audley insists, 'I haven't read ... Wilkie Collins for nothing' (342). And Robert debates with George and Alicia about the 'exaggerated' pre-Raphaelite portrait of Lucy, a work of art that mirrors the exaggerated sensation novel (66). Robert finds 'something odd about it' and Alicia agrees, surmising that it is not a realistic depiction of Lucy, even if 'she *could* look so' (66). I began to notice such self-reflexivity everywhere, thus coming to see Victorian sensation novelists as both affect theorists and narrative theorists. This matters because even though criticism on sensation novels has expanded radically in the past few decades, scholars still too often mine these novels for their cultural representations, while their playful narrative and formal devices go overlooked.

Indeed, the majority of scholarship on Victorian affects and embodiment has ignored sensation fiction, focusing instead on writers such as George Eliot, Thomas Hardy and Henry James. Yet if we truly want to understand the nineteenth-century novel's innovations with regard to feeling, we must include these popular novels in the conversation. Take, for example, this passage from Ellen Wood's *East Lynne* (1861). When Isabel Carlyle is on holiday with her husband, she looks out of her hotel window and finds herself thinking of the man who will later become her lover:

> Looking at [the crowd] with her eyes, not with her senses; her senses were holding commune with herself, and it was not altogether satisfactory. She was aware that a sensation all too warm, a feeling of attraction towards Francis Levison, was working within her; not a voluntary one; she could no more repress it than she could repress her own sense of being. (211–12)

This notion that Isabel's senses have a kind of agency is typical of sensationalism: her sensations are not 'voluntary', 'hold commune with herself' and 'work within her'. When I offer this as an example typical of the language of sensation fiction, you might think: but similar descriptions happen in novels by Dickens or Trollope. But that is precisely my point. Even if there is a genre called the sensation novel, sensationalism – the detailed and self-conscious expression of bodily sensations and how they circulate – can be found across Victorian literature. And I argue in *Narrative, Affect and Victorian Sensation* that while the sensation genre is the most pointed expression of this tendency, sensationalism is not limited to these texts alone. Again, there is much existent Victorian scholarship on embodiment and feeling (especially sympathy). But what happens to our understanding of Victorian texts, as well as to theories of affect and narrative, when we truly put sensationalism at the centre of our reading? This is my primary question in this book.

Tracing sensationalism has guided me beyond a corpus of novels consistently labelled 'sensation fiction' to domestic realists like Charlotte Yonge, canonical authors like Charlotte Brontë, Charles Dickens and Hardy, and even spasmodic poets. By discussing what nineteenth-century readers actually read, I am able to track the embodied nature of sensationalism through forgotten popular literature and canonical realist novels alike, exposing a more varied school of sensation writing than has been studied thus far. Marlene Tromp has recently argued that Victorian scholars would do well to emphasise the porousness between sensation and realism rather than their difference. Viewing the dramatic events described in sensation novels – murder, infidelity, abuse and secrecy – as unrealistic risks dismissing or delegitimising these experiences, so often linked to female trauma and to women's bodily agency. Tromp explains, 'The real has much more of the sensational than we have allowed and opening ourselves to its meaning may help us read not only the fictional, but the social politics of the period, in new ways' ('Sensation' 860). I take seriously her claims about generic hierarchies and porousness – indeed, supposedly realist authors often turn to sensationalism to articulate female trauma, shared feelings, or not-quite-nameable emotion states.

I also find Tromp's comments resonating in unexpected ways in 2023. The past few years have been very sensational, as we have lived through a global pandemic that has radically changed the way many of us write, think and teach. Sensational narratives make the claim that feelings are not bound to a single body and that bodies generate meaning when they are put in relation to other bodies and systems of knowledge. These claims read as truisms, as many of us have experienced collective emotions – anxiety, fear, relief – in new and heightened ways. More than ever, the history of feeling, and especially the history of how we understand and evaluate the affective transmission of and between bodies, matters. And the sensation novel shows how popular fiction is a vital part of such history.

Introduction: Hyperrealism and Victorian Affects

In Wilkie Collins's sensation novel *The Woman in White* (1859–60), the villainous Count Fosco articulates the materialist qualities of the genre when he claims, 'Mind, they say, rules the world. But what rules the mind? The body' (617). Victorian sensation novels are filled with detailed descriptions of bodies that affect and are affected by others. A familiar example is the meeting of Anne Catherick and Walter Hartright in Collins's novel. As Walter walks along London's Finchley Road near midnight, he is interrupted by 'the touch of a hand laid lightly and suddenly on my shoulder from behind me' (20). Prior to their meeting, Collins stresses Walter's cognitive vacuity: 'my mind remained passively open', Walter records, 'I thought but little on any subject – indeed, so far as my own sensations were concerned, I can hardly say that I thought at all' (19). Walter's unthinking body is set to receive 'sensations', and the passage continues as follows: 'I had mechanically turned . . . and was strolling along the lonely high-road – idly wondering, I remember, what the Cumberland young ladies would look like – when, in one moment, every drop of blood in my body was brought to a stop by the touch of a hand laid lightly and suddenly on my shoulder from behind me' (20). Walter turns 'on the instant' to see 'the figure of a solitary Woman, dressed from head to foot in white garments', her 'hand pointing to the dark cloud over London' (20). The affective transmission between these two characters is brought about by touch, as critics from Margaret Oliphant to D. A. Miller have emphasised.[1] Walter does not first see Anne but feels her, an aspect of this encounter that he remarks upon as odd: 'Steal after me and touch me? Why not call to me?' (22). Collins imagines skin not as a barrier between individuals but as a porous surface through which sensations pass.[2] Additionally, Collins emphasises how Walter's body acts independently of his mind. He 'mechanically' turns in the direction of London, just as he finds Anne's voice to be 'mechanical in its tones' (20, 21). His legs move involuntarily, 'on the instant', and Anne, initially, is simply a disembodied hand (20). Walter's passive mind, the tactile quality of this encounter and their automatic movements are some of the ways in which Collins theorises how the transmission of affect occurs between these two characters.

This confrontation between Walter and Anne is at once a typical and exemplary instance of sensationalism. Janice Allan calls it '*the iconic moment of sensationalism*' (99). In what follows, I argue that sensation novelists such as Mary Elizabeth Braddon, Rhoda Broughton, Collins, Charles Reade, Ellen Wood and others theorise how affects are transmitted through bodies as well as through narratives. As Walter recalls meeting Anne in the passage above, he also records his own affective responses: 'I tremble, now, when I write' (23). Through self-reflexive moments that explore what it means to be moved by a narrative, whether fictional or real, sensation novels develop theories of *narrative affect*, our embodied responses to reading, imagining and even writing a narrative. The sensation novel should thus be understood as a key contribution to the novel's assessment of its own workings, especially the ways in which reading and writing figure as affective acts. While associations between the genre and embodied reading are well documented, scholars have tended to employ the accounts of scandalised reviewers rather than mine the novels themselves for theories of affective transmission. *Narrative, Affect and Victorian Sensation* recentres this popular form within the growing body of work on Victorian feeling and within the Victorian canon more broadly, an impulse that began in the 1980s and 1990s but which remains unfinished. I highlight the self-consciousness and narrative complexity of a genre long dismissed as plot-driven, silly and feminine.

A second, and no less important, aim of this book is to radically expand the field of sensationalism. I discuss lesser-known female sensation authors like Caroline Clive, Amelia Edwards, Annie Edwards and Florence Wilford, and read them alongside domestic realists, canonical authors and popular novelists including Charlotte Brontë, Charles Dickens, Thomas Hardy, Margaret Oliphant and Charlotte Yonge. My variety of texts approximates what many Victorian readers read, and by discussing such a range of novels, I am able to trace a broader field of sensation writing than has been studied to date. I read across texts, including those not conventionally labelled 'sensation fiction', identifying detailed descriptions and theorisations of bodily affects.[3] I discuss not Ellen Wood's *East Lynne* but her diatribe against trade unions, *A Life's Secret* (1862), and not Charles Reade's *Hard Cash* (1863) but his study in jealously, *Griffith Gaunt* (1866). Through such readings, sensationalism becomes not a minor group of texts that faded in the 1870s but emerges as an influential novelistic language and style for discussing the impacts of reading, free will and what we now call affect.

Although scholars have identified an 'affective turn' impacting cultural studies in the early twenty-first century, this phenomenon might be best understood as an affective return. There is much to learn from sensation authors' theorisations of affect, a concept that has proven to be challenging for literary and cultural critics since the circulation of affect is at once the most ordinary of human phenomena and yet difficult to put into words. Contemporary theorists speak of affect as an intensity, flow or impression, which can circulate, stick or be transmitted between bodies. Teresa Brennan offers an everyday example of the transmission of affect, asking, 'Is there anyone who has not, at least once, walked into a room and "felt the atmosphere"?' (1). Brennan, in 2004, bemoans a reluctance to acknowledge the transmission of affect in much contemporary thought since the idea challenges the concept of 'the emotionally contained subject'. Yet she admits that 'this reluctance, historically, is only recent' (2). Indeed, the Victorians had a range of terms for affect and its circulation, such as 'influences', 'strange sympathies' and 'sensations'. We find descriptions of affect in Victorian fiction when a narrator's body wilfully intrudes upon their writing, when characters read one another's bodies for meaning, or when a character or narrator tries to articulate a feeling or sensation that does not cohere to a nameable emotion. Although Victorian literature is filled with attempts to acknowledge and narrativise affective experience, sensationalism is the most visible expression of such attempts.

While I expand the reach of sensationalism, I also understand sensation fiction to be a definable genre. Popular British fiction of the 1860s and 1870s, sensation novels were so called because of the sensational events they described but also because of the physical sensations they were thought to encourage in the bodies of susceptible (female) readers. In her oft-quoted review of *The Woman in White*, Margaret Oliphant claims that the reader is 'chilled by a confused and unexplainable alarm' and that her 'nerves are affected' like those of Walter's ('Sensation Novels' 572). Such physical responsiveness was supposedly encouraged by the texts' withholding and then exposure of shocking information, as well as the emphasis on characters' bodies and nerves. In a culture that valued reading as a wholesome family activity, sensation fiction challenged the British novel and the British home. The genre additionally challenged 'the emotionally contained subject' as the novels themselves imagine a world in which affects move indiscreetly between bodies, both fictional and real. In framing the genre in this way, I build on the work of Ann Cvetkovich and Pamela Gilbert, whose formative studies of sensation novels in the 1990s attend to their affective and embodied politics. More recently, nineteenth-century scholars, including Gilbert, have claimed that the mid-century European novel did not in fact prioritise interiority but rather crafted a materialist self. In *Victorian Skin*, Gilbert argues that 'affect – and the uncertainty that the term implies – became central to the novel and to realism more broadly' in mid-century Europe. She suggests that realism became more about assessing the surfaces of characters' bodies than assessing story and predicting plot (65). Frederic Jameson makes similar claims in *The Antinomes of Realism* when he argues that it is 'appropriate to associate the rise of affect with the emergence of the phenomenological body in language and representation' in mid-century European literature (32). He highlights Flaubert and Balzac as authors who took on the task of articulating affect. I argue, however, for the importance of reading so-called feminised, popular forms like the sensation novel. If realist narratives emphasise a surface self, as Gilbert claims, then sensational narratives emphasise a transpersonal self, one that influences and is affected by other bodies and atmospheres. In these novels, the act of reading another's body for meaning leaves open the possibility 'that the emotions or affects of one person, and the enhancing or depressing energies these affects entail, can enter into another' (Brennan 3).

The qualities that make sensation novels so important to the history of feeling are also what made them so detestable to Victorian reviewers. A reviewer in the *Christian Remembrancer* complained that sensation novelists' investment in feeling demanded a 'whole set of new words' (108). In these novels, 'the victim of feeling ... sinks at once into the inspired or possessed animal, and is always supposed to be past articulate speech; and we have the *cry*, the *smothered cry of rage*, the *wail*, the *low wailing cry*, the *wail of despair*, with which, if our readers are not familiar, *ad nauseam*, we can only say that we *are*' (109). Such language is borrowed from sentimental fiction, but it is also characteristic of the way in which sensation fiction developed a vocabulary to describe wilful bodies that betray the conscious mind. In Wood's *East Lynne*, when Isabel learns of her father's death, the narrator doesn't convey her mental state but allows her body to speak for her: 'a low wail of anguish broke from her, telling its own tale of despair' (88). Sensation authors develop theories about bodies and their affective transmission, and they are especially attentive – though not always in ways aligned with contemporary thought – to female bodies, racialised bodies and working-class bodies. Mary Ann O'Farrell has suggested that the blush in the nineteenth-century novel functions as an 'invitation to narrative' (4). In sensation fiction, all affective descriptions figure as narrative invitations as narrators self-consciously express how affects 'work to shape the "surfaces" of individual and collective bodies' (Ahmed, *Cultural Politics* 1).

In addition to the haptic and mechanical qualities of the scene between Walter and Anne, what is significant is the manner in which Walter, the novel's narrator and editor, describes and attempts to process his affects in such detail. This self-reflexivity is key to understanding sensationalism's specific innovations to the mid-century novel. Again, Walter's self-conscious descriptions of his 'own sensations' – his attempts to narrativise his affects – are what make this such a sensational scene (19). After Anne leaves, Walter is 'mechanically walking forward a few paces; now stopping again absently. . . . I was conscious of nothing but the confusion of my own thoughts' (27). This description, with its shifts from present to past tense, emphasises the immediacy and intensity of the encounter. Walter's attention to bodily detail is characteristic of sensationalism and what I call *hyperrealism*. Sensation fiction should not be understood as anti-realist but rather as 'hyperrealistic', a term that Jennifer Phegley uses to describe lowbrow Victorian forms (26). Phegley does not explore the term at length but employs it in a list to categorise typically sexist nineteenth-century reviews of fiction. If 'high culture' forms were seen to be masculine, realistic, idealistic and cerebral, then 'low culture' forms were feminine, sensational, hyperrealistic and physical (26). Phegley equates hyperrealism with 'detailism', noting that women who wrote sensation fiction 'were seen to be lost in details of a more bodily and disruptive kind', in contrast to those who described domestic scenes or environments (25). Lyn Pykett also describes sensation as 'a riot of detail and promiscuous emotion' (27). While Phegley and Pykett rightly highlight the misogynistic nature of these 'low culture' categorisations, I reclaim hyperrealism as a useful term, one that gets at the intensity, detailed bodily descriptions and self-consciousness of sensation fiction – the way in which it is often transparent about the machinations of realist representation. Note that the prefix *hyper* in Greek means to go over, beyond or surpass.[4]

For instance, Annie Edwards playfully references assumptions about sensation and detailism in her novel *Miss Forrester* (1865). Her narrator invokes George Eliot's use of Dutch paintings in *Adam Bede* (1859) to reference a certain type of realistic representation:

> A defter hand than mine would put all the picture before you of this assemblage; every detail clear, sharp, telling as the finish of a Dutch painting. But such capacity is not mine. I might elaborately describe the low grey manor-house, its pointed slate roof, and mullioned windows shining in the noonday sun, and with its two giant cedars casting dense and fragrant shade upon the new-mown grass . . . . But when I had given you such a catalogue . . . by how much would you be furthered in your interest concerning what I have really got to say? None of these people interest me; none of them have a hold upon my imagination; while, in sharp contrast, two figures rise clear, vivid, living before my sight[.] (140–1)

The 'figures' that arise are both figures of sensation, the titular Miss Forrester and Mr Stretton, whom, the narrator tells us, 'You associated . . . at once with the lowest grade of book-making men at races' (141). What emerges here is an assessment of 'your interest' and the narrator's 'interest'. She implies that a list of details about the environment (which she does ironically provide) is boring, and she prefers to detail what will engage her readers affectively. Sensation narrators frequently describe the act of writing in such explicit ways, calling attention to their narrative choices in the manner of Edwards's narrator, or, more materially, to their paper or tears as they write. Collins's Walter records, 'I trace these lines, self-distrustfully, with the shadows of after-events darkening the very paper I write on' (23). Such self-reflexivity is fundamental to sensationalism's formal effects.

Walter is not only influenced by Anne's physical presence but by the story that she tells. She says, 'I have met with an accident – I am very unfortunate in being here alone so late' (21). Anne's explanation meets James Phelan's definition of a narrative: 'somebody telling someone else on some occasion and for some purpose(s) that something happened' (18). This flexible, rhetorically focused definition is useful for the sensation genre, which tends to feature gossipy third-person narrators or multiple first-person character-narrators. Although Walter Hartright is the editor, *The Woman in White* is told by many different narrators – and even one object, 'The Narrative of the Tombstone' – Collins seeming to realise that a story about collective affects is best told by a collective of voices. In this novel and others, sensation narrators exhibit a knowingness, and sometimes even a wariness, about sensational stories and the shocks that result from them, often commenting explicitly on the limitations of sensationalism as a form. Mary Elizabeth Braddon's *The Doctor's Wife* (1864), for instance, features a sensation novelist as character, a heroine whose reading is compared to opium eating and a narrator who wryly claims, 'This is *not* a sensation novel' (358). Built into the very form of the genre, then, are self-reflexive and parodic commentaries on the novel and the feelings associated with reading. These novels detail how reading, to borrow from Robyn Warhol, 'always happens in and to a body' (*Having* ix).

The genre is thus both metafictional and materialist, defined as it is by the prevalence of reading and writing bodies and by narrators and characters who are compelled to read and feel the bodily affects of characters for meaning, enacting a model of close reading as body reading that I establish in the pages that follow. These two aspects of my argument – that sensation novels were self-reflexive and that they were deeply affective – might seem at odds with one another. Yet like theorist Sara Ahmed, I contest an 'understanding of emotion as "the unthought", just as we need to contest the assumption that "rational thought" is unemotional, or that it does not involve being moved by others' (170).[5]

Furthermore, the fluctuation between so-called detached reflection and immersive experience that is represented and elicited by sensationalism suggests that these states are not necessarily opposed but can operate on a kind of oscillating rhythm. Each chapter of the book focuses on one way in which sensation authors theorise the transmission of narrative affects: how so-called fictional affects bleed into characters' lived realities (Chapter 1), how reading and writing sensationalism was associated with 'morbid' feelings (Chapter 2), how narratives conveyed via newspapers, courtroom trials and gossip function, like sensationalism, to disrupt conceptions of public and private feelings (Chapter 3), how affective contagion is both dangerous and 'natural', whether in a crowd or when directed by a narrator (Chapter 4), and finally, how feeling along with others, whether real or fictional, can be pleasurable and even healing (Chapter 5 and Coda). All of these theories underscore affect's transpersonal qualities.

It is worth clarifying my use of terminology: in contemporary terms, while affects are akin to physical sensations or bodily feelings, emotion, by contrast, signifies a conscious state that can be named. I follow Rei Terada in understanding the emotion–affect divide in this way: 'by *emotion* we usually mean a psychological, at least minimally interpretive experience whose physiological aspect is *affect*' (4). Put another way, emotions are 'feelings that have found the right match in words', while affects are more embodied and not necessarily bound to a single body (Brennan 5). I use the word *feelings* more broadly, understanding it to refer to both the physiological and the psychological. While contemporary affect theory and narrative theory are useful tools for reading these novels, rather than simply applying these contemporary theories to the novels I discuss, I use them as catalysts for tracing the already-existing theories, terms and narrative techniques at play in these historical fictions. Sara Ahmed's concept of the 'affect alien', for instance, leads to me the Victorian use of the term 'morbid'. Lisa Zunshine's work on Theory of Mind allows me to see how sensation fiction foregrounded the complexity of body reading. My approach may often seem more reading-focused than historicist as I work to trace the terminology and theories present in these novels, but my readings are also informed by the ways in which philosophers, scientists and other writers theorised affect and emotion in this period. Again, the chapters discuss well-known sensation writers, realist authors who experimented with sensationalism, American authors and spasmodic poets. In preparation for these readings, the remaining four sections of the introduction define the sensation genre and hyperrealism, position sensationalism alongside Victorian theories of free will and embodiment, and then situate it within the fields of affect theory and narrative theory, respectively.

Defining sensation and hyperrealism

While sensationalism seemed to suddenly appear in England in 1860 as a fully formed genre, this was of course not the case. Novels similar in style were published throughout the 1850s in England, and these novels were not merely a phenomenon in the United Kingdom but also in America, with writers like Louisa May Alcott and E. D. E. N. Southworth penning sensational stories. That said, a specific and substantial group of texts were published in England, Scotland and Ireland in the 1860s and 1870s that have both melodramatic plots and an embodied vocabulary. I differ from some early scholarship on sensation fiction in defining it as a distinctive genre. Ann Cvetkovich finds, much like Pamela Gilbert, that 'the sensation novel is not really a distinct genre [since] it resembles other popular and mass-produced subgenres of the novel that appeared during the rise of capitalism' (14).[6] My attention to a wide range of novels, however, indicates clear patterns in narrative technique and content. Since Gilbert and Cvetkovich's works were published in the 1990s, the digitisation and free online access of texts through sites like Google Books, Archive.org and Project Gutenberg has allowed scholars to access a far wider range of sensation novels. It is now possible to read sensation writers whose work has not been re-published in contemporary scholarly editions and thus develop an even more comprehensive picture of the genre. The novels frequently feature a woman who transgresses against her husband or the institution of marriage more generally. A familiar sensation plot might be: a woman marries (forcibly or naively), regrets her decision, and leaves or murders her husband.[7] Such a plot demands extended discussions of the heroine's feelings, sexual desires and bodily sensations.

Sensationalism can be understood as an extension of early nineteenth-century gothic forms, but its emphasis on the material rather than the spectral is an important distinction between these genres. In *Lady Audley's Secret*, Robert jokes, 'I believe all ghosts to be the result of damp' (69). In sensation, the body holds the clue: 'You sleep in a damp bed – you awake suddenly in the dead of the night with a cold shiver, and see an old lady . . . sitting at the foot of the bed. The old lady is indigestion, and the cold shiver is a damp sheet' (69). Further, while gothic fiction was typically set in the past and on the continent, sensation fiction was defined by proximity of time and place. Commenting on both physiological and temporal notions of proximity, Henry Mansel, one of the genre's more vocal critics, wrote, 'a tale which aims at electrifying the nerves of the reader is never thoroughly effective unless the scene be laid in our own days and among the people we are in the habit of meeting' (488–9). Sensation fiction was consistently marked as a 'modern' genre for its reference to new technologies; the novels are filled with characters sending telegraphic messages and taking trains. Nicholas Daly has linked the practice of riding the train to the experience of reading sensation fiction. The railway carriage was 'envisaged as a "framework of bones without muscles"', and so the 'traveller's body was imagined as supplying the missing shock-absorbing connective tissue' (43). Thus, both riding the train and reading these novels were acts that battered the nervous system, resulting in a specifically modern sensory experience. Daly's understanding of train travel as causing its passengers to be 'locked in an iron cage' encapsulates an anxiety that was rampant in mid-century thought about losing control of one's will or body, and which was articulated in critiques of sensationalism (45).

There was perhaps no Victorian writer seemingly more scandalised by the genre and its associations with speed and modernity than Margaret Oliphant. Her two oft-cited articles in *Blackwood's*, 'Sensation Novels' (1862) and 'Novels' (1867), register her concerns that serial publication encouraged nervous excitement in readers and that sensation novels were unfit reading material for women. Oliphant's 1862 essay in particular has been the standard for critics looking for early definitions of the sensation novel. While later in the decade sensationalism would become more associated with women writers and readers, Oliphant spends much of the review discussing Collins and Dickens. She emphasises the genre's distortion of realism: in contrast to realistic fiction, she finds sensation fiction to be too fast and too eventful. She blames serial publication, specifically '*weekly* publication, with its necessity for frequent and rapid recurrence of piquant situation and startling incident', for contributing to bad forms of writing and reading

(568). She spends much of the review condemning a new 'sensation novel', Dickens's *Great Expectations* (1860). She claims that in this novel, Dickens 'has hurried aside into regions of exaggeration' and has 'no longer patience' to perfect his characters (574, 575). The idea that sensation authors were quickly and thoughtlessly turning out books for a profit was a well-known criticism. Oliphant equates the supposed speed and excess of the narrative with its unrealistic representation. In 'books abounding in sensation ... the effect is invariably maintained by violent and illegitimate means, as fantastic in themselves as they are contradictory to actual life' (565).

Despite the vitriol she reserves for Dickens, Oliphant praises *The Woman in White* and Collins's 'laborious reticence' (566). Collins's novel appeared immediately following the serialisation of Dickens's *A Tale of Two Cities* in *All the Year Round* in November 1859 and so comparisons between the two friends and collaborators were almost inevitable. Oliphant writes of Collins, 'We cannot object to the means by which he startles and thrills his readers; everything is legitimate, natural, and possible; all the exaggerations of excitement are carefully eschewed, and there is almost as little that is objectionable in this highly-wrought sensation-novel, as if it had been a domestic history of the most gentle and unexciting kind' (566). Collins's supposedly tempered sensationalism means that his novel, for Oliphant, comes admirably close to being an 'unexciting' domestic tale (praise that may not have thrilled him). There is a preoccupation in the review with legitimacy and naturalness. The effects of sensation novels, *The Woman in White* notwithstanding, are 'illegitimate' because they are so unlike actual life. Oliphant thus makes an assumption about what good books should do – mimic life – but she also makes an assumption about life itself, namely that for most people it does not abound in strong feelings. Winifred Hughes has argued that we might understand sensation authors as narrating a 'certain kind of experience that the realists overlook', perhaps one that acknowledges the intensity of modern life (65).[8] Daly's concept of the sensation novel as 'synchroniz[ing] its readers with industrial modernity' (37) is relevant here, as is Dehn Gilmore's argument that the sensation novel borrowed from the modern exhibition 'a way of thinking through and framing a self-conscious experience of modern life and its sensory onrush' (89).

Sensationalism's exaggeration and 'sensory onrush' returns me to hyperrealism. My understanding of hyperrealism builds on the affective 'detailism' present in these texts but also on Janice Allan's framing of sensationalism as like a 'performance in drag' since it renders transparent the values and tropes behind Victorian realism (107).[9] Allan argues that 'sensationalism's exaggerated and self-conscious incorporation of the factual and the true effectively turns realism into a spectacle' (106). We might recall here the way in which sensation novels not only used the 'found document' trope of gothic novels but also incorporated playful mixes of diary, letter or telegraph, as well as the use of authorial prefaces in which stories were claimed to be ripped from newspaper headlines. Hyperrealism thus results from detailed accounts of bodily sensations, but also from calling explicit attention to the processes behind the narrative act, both of which lay bare the limits of realistic representation. How do you narrate unnameable bodily states? When does verisimilitude become metafiction?

Lucy Audley's pre-Raphaelite portrait in *Lady Audley's Secret* provides an example of hyperrealism. Pre-Raphaelite paintings would have recalled for Braddon's readers brightly coloured portraits of women by artists such as Dante Gabriel Rossetti, John William Waterhouse and John Everett Millais, which combined realism with symbolism. In Braddon's novel, the artist 'painted, hair by hair, those feathery masses of ringlets with every glimmer of gold, and every shadow of pale brown' (65). It is not just detailed but exaggerated, hinting at a darkness behind the supposedly sweet Lucy Audley: 'No one but a pre-Raphaelite would have so exaggerated every attribute of that delicate face as to give a lurid brightness to the blonde complexion, and a strange, sinister light to the deep blue eyes' (65). Like the painting, the scene itself is exaggerated, as Robert and George travel through a secret passageway to inspect the paintings in Lucy's room. Alicia tells them that they will have 'twenty minutes for [their] inspection of the paintings – that is about a minute apiece' (63). When they enter, however, both are transfixed by Lucy's portrait; they regard it one at a time, in solitude and by candlelight. This scenario is a plot device – George is Lucy's long-lost husband and recognises her – but it is also a hyperbolic example of body reading, the watchful examination and reception of another's body for meaning. Robert first examines the portrait and then watches George watching it. George 'sat before it for about a quarter of an hour without uttering a word – only staring blankly at the painting' (65). Robert misreads George's affects, first assuming that he has fallen asleep and then that he has caught a cold; he doesn't understand that George has, in effect, seen a ghost. Despite Robert's misreading, the men figure as model sensation readers in that they are close readers and slow readers, taking in all the details of Lucy's portrait for meaning. It is worth noting that Oliphant's links between sensation fiction and speed are misleading as these novels consistently value slowness and attention.[10]

The scene then evolves into a debate about authentic representation, highlighting how hyperrealism 'turns realism into a spectacle'. While the painting renders George inert, it unnerves Robert, who finds 'something odd about it' that he cannot quite name. Alicia agrees: 'We have never seen my lady look as she does in that picture; but I think that she *could* look so' (66). Robert challenges this reading and insists that the actual woman and the portrait are distinct: 'the picture is – the picture: and my lady is – my lady' (66). Yet the canny reader likely isn't so sure. As the narrator explains, 'It was so like, and yet so unlike. It was as if you had burned strange-coloured fires before my lady's face' (65). The novel invites comparisons between the painting and the emerging genre, since both expose Lucy's doubleness and illegibility (107). Along with such commentary about realistic representation, intertextual and metafictional references are common in these novels. While metafiction is certainly not an invention of postmodernism – historical examples include Shakespeare's *The Tempest* (1611) or Laurence Sterne's *Tristram Shandy* (1759) – much scholarship on metafiction tends to read it as synonymous with modernist and postmodernist writing. Even Jenny Bourne Taylor, attempting to characterise Wilkie Collins's 'dialogic and self-reflexive' writing style, refers to him as 'one of the most "modern" (even postmodern) of nineteenth-century novelists' (1). Yet what if we saw his 'self-reflexive' style as not postmodern or ahead of his time, but very much of his time? Elaine Freedgood has recently encouraged critics to unthink the so-called classically realist Victorian novel – an idea formulated by critics of the 1970s and 1980s – and instead to embrace the nineteenth-century novel's 'full oddness', 'self-reflexivity' and 'formal hijinks' (x). The sensation novel and its hyperrealistic form supports the claim that the Victorian novel is more metafictional and metaleptic than scholars have previously acknowledged.

While these self-reflexive tendencies can be seen in the earliest of sensation novels, second-generation sensationalism, novels published in the mid-1860s and beyond, are even more overt in their uses of parody and hyperrealism. Braddon, in particular, has garnered scholarly attention over her parodic narrative voice.[11] A number of critics have discussed Braddon's generic experimentation in *The Doctor's Wife* (1864) in particular.[12] The novel is a revision of Gustave Flaubert's *Madame Bovary* (1857), and Braddon uses the sensation author-character Sigismund Smith to poke fun at her own literary borrowing: Smith 'put neat paraphrases of Bulwer, or Dickens, or Thackeray' into his heroes' mouths (28). Braddon also references the popular assumption that there was an addictive quality to these novels when Smith compares his readership to 'a man who's accustomed to strong liquors, and to whose vitiated palate simple drinks seem flat and wishy-washy' (47). Both Braddon and her characters are hyper-aware of their place in literary culture. It is worth noting that Braddon's reader is only in on these jokes if she has an awareness of Braddon's authorial position and the cultural discourse surrounding sensation fiction. These metafictional moments in sensation novels can thus challenge how we understand nineteenth-century popular women's fiction, as they are evidence of both sophisticated narrative techniques and a skilled readership.

Free will and embodiment

Earlier in the introduction, I referenced one Victorian reviewer's complaint that sensation novels demanded a 'whole set of new words'. Ellen Wood, for instance, frequently uses the term 'rebellious' to describe Isabel's affective state as she sheds 'rebellious tears' (118), displays 'rebellious emotion' (91), has a 'rebellious heart' (214) and has a body that 'throbbed rebelliously' (301). Wood seems to have struck on a term that allows her to describe a body that betrays the conscious mind. History of emotions scholar Thomas Dixon has argued that due to the influence of Charles Darwin and others, the nineteenth century witnessed a cultural shift in understanding human subjectivity, as human beings seemed to move from 'a state of extensive voluntary control over our bodies and behaviours ... to a state of enslavement to useless physical urges that are disobedient to our wills' (176). At the same time that Darwin's evolutionary theories appeared, sensation authors experimented with a language and form to describe such disobedient, wilful bodies.

The appearance of sensation fiction can be situated alongside a series of publications from 1859 that debated the 'Free-will controversy', a debate significant to the history of affect, although no scholars have yet contextualised it as such (Bain iv). This year, in which Collins published the first instalment of *The Woman in White*, also saw the publication of Alexander Bain's *The Emotions and the Will*, Darwin's *On the Origin of Species*, John Stuart Mill's *On Liberty* and Samuel Smiles's *Self-Help*. The late 1850s was thus a moment of convergence for writing on free will and feeling. While sensation fiction didn't fully take shape until the 1860s, novelists writing in the late 1850s were certainly experimenting with sensational devices, and this is also when writers like Collins and Wood began their careers. All of these 1859 publications emerge from radically different perspectives, but they similarly ask: Do human beings really have free will? Are we more than our bodies or our impulses? What differentiates humans from animals or machines? These questions drive sensation novels as well. Discussions of free will are always discussions about our abilities to control our bodily affects and the labelling of specific emotions as socially productive or disruptive.

Rick Rylance has explained that the concept of the will was vital for the Victorians on religious, ethical and ontological grounds.[13] The will was also central to Victorian notions of economic success, particularly in the context of Smilesian notions of the self-made man (194). Smiles, in what is arguably the first modern self-help book, and Mill, in his treatise on liberty, both emphasise the power of what they variously call 'will' or 'desire' in forming the Victorian subject. Smiles stresses the value of individual determination: 'It is *will*, – force of purpose, – that enables a man to do or be whatever he sets his mind on being or doing' (226). Mill also emphasises the importance of personal autonomy: 'A person whose desires and impulses are his own ... is said to have a character. One whose desires and impulses are not his own, has no character, no more than a steam-engine has a character' (62). For both Smiles and Mill, the Victorian subject is implicitly a white subject (and for Smiles, a white male subject). Mill makes this clear when he explains that his doctrine of liberty leaves out 'those backward states of society' (18). In chapter 1 of *On Liberty*, as Lisa Lowe notes, Mill argues for 'the imposition of despotic government on those "unfit" for self-government', specifically referencing Colonial India (113–14). Mill's ideas of the will are thus inseparable from colonial ideology.

By contrast, Darwin and Bain question the possibility of true self-determination and underscore somatic agency, much like sensation novels; and they do so in ways that can even challenge white male British exceptionalism and individuality. Darwin, in a chapter on 'Instinct', stresses the manner in which the lives of all humans (and animals) are dictated by unconscious habitual actions that are often 'in direct opposition to our conscious will' (190). He further emphasises the interdependence of all beings, noting that the idea 'that each species has been independently created – is erroneous' (15).[14] Bain, too, constantly emphasises interconnection and affective transmission. His book sets up an associationist relationship between emotions and the will, arguing that the will emerges not from the mind but from the entire organism: 'Our consciousness in this life is an *embodied* consciousness' (436).[15] Along with Darwin and Herbert Spencer, Bain was a key figure in pioneering the belief that the science of the mind should be a science of matter (Dixon 141). In his later *Mind and Body: The Theories of their Relation* (1873), Bain argues that it is impossible to 'speak of mind apart from body' since we cannot 'perceive a mind acting apart from its material companion' (130). He rejects a notion of the mind using the body 'as its *instrument*', instead defining the human being as 'an extended and material mass, attached to which is the power of becoming alive to feeling and thought' (132, 137). Darwin and Bain thus emphasise the interdependence of the environment and the human body.

Relevant to the 'Free-will controversy', and its relationship to colonial ideology in particular, was the Indian Uprising. Sometimes called the Sepoy Rebellion and, formerly, the Indian Mutiny, the uprising was arguably the biggest threat to English imperial rule in the nineteenth century and a radical turning point in national and global relations. I do not intend to make this geopolitical catastrophe a mere example of a philosophical dispute but to suggest, rather, that the way in which the Victorians discussed free will in this period was impacted by this historical event. In turn, the way in which the Indian Uprising was discussed by the press reveals how assumptions about emotions and the will work to reinforce or shape cultural narratives, recalling Ahmed's claim that 'emotions operate to "make" and "shape" bodies as forms of action' (*Cultural Politics* 4). The revolt began on 10 May 1857 when Indian soldiers (or sepoys) in Meerut were required to bite off the ends of rifle cartridges greased with pork and beef fat, taboo for both Hindus and Muslims; their response was also likely due to both growing resentment and rumours that British forces were coming to attack (Herbert 3). British officers and their wives and children were murdered, and more massacres followed, leading up to the notorious Massacre at Cawnpore in which Indian forces, led by Nana Sahib, murdered over 100 British women and children, throwing their remains into a well. British soldiers arrived the following day to witness the scene, and candid descriptions of the massacre soon followed in the British press. Saverio Tomaiulo has compared the '"sensational" narration of colonial atrocities' to the textual strategies used in sensation novels, claiming that the 'presence of (prevalently) male villains of foreign origin, the depiction of physical pain and the reiteration of terms such as "horror"' serve to recall sensational strategies and worked to justify colonial order (115). Colonial law was quickly restored with the 1858 Government of India Act, but the Rebellion nonetheless shocked the British public and forced them to question their national optimism, if not to radically revise the colonial mission. Christopher Herbert links the timing of the Rebellion with the rise of sensational popular narratives, asking, 'was the sudden appearance of "sensation" fiction in the Victorian literary marketplace itself a marker of the "terrible break" in British life that the Mutiny was said to have produced?' (242). The Rebellion, and the media coverage of it, upended the kinds of hierarchies that Smiles and Mill attempted to maintain. While I do not wish to collapse cultural narratives about scandalous novels and the psychic and physical violence associated with colonialism, I do want to emphasise that the sensation novel and the Rebellion figured as sensational precisely because they were about volatile bodies and the limits of the will, narratives both terrifying and thrilling to the Victorian public.

Yet why this obsession with free will, a term likely popularised by Bain, even if the phrase had been in use in religious argument long before 1859? It might be best understood as a response to the myriad of cultural changes that seemed to coalesce in the late 1850s and the years following. Human beings now had to demonstrate what made them distinct from both animals and machines as a likeness to either might suggest that their behaviours were more instinctual or mechanical than they would like to think. Britons also attempted to demonstrate what made them distinct from their colonial subjects. As early as the 1830s, many British citizens began to consider '"unnatural" anything human that partook of mimicry or seemed in any way mechanical or constructed', as

Rebecca Stern has shown (425–6). Mill's comparison of the characterless man to a steam-engine is thus part of a larger cultural discussion about mechanistic behaviour. Stern argues that a range of writers tried to maintain a sense of the naturalness of human subjectivity by condemning artifice and promoting sincere identity, even as authors of conduct books ironically instructed their readers in the act of 'natural' performance. The danger lay not so much in the way that human behaviour could be simulated but rather when this mechanised behaviour was exposed as such: 'If one's "act" was too visibly rehearsed, the repetitions that made up proper, coherent identity were too reminiscent of the machines that had come to threaten nature in a more literal sense' (426). Industrialised society – and I would add post-Darwinian society – put more pressure on ideas of free will and one's ability to control her feelings. Yet bodily reflexes like yawns or flinches reveal that strength of will only goes so far.[16] Debates about free will, then, were not only about distinguishing human beings from machines, animals or other human beings, but about exploring Victorian subjects' comfort with somatic agency and transpersonal experience.

Sensationalism explores ideas about both mechanised behaviour and permeable bodies in fictional form. It is useful to return to Walter and Anne's meeting in *The Woman in White*. Benjamin Morgan, too, sees this encounter as representative of sensation fiction, noting that even more scandalous than the erotic elements of sensationalism 'was the way in which [sensation authors] call attention to the mechanical actions of human bodies' (142).[17] Despite this focus on the narration and representation of nervous bodies and mechanical actions, sensation fiction has been largely absent in studies on Victorian embodiment. In Mary Ann O'Farrell's *Telling Complexions* (1997), she positions the blush in the nineteenth-century novel as a 'demand for interpretation' (4). While her work presents a useful model for sensation fiction, she focuses on canonical writers like Austen, Eliot, Dickens and Gaskell.[18] William Cohen's excellent *Embodied: Victorian Literature and the Senses* (2008) argues that many Victorian writers challenged Enlightenment ideals in favour of stressing the material existence of the human body. While Cohen observes that the 'several meanings of *sensation* pertinent to the fictional subgenre designated by this name make it an especially apt object for inquiry', he only includes a brief discussion of Collins's *Poor Miss Finch* (1872) (13). Similarly, Nicholas Dames, in *The*

Physiology of the Novel: Reading, Neural Science, and the Form of Victorian Fiction (2007), presents what he calls physiological novel theory, developed by Victorian thinkers like George Henry Lewes, E. S. Dallas and Bain. He explains that he will not look to 'any sensation novelists of the 1860s and 1870s', instead discussing 'more self-conscious and detached (if currently more canonical) novels' (13). This distinction takes for granted that sensation authors were not self-conscious about their own methods and techniques, an assumption that I challenge. Finally, and most recently, Morgan's *The Outward Mind: Materialist Aesthetics in Victorian Science and Literature* (2017) devotes just a few pages to sensation fiction. He records that the critical tendency to read these novels as supplying ideologies of gender and mental health is partly due to the fact that their critical reassessment took place alongside a period in literary criticism 'that drew on Foucault's conception of bodies as sites of textual inscriptions of legal, sexual, and psychiatric power' (140). The very qualities that made sensation novels such a fruitful site for Foucauldian critics, he argues, can also make them rich sources for newer approaches to materialism and ontology (140–1). Indeed, this book is an attempt to fill that critical space.

These studies show that discussions of somatic agency and materiality are relevant across a wide range of Victorian literature. However, attention to bodily affects is not merely one metaphorical or representational strategy in sensation novels but the very basis of characterisation, plot and narration, as Ann Cvetkovich and Pamela Gilbert recognised decades ago. In addition to Gilbert's recent *Victorian Skin*, her earlier *Disease, Desire, and the Body in Victorian Women's Popular Novels* (1997) was an important early intervention in Victorian studies and the history of embodiment. She draws from a range of theorists, including Bakhtin and Foucault, to analyse metaphors of reading and the body in periodical reviews and in novels by Braddon, Broughton and Ouida. While Gilbert's focus on the rhetoric of contamination and disease differs from my own, I am compelled by her claim that the body is 'ineradicably entwined in subjectivity' in these novels, an idea that she expands upon in her later work (15). And Cvetkovich's *Mixed Feelings: Feminism, Mass Culture, and Victorian Sensationalism* (1992) explores the politics of affect in sensation novels, suggesting that affect functions as a source of 'both social stability and social instability' for middle-class female characters (6). A major focus of her book is the way in which the middle-class woman is constructed as a mysterious or suffering woman in sensation fiction, a topic that I develop and revise in Chapter 3 by showing how Collins and Oliphant recognise that very construction and work to challenge it. While Cvetkovich claims that sensation novels construct 'physical experiences' as 'immediate and natural', I emphasise, in contrast, the ways in which sensation characters and narrators question what appears to be 'natural' as they self-reflexively process their feelings (24).

Excepting the efforts of Cvetkovich and Gilbert, it is striking how scholarship on embodiment and feeling so consistently ignores sensation novels, as if the authors' direct engagement with such topics makes them too obvious to consider. Marlene Tromp notes that while 'sensation often supplies the leverage to read against the grain, we often (perhaps unconsciously) return it to its generic box when we have completed the task' ('Sensation' 858). The use of sensational language and techniques by such a wide range of authors in this period encourages me to not 'return it to its generic box'. Additionally, I concur with Tromp's insistence that attending properly to sensationalism can help scholars to read both the fiction and the politics of the period in new ways (860). Sensationalism's utter acceptance of wilful bodies and affective co-experience is striking given the timely debates about free will and further implies that many Victorian audiences were hungry for such narratives of the body.

Theorising Victorian affect

This self-conscious theorising present in sensationalism is why I read what scholars have called the 'affective turn' as an affective return, a return to earlier ways of thinking and being in the world. In this section, I propose that contextual affect theory can offer a useful lens through which to read sensation fiction, but I also suggest that contemporary affect theory can benefit from engaging with historical understandings of affect. Teresa Brennan's work is helpful here as she recognises that in 'other cultures and other times, there are – or have been – different, more permeable, ways of being' (11). Brennan maps resistance to the transmission of affect – and the related concept of 'entrainment', the process whereby one person's nervous system, or a group's, is brought into alignment with another's – due to a long-standing attraction to a model of the subject whose 'emotions and energies are naturally contained' (2). Yet this model must be historicised. She explains that the influence of the emotionally contained subject means that scholars who accept notions of affective transmission often emphasise that it functions via sight, rather than, say, touch or smell. Brennan explains how a reliance on sight, which she argues took hold as the key sense in the eighteenth century, is intimately related to ideas of distinct personhood: 'If entrainment is effected by sight, then on the face of it, our boundaries stay intact. We become like someone else by imitating that person, not by literally becoming or in some way merging with him or her' (10). Yet Victorian sensation fiction, despite being produced in an era that predominately privileged sight, experiments with moments in which boundaries blur and identities merge. While the last section set up why so many Victorians were obsessed with wilfulness and embodiment, this section explores how they described and understood such transpersonal, affective experiences. It does so by first addressing that most common of Victorian emotion words: sympathy.

For many Victorian writers, sympathy was the term they used to refer to the transmission or circuit of affect. While it was employed to describe a conscious feeling of compassion for another, it could also refer to shared, involuntary bodily affects.[19] Scholars working on nineteenth-century literature have long been invested in an idea of sympathy as a cognitive and ethical response to reading, one outlined by George Eliot below. In this letter from July 1859, Eliot imagines that art should extend our 'sympathies':

> If Art does not enlarge men's sympathies, it does nothing morally ... the only effect I ardently long to produce by my writings is, that those who read them should be better able to *imagine* and to *feel* the pains and the joys of those who differ from themselves in everything but the broad fact of being struggling, erring, human creatures. (*Letters*, vol. 3, 111)

Eliot's sentiment is a compassionate model of the power of fictional narratives, one that holds weight in contemporary scholarship, where the importance of sympathy to the development of nineteenth-century subjects and the novel as a genre has been well established. Along these lines, most critics tend to understand sympathy as cognitive or as a kind of mental feeling. In *Scenes of Sympathy*, Audrey Jaffe draws from Adam Smith's *Theory of Moral Sentiments* (1759) when she explains that 'sympathy "does away" with bodies in order to produce representations, replacing persons with mental pictures, generalized images of ease and of suffering' (11). Yet if in Eliot's terms sympathy takes into account imagining the feelings of other people and as a result actually *feeling* the pains and joys of others, then this understanding of sympathy tells only part of the story. I thus want to make a case for a way of thinking about Victorian sympathy that does not 'do away' with the body.[20]

Why might this use of terminology matter? And what does it mean to read literary texts alongside a more embodied and ambiguous understanding of Victorian sympathy? Recognising sympathy as embodied can allow us to reconsider historical feelings, since embodied sympathy serves to break down the emotion–affect binary. In texts ranging from folk psychology to scientific writing to sensation novels, we see mid-Victorians understanding sympathy as both emotion and affect, cognitive and embodied, and personal and transpersonal. For instance, Henry George Atkinson, writing to Harriet Martineau in *Letters on the Laws of Man's Nature and Development* (1851), calls sympathies between individuals 'the influences of one organized body upon another', in what could be understood as an early expression of affect (117–18). Atkinson and Martineau's fascinating book caused a stir upon its publication, both for Martineau's atheism and for Atkinson's interests in mesmerism and clairvoyance. The book consists largely of Martineau asking Atkinson questions and his lengthy responses. Atkinson was not a trained scientist but wrote extensively on mesmerism, phrenology, materialism and spiritualism; he claims that the notion that the 'mind [is] entirely independent of body' is a 'mere delusion', as is the concept of 'free will' (1851, 6). Given his effort to trace all emotions to physical causes, it is not surprising that he understands sympathy as deeply material. In a passage relating mesmerism to sympathy, he explains that 'some mesmerized persons are able to describe the condition of others by sympathetic sensations, occurring in themselves' (37). While this 'sympathetic condition' can exist within anyone, some people are particularly susceptible to the feelings of others, and he notes that this condition is common in those who mesmerise: 'While mesmerising, they will feel pain in the part affected in the patient; and, in some instances, imbibe the disease' (37–8). Sympathy here is a sharing and transference of affect, registered via 'sensations'. The notion that the hypnotist can feel the pain of the patient and even take on a physical ailment implies a porous understanding of the human body. This is a significant departure from the cognitive understanding of sympathy which was imagined to be processed through one's mental modelling and judgements, and was thus more rational, regulated and less affective.

Similar notions of sympathy were echoed by psychologists and philosophers in the period. For instance, Bain and Darwin, whom I referenced in the previous section as promoting a materialist understanding of human subjectivity, understand sympathy as the drifting of affect from one body to another or between various bodies. Darwin offers everyday occurrences, which 'seem to be due to imitation or some sort of sympathy' – note his use of 'imitation' and 'sympathy' as almost interchangeable terms (40). He offers a number of examples of sympathy between bodies: when a singer becomes hoarse, audience members might sympathetically clear their own throats, or 'at leaping matches, as the performer makes his spring, many of the spectators, generally men and boys, move their feet' (40–1). Contemporary cognitive science in fact supports these early observations of Darwin's. We now know that when we see an action performed, like a jump, it activates the same neural networks as if we were to perform it ourselves and we may even experience what it feels like to perform the action: we might feel our own body strain or stretch while watching another jump (Gibbs 197). In a related example – one that seems particularly appropriate for Victorian society – Darwin writes, 'So strong, also, is the power of sympathy that a sensitive person, as a lady has assured me, will sometimes blush at a flagrant breach of etiquette by a perfect stranger, though the act may in no way concern her' (332). This extends the notion of feeling along with someone to feeling in the place of someone else.

Bain goes further in defining how he imagines the process of sympathy to work in individual bodies. In *The Emotions and the Will*, Bain defines sympathy as a process by which 'one individual ... fall[s] in with the emotional or active states of others' (211). There are two steps to reaching sympathy: the first is imitation or the 'tendency to assume a state, attitude, or movement, that we see enacted by another person'; the second is 'the assumption of a mental state or consciousness, through the occurrence of the bodily accompaniment' (212, 215). In Bain's understanding, sympathy with other people begins in the body, with physical imitation, and then moves into the mind. In our contemporary terminology, this might be a process of empathy followed by sympathy, or an experience of affect followed by the recognition of an emotion. Again, such feelings are transpersonal: he describes emotions as 'waves' that can 'inflame' other bodies (177–8). He notes that in the process of 'mutual sympathy', individuality is 'softened down into uniformity' (182). And he extols this anti-individualist element of sympathy, insisting that 'the taking one out of one's self may be a positive advantage, even at some cost' (180). So, while sympathy may be sacrificial, it also comes with pleasures and moments of deep connection.

Martineau and Atkinson, Darwin, and Bain thus variously equate sympathy with a form of imitation, a sharing of affects, or in Atkinson's case, a heightened sensory intuitiveness. Sensation novels, too, are replete with examples of bodily sympathy. For instance, in *East Lynne*, Isabel has all of 'her sympathies awakened' when she learns of the poverty of the local piano instructor, Mr Kane (69). When Isabel tells Kane that she will help him, the narrator articulates their feelings as shared and embodied: 'The tears rushed into Mr Kane's eyes: Isabel was not sure but they were in her own' (70). Again, for many Victorian writers, 'sympathy' encompassed our current concepts of both sympathy and empathy. Suzanne Keen distinguishes between our contemporary usage of the terms 'sympathy' and 'empathy' by explaining that sympathy is a supportive emotion about another's feelings ('*I feel pity for your pain*') while empathy is actually feeling what another is feeling ('*I feel your pain*') (5). Keen defines empathy as a 'vicarious, spontaneous sharing of affect, [which] can be provoked by witnessing another's emotional state, by hearing about another's condition, or even by reading' (4). Thus, empathy is not always a compassionate emotional response as it can describe anything from the sharing of sexual arousal, anxiety or anger moving between bodies. So, too, with Victorian sympathy. Tracing Victorian bodily sympathy thus allows for a pre-modern genealogy of both empathy and the transmission of affect, and it is just one example of the way in which Victorian understandings of feeling were far more embodied than they are typically understood to be. I explore the notion of bodily sympathy in greater detail in Chapters 4 and 5.

This, however, is not a book primarily about Victorian sympathy but Victorian affect, and sympathy offers just one way in which affective transmission may take shape. While affect is a contemporary term not used in the Victorian period, I employ it throughout because it is usefully inclusive. Additionally, sympathy and empathy have dominated work in the field, but they rely upon sameness or a (perceived) sense of recognition or understanding. The transmission of affect, in contrast, suggests that we are physically impacted and influenced by other bodies but not that we always share the same emotion states – or indeed that we can even know what another is feeling. Someone else's anger expressed via an angry tone or facial expression might cause me to be angry or, depending on the context, it might instead cause me to me to cry, run away, want to calm them down or roll my eyes. Bain notes that while it is 'easy enough to chime in with the current of the ordinary emotions, pains, and pleasures of those around us, many cases arise where a laborious effort is requisite to enable us to approach in our own feelings the state of mind of another person' (183). Sympathy might not be attained due to 'disparity of nature', such as when people's personalities are so different that it is impossible to sympathise, or because of antipathy, 'the deathblow to fellow-feeling' (183). Bain likens antipathy to disgust or abhorrence and discusses it in very specific social contexts, referencing the 'antipathy of the white population of the United States to the persons of the free blacks' (277). He explains that antipathy frames class systems and relationships to foreign bodies (279). Using affect as a framework thus allows me to examine not only moments of sympathy, then, but moments of antipathy, as well as moments of affective dissonance, in which characters struggle to make sense of their conflicting feelings.

Bain's comments on affects and racism further show how deeply context matters when it comes to affects. Indeed, this is why Victorian writers have affinity with contextual affect theorists, who reject the notion of affect as devoid of identity or environment. Contextual affect theorists challenge scholars like Brian Massumi who tend to situate affect as outside of language and social context. Massumi defines affect as 'a prepersonal intensity corresponding to the passage from one experiential state of the body to another and implying an augmentation or diminution in that body's capacity to act' (xvii). Eric Shouse builds on Massumi to argue that, unlike emotion, affect 'cannot be fully realised in language ... because affect is always prior to and/or outside of consciousness' (para. 5). Yet if affects are outside of consciousness and language, then how can scholars critically interpret them?

Clare Hemmings's 2005 intervention into the field rejected 'the contemporary fascination with affect as outside social meaning' (565). Hemmings argues that 'affect might in fact be valuable precisely to the extent that it is not autonomous' (549, 565). Bodies and their affects only fully take shape when they are placed within cultural contexts, as scholars like Cvetkovich, Gilbert, Sarah Ahmed, Lauren Berlant and Sianne Ngai also insist, whether that context be mid-Victorian literary culture, 'women's culture' in the United States, twentieth-century debates about asylum-seekers in the contemporary United Kingdom, or American abolitionist writing. This strain of contextual affect theory is most productive for mining Victorian understandings of affect, not only because of the historical context demanded by such writing but because mid-Victorians themselves largely understood affect within specific social and cultural scenarios. For instance, part of the shock of Walter's encounter with Anne is not merely that she touches him, but that she is a woman alone on the street at night.

Furthermore, Victorian theories of affect can challenge a radical separation of mind and body, a critical tendency seen in the work of affect scholars like Massumi. Recall that Bain insists that we cannot 'perceive a mind acting apart from its material companion' (130). Scholars such as Ruth Leys and Linda Zerilli find that affect theorists who insist that affect is independent of signification or meaning rely too heavily on a classic dualism of mind and body. Massumi, Leys claims, idealises 'the mind by defining it as a purely disembodied consciousness' (456). Instead, we must understand that affect and cognition are 'radically entangled' (Zerilli 282). Mid-century Victorian writers did not always rigidly separate affect and emotion, body and mind, as their flexible use of the term 'sympathy' demonstrates. Other feeling states also demonstrate this point, however. For example, in *Griffith Gaunt, or Jealousy*, Charles Reade's very title demonstrates the way in which his character study is also a study of an emotion. The first time that Griffith is noticeably jealous, his would-be lover, Kate, sees it expressed through his body: 'she witnessed the livid passion of jealousy writhing in every lineament of a human face. That terrible passion had transfigured its victim in a moment' (7–8). His face 'discolored, and convulsed, and [became] almost demonical' (8). Jealousy is a nameable emotion, but it is recognised and realised through Griffith's physical transformation. Kate understands his intense reaction to be different from 'petty jealousy', which she has detected 'pinching or coloring many a pretty face that tried very hard to hide it', the emotion here interchangeable with its associated affects (8). As Darwin would later explain in his 1872 *The Expression of the Emotions in Man and Animals*, most of our emotions 'are so closely connected with their expression, that they hardly exist if the body remains passive' (217).

While I reference contemporary affect theorists throughout the book, I do so with an awareness that scholars in this field have tended to be rather presentist in their source material. Yet I argue that affect theory, with its emphasis on materiality and permeability, can be useful for historical readings of emotions, reminding us to return to descriptions of the body. Two recent collections are evidence of the ways in which affect theory can productively be put in conversation with historical texts: *Affect Theory and Early Modern Texts: Politics, Ecologies, and Form* (2017), edited by Amanda Bailey and Mario DiGangi, and *Affect Theory and Literary Critical Practice: A Feel for the Text* (2019), edited by Stephen Ahern and which features an essay of mine that is an early thinking through of this book. Both collections have the aim of challenging the presentism that has marked the field, and they demonstrate ways in which 'affect can shed new light on the formal elements of literary texts' (Bailey and DiGangi 6). As Ahern explains, 'Affect theory offers up to the critic rich accounts of the phenomenology of felt experience that can help us better grasp what's at stake' in historical texts (5). Furthermore, an alignment of affect theory and the field known as the history of emotions, which situates discourses of emotion in specific socio-historical moments or contexts, can productively extend both fields. The history of emotions offers scholars working historically a sense of defamiliarisation, a reminder that my terms might not match the period that I am exploring and that all emotional terms are historically and culturally situated. It is a challenge getting outside of our own emotional ideologies and vocabularies. Barbara Rosenwein notes that exercises like word counts can only get us so far as we then have to place emotion words as part of a larger whole or ask how emotions were expressed physically in the past (16). Even though they are written texts, sensation novels, because of their embodied vocabulary, provide one way to do so, and scholars such as Janice Allan and Mario Ortiz-Robles have productively read affect alongside sensation fiction.[21] In addition to arguing for the benefit of affect theory and the history of emotions to the study of these novels, I argue that the fluid approaches to emotion and embodiment exhibited by Victorian writers can provide us with compelling models for theorising affect today.

Narrating affect

Yet what tools can we use in order to read affect in and across sensational narratives? Sensation authors' theorisations of affect are most obvious in their strategies for encouraging readerly feeling and in their techniques for narrating characters' affective experience. While the sensation novel has been integrated into more Victorian scholarship in recent decades, the formal experimentation of these authors is still underexplored likely because the genre remained, for so long, in the shadow of sexist and classist Victorian reviewers and, later, dismissive twentieth-century scholarship, which understood it merely 'in terms of the cultural fears and anxieties that it (unconsciously) expresse[d]' (Badowska 158). In 2013, I co-edited a special issue of *Women's Writing* on female sensation authors with Anne-Marie Beller. In the introduction, we claimed that recent scholarship, including that in our issue, had begun to show that sensation novelists were 'more sophisticated in their textual strategies than previously credited, thereby justifying literary-critical attention to the aesthetic and formal aspects of their fiction' (144). Narrative theory, with its focus on the *how* of narratives over the *what*, is key to this work.

As with affect theory, sensation novels have much to offer to the field of narrative theory as they put some stress on the body in Phelan's 'somebody telling someone else on some occasion and for some purpose(s) that something happened' (18). The genre can help inform what Susan S. Lanser calls a more 'corporeally thoughtful' narratology (127). We find, in these novels, narrators who stop to process their feelings (or those of their characters) in what may seem like interruptions but are themselves narrative events. Such moments are where I locate affect in these texts – as well as in descriptions of characters' bodily movements, reflex actions or shifts in atmosphere between and among characters. In the opening of Amelia Edwards's *Barbara's History*, the narrator notes that her own words 'have power to arrest my pen, and blind my eyes with unaccustomed tears' (1). Barbara's affects obscure her words and stall the narrative that she attempts to write, but they also afford the occasion for her writing. Indeed, 'Affect is what makes events reportable by any narrator' (Shuman and Young 413). Again, such moments are not divergences from the plot but are precisely what constitute sensational plotting. Furthermore, narrators' affective responses and their anticipation of readers' affects work to stage an interactive experience in these novels. Wood's narrator in *East Lynne* urges her reader to 'cool your anger. I agree with you that [Isabel] ought never to have come back; that it was an act little short of madness: but are you quite sure that you would not have done the same, under the facility and the temptation?' (591). This confrontational metaleptic address collapses worlds and feelings as Wood's narrator suggests that readers not think themselves entirely removed from the narrative they are reading. A narrative theory informed by affect should be particularly attentive to metalepsis, what Gerard Genette calls a breach of 'a shifting and sacred frontier between two worlds, the world in which one tells and the world of which one tells', since the transmission of affect effectively breaches these two worlds (xv).

Additionally, sensation novels employ the following techniques in order to create an affective and engaged reading experience: first-person character narrators who purport to tell the truth; use of present tense to convey a sense of immediacy; narrators who urge readers to look at and evaluate characters' bodies and affects (especially blushes); and references to the acts of reading and writing. The work of narrative theorists Robyn Warhol and Suzanne Keen, who discuss narrative emotions, as well as that by cognitive narratologists, is helpful in understanding the narrative devices at work in the novels and how they relate to affect. I take seriously Warhol's claim in *Having a Good Cry: Effeminate Feelings and Pop-Culture Forms* (2003) that we should think of narrative structures 'as devices that work through readers' bodily feelings' (8).[22] Warhol attempts to develop 'a language for talking about the reader's body', and she looks at popular forms such as soap operas and serialised fiction, noting that they all follow established conventions for encouraging specific feelings at key moments (ix). And Keen's work on empathy also explores readerly feeling, suggesting that we may respond with greater empathy to fictional characters and situations than real ones because their protective fictionality releases 'readers from the obligations of self-protection through skepticism and suspicion' (xii). In other words, we are free to feel without fear of judgement or ramification within a fictional context; this explains how metafiction can in fact support rather than challenge affective responses in readers.

Finally, an important feature of sensation's attention to affect is the genre's emphasis on mind reading. Mind reading, applied interchangeably with the phrase Theory of Mind, is used by cognitive psychologists to describe our ability to assign states of mind, feelings and beliefs to others. Theory of Mind (ToM) became popular with a range of narrative theorists in the early 2000s, including but not limited to Alan Palmer, Alan Richardson, Blakey Vermeule and Lisa Zunshine. In Zunshine's words, we take part in mind reading when 'we ascribe to a person a certain mental state on the basis of her observable action' (*Why We Read* 6). Intuiting others' states of mind is how we navigate our social environment as human beings, and ToM allows us to understand fictional characters in the same way. We, however misguided, invest fictional characters with 'an inexhaustible repertoire of states of mind' and receive pleasure in testing our own mind reading capacities under fictional circumstances (20). The role of ToM in canonical nineteenth-century fiction has already received much attention – all of the theorists that I name above gravitate towards Jane Austen, crediting her with the development of new narrative techniques for representing consciousness – but few scholars have linked mind reading to sensation fiction.

Emphasising the importance of mind reading within sensation fiction might seem counter to my claim that sensation novels locate the essence of human subjectivity in the body, but I stress throughout the book that mind reading happens in and through the body. Even in Austen's work, as Richardson notes, characters must pay special attention to one another's bodies in an era in which reticence was required 'in relation to erotic matters and "courtship" in general' (86). And Zunshine explains that our evolutionary history as a social species 'ensures that you intuitively expect me to read your body as indicative of your thoughts, desires, and intentions, and that my reading of your body will be crucial for the outcome of our communication' (*Getting Inside* 13–14). Given the fact that bodies are both 'the best and worst source of information about people's thoughts and feelings', we frequently misread one another's intentions and emotions, but misreading is still mind reading (13). Misreading bodies and distrusting the performative nature of certain bodies is the very stuff of sensation fiction. In *Social Minds*, Palmer briefly mentions Collins's work, noting that he is similar to Dickens in his emphasis 'on the surface: the looks, facial expressions, bodily movements, and sign language by which characters communicate with others' (165). He finds that in *No Name*, there is almost no 'direct report of internal thought' but a great deal of what he calls 'highly visible thinking' (166). In fact, all sensation novelists rely on visible thinking – or visible feeling – in their depictions of mind reading. Additionally, a key feature of the sensation novel is that narrators frequently call attention to mind reading not only in relation to courtship but between married characters who are uncertain or suspicious about one another's motives and emotions.

Another feature of sensationalism is the way in which mind reading is foregrounded as difficult and often troubling. Maria K. Bachman, one of the few critics to discuss sensation fiction in the context of ToM, argues that while 'reading novels may very well exercise our ToM, reading a novel such as *The Woman in White* tests our cognitive limits' (78). Sensation fiction, with its constant spying, eavesdropping and dramatic revelations, 'engages its readers in a kind of ToM marathon' as we work to make sense of the characters' mysterious actions and affects (94). Sensationalism also engages characters in such marathons. After Anne touches Walter, he must process what has just happened to him. He does so not by speaking to Anne (since he is 'too seriously startled'), but by looking at her body (20). He finds that she has 'large, grave, wistfully attentive eyes; nervous, uncertain lips .... There was nothing wild, nothing immodest in her manner: it was quiet and self-controlled, a little melancholy and a little touched by suspicion' (20–1). By reading her eyes, lips and 'manner', which is synonymous with her affects, Walter intuits that she must be both melancholy and suspicious. Yet he is also stumped: 'What sort of a woman she was . . . I altogether failed to guess' (21). This is not surprising, since the scene emphasises reflex action over conscious thought. Indeed, what frequently happens in sensation novels is that characters simply cannot read others. Sensationalism thus emphasises the difficulty of easily correlating physiological affects with understandable emotions, as characters observe and respond to another's body and behaviour but often get stuck in the (conscious or unconscious) process of assessing another's mental state.

The manner in which ToM is foregrounded in sensation is not surprising or anachronistic, since Victorian writing on emotion shows that ToM was being negotiated in this period even though it was not named as such. Herbert Spencer's 'The Physiology of Laughter', published in *Macmillan's Magazine* in March 1860 (and followed by an excerpt from Smiles's *Self-Help*), notes the manner in which we assign mental states based on the observation of others' bodily movements, whether those movements are conscious or not. He explains that 'external actions, *through which we read the feelings of others*, show us that under any considerable tension, the nervous system . . . discharges itself on the muscular system . . . with or without the guidance of the will' (395; emphasis added). He records that emotions are betrayed by the body – 'joy almost universally produces contraction of the muscles' – and then interpreted by others, in what can be understood as an early expression of mind reading (396). While reading or looking may seem to emphasise vision and physical separation, such activities can be deeply affective as we also feel another's affects or the atmosphere created by various bodies.

***

Chapter 1 of *Narrative, Affect and Victorian Sensation* explores the theorisation of narrative affects via fictional readers, specifically the depiction of female readers in Amelia Edwards's *Hand and Glove* (1858) and *Barbara's History* (1863) and Rhoda Broughton's *Cometh Up as a Flower* (1867). My focus moves beyond the moment of affective reading to explore the experience of emplotment in these characters' lives as they follow the scripts laid out in the pre-sensational forms that they are reading: French romance novels, gothic fiction and spasmodic poems. The characters narrate the experience of engaging with fictional worlds and their place within them, an educational process that has high stakes for young, desiring women. They also narrate their affective dissonance as they recognise the risks involved in passively giving way to their bodily pleasure. These are narratives of development that theorise the messiness of inhabiting fictional worlds and actual bodies.

Chapter 2 turns to the affects that stick to the sensation author, using the periodical press's conflation of the supposed immorality of female sensation writers and their characters as a starting point. The chapter focuses on Florence Wilford's *Nigel Bartram's Ideal* (1869), a little-known novel about a sensation writer reformed of her 'morbid' influences. Morbid was an important emotion word used to describe someone (especially a woman) who was considered a threat to the social order, but it could also mean someone who became too absorbed in her own feelings. Wilford shows how the author's work and body figure as barometers for her morality. I relate Wilford's narrative to a range of texts that similarly associate writing sensational narratives with morbidity: Charlotte Yonge's domestic realist novel *The Clever Woman of the Family* (1865) and American Louisa May Alcott's *Behind a Mask: or, A Woman's Power* (1866) and *Little Women* (1868–9). Yet Wilford's novel also details its protagonist's transformation from morbid woman to 'clever woman', a state I liken to Sara Ahmed's 'affect alien' but which offers more hopeful possibilities for community and connectivity.

Chapter 3 discusses narrative affects in Oliphant's *Salem Chapel* and Collins's *Armadale* (1866) by way of sensational newspapers, trials and gossip. What can the transmission of these sensational narratives tell us about public and private feelings? I employ Zunshine's notion of embodied transparency to argue that in both public and private spaces, the body becomes a site of emotional legibility. Yet Oliphant and Collins expose that very invitation, so vital to the form of sensationalism, as violating. In *Salem Chapel*, Oliphant questions sensationalism's reliance on voyeuristic thrills, and specifically its treatment of women's bodies as the source of such voyeurism. While *Armadale* betrays an anxiety about a mass of readers hungry for sensational stories, the novel also, through Lydia Gwilt, explores the possibilities of playful narrative self-construction. Lydia, a villainess who revels in her skills of disguise, becomes a fictional character when she is written about in the newspaper. Her reaction to reading her own diary – 'It makes my heart beat, it makes my face flush, only to read about it now!' – suggests that she is equal parts sensation character, reader and writer (662). While Oliphant's novel seems to recommend seclusion as the only form of self-preservation, Collins's characters adopt more flexible models of sensationalism and selfhood.

Chapter 4 explores differing ways in which bodily sympathy takes shape in sensation fiction, specifically linking this understanding of sympathy to crowd behaviour. While late Victorian crowd psychology and some concepts from contemporary affect theory imply that the crowd offers a release from social hierarchies, Victorian fiction shows the crowd, and especially the mob, as a site in which social distinctions matter and become visible. The chapter focuses on crowds in the work of Ellen Wood and

Caroline Clive, an early sensation author whose work deserves more attention. Wood represents the dark side of contagious feeling in her depiction of a mob in *A Life's Secret*, a novel that features both a sensational plot and a critique of what Wood saw as immoral Trade Unionists. In a striking convergence of fictional and actual bodies, the serial publication of the novel led to an actual mob, in which rioters protested her anti-union stance. Clive depicts the mob differently in her proto-sensation novel *Paul Ferroll* (1855): she understands the mob as an innately human phenomenon and uses it to highlight her protagonist's disturbingly incongruous affects. Throughout, I link their depictions of shared feeling to the ways in which the narrators direct our sympathy towards (or away from) certain characters.

The final chapter further explores embodied theories of Victorian sympathy but focuses more on characterisation than narration. Sensation fiction encouraged readers to experience characters' lives as though they were their own, and this scenario was seen as particularly problematic for female readers who somehow risked becoming the characters about whom they read. I explore this scenario in Collins's *The Woman in White*, Thomas Hardy's *Desperate Remedies* and Charles Reade's *Griffith Gaunt* through depictions of female doubles. Unlike gothic narratives, sensation novels rewrite the double not as a harbinger of death but as a sympathetic figure. As characters confront possible future or past versions of themselves in the form of a double, one's counterfictional life becomes not just a theoretical concept but a living, breathing being. The chapter briefly extends this argument to male doubles with a discussion of Collins's *Armadale* and *Poor Miss Finch*. These plots suggest that physical susceptibility to others – the kind of susceptibility that permitted such nervousness in sensation readers – was not inherently harmful or disturbing but might be exciting or even healing.

The brief coda attends to the affective pleasures of sensational reading but also the pleasures of not reading, exploring the affects associated with distracted reading and pauses in serial reading. Throughout the book, I ask what knowledge the sensorial, emotive and playful world of sensationalism offers up to its readers. What emerges is that sensation authors, in these popular novels, theorise ways in which our bodies respond to differing narratives and how our interconnected bodies themselves become sites for narrative interpretation, even as they continually resist and challenge such interpretation.

Notes

1 Oliphant, in her 1862 review, praises the effectiveness of this scene: 'Few readers will be able to resist the mysterious thrill of this sudden touch. The sensation is distinct and indisputable' (571). D. A. Miller, in his early and important analysis of the novel, notes that this scene is first and foremost about affective transmission via touch (even as he also highlights the gender dynamics): 'Released from – and with – the Woman, nervousness touches and enters the Man: Anne's nervous gesture is at once sympathetically "caught" in Walter's nervous response to it' (110–11).
2 Dehn Gilmore has challenged the critical emphasis on touch in sensation fiction, specifically countering Miller's reading. She says that the Victorian reader's experience of the sensational was as much about sight as it was about touch, leading her to equate the experience of the sensation reader to an exhibition attendee (88). Admittedly, sight is hugely important in these novels, which demand that readers watch and read other bodies, but I would qualify her argument to point out that exhibition-goers were also stimulated by interactions with other bodies, sounds, smells and tastes. Gilmore presents a brilliant reading of Mr Fairlie's room as similar to a bewildering exhibition, but it is worth noting that he is especially concerned about loud noises and people's bodies coming too close to his own. What I take from Gilmore's creative reading is that the sensation novel is concerned with (and offers strategies for) the 'over-stimulated' body more generally (89).
3 I am influenced by Maia McAleavey's claim in *The Bigamy Plot* that 'focusing on plot illuminates unexpected relationships between canonical and popular texts, allowing us to imagine new literary-historical genealogies' (13). I focus not only on plot in what follows but on the use of affective and melodramatic language – and the self-reflexivity that accompanies such language – across canonical and popular texts.
4 John R. Reed also uses the term in *Dickens's Hyperrealism* (2010). He borrows the term *hyperreality* from Umberto Eco to refer to 'Dickens's ability to convey a sense of the everyday world while at the same time almost magically transforming it' (4). I consider many of Dickens's novels to be sensation novels – as did Victorian reviewers – and thus Reed's understanding of hyperreality as exaggerated reality is similar to how I am employing the term here. Where we depart is in his positioning Dickens as 'nonrealist' or as

directly opposing realism (106). Instead, I understand hyperrealism as exaggerated realism, and I thus have a more flexible understanding of realism.

5 Ahmed further argues in *The Cultural Politics of Emotion* that knowledge cannot be separated from feelings or sensations since knowledge is bound up with 'all those feelings that are crucially felt on the bodily surface, the kind of surface where we touch and are touched by the world' (171).

6 Gilbert includes a lengthy, thought-provoking section on genre in her book. She says in the introduction, 'Genre is a category that has less to do with intrinsic properties of particular texts than the needs and concerns of readers reading those texts – a particular era and cultural group, its concatenation of fears and desires and market forces which take shape from and feed those trends' (3–4).

7 McAleavey notes that while the sensation novel was nearly synonymous with the bigamy plot for a time, traces of this plot are in fact present in 'many of the period's best known and most respected novels' (3).

8 Many sensation authors, especially Charles Reade, attempted to combat arguments that their books were unrealistic by explaining that their stories were lifted from newspaper accounts. In his 1868 preface to *Hard Cash*, he writes that the novel is 'a fiction built on truths; and these truths have been gathered by long, severe, systematic labour, from a multitude of volumes, pamphlets, journals, reports, blue-books, manuscript narratives, letters, and living people' (3).

9 Again, hyperrealism is not a rejection of realism since realism is defined by a degree of self-consciousness. George Levine of course claims that nineteenth-century novelists were 'self-conscious about the nature of their medium' (4). And Tabitha Sparks argues that 'the presence of a self-referential narrator and frequent allusion to art, fiction and their relationship to life' are part of the 'metafictional narrative techniques' that we can locate in Victorian realism ('Sensation Intervention' 156).

10 I discuss speed and sensation in my recent article, '"I veer about between hope and despair": Utopian Visions in Victorian Sensation Fiction'. Critics linked sensation novels' fast pacing to the idea that they were quickly written, cheap and disposable; they were also called 'fast' due to their scandalous content. Yet speed within sensation novels is typically marked as terrifying by characters. And, in turn, slow and careful watchfulness is vital to solving mysteries.

11 Beth Palmer argues that Braddon, along with Florence Marryat and Ellen Wood, 'consciously highlight[s] sensation as performative by repeating or ironizing aspects of it, and by attempting to foster a consciousness of that performance in the readership or audience' (13–14).
12 On *The Doctor's Wife*'s generic hybridity, see Gilbert (1997), Golden (2003) and Sparks (2000). Braddon's lesser-known novels have received attention for their metafictional qualities as well. Anne-Marie Beller finds in Braddon's later-century novel *Vixen* (1879) a 'satirical treatment of the aspiring "woman of letters"' ('Popularity' 250). Lyn Pykett notes that *Eleanor's Victory* exhibits a 'highly developed self-reflexivity about its own fictional mode' ('Mary Elizabeth Braddon' 127).
13 Rylance explains, 'It was important to religious experience, because of the stress placed on the effort to salvation through individual striving and worth, and because contemporary theological argument held that the will was an indication of the special distinction between man and brute. It was important in ethical argument, because it justified ethical prescriptions and rewards. It was important in ontological arguments, because it declared man to be more than the sum of his determining causes' (194).
14 For a discussion of the relationship between sensation and Darwin's ideas, see Susan David Bernstein's 'Ape Anxiety: Sensation Fiction, Evolution, and the Genre Question'. She links *Origin of Species* with *The Woman in White*, noting that both 'Darwin and serialized scandalous novels of the decade' possessed 'an underlying anxiety about ambiguous boundaries' (250–1).
15 Bain was close friends with Mill but his consistent emphasis on the human body means that he approaches questions of the will from this materialist lens. Bain assisted with Mill's *Systems of Logic* (1843), and Mill wrote a complimentary review of Bain's work in 1859. Bain's earlier *The Senses and the Intellect* (1855) included a section on will that he redrafted multiple times and was never completely happy with. George Henry Lewes and Spencer nonetheless praised his early analysis of 'the formation of the will from reflex action' (Rylance 195).
16 Tiffany Watt Smith has argued for the flinch as a way to explore growing concerns in the mid-Victorian period that complex emotional experiences were being overturned in favour of bodily reflexes. A flinch 'suggests porous ways of being, pointing up visceral co-experience and the wandering of bodily affects' (19).

17 Along similar lines, Nicholas Dames calls attention to the scene's 'automatic, physical responses', and claims that sensation fiction made visible 'a dynamic that mainstream, Victorian fiction grappled with in its own ways: the developing sense that consciousness was at least partly comprised of, and possibly even dominated by, the formerly debased realm of automatic, nervous functions' ('1825–1880' 215–16, 218).
18 I discuss the use of the blush in sensation fiction in Chapters 1 and 2.
19 Suzanne Keen observes that in the eighteenth and nineteenth centuries terms such as sympathy and 'fellow feeling' had meanings similar to our contemporary understanding of empathy (42–3).
20 In *Victorian Skin*, Gilbert discusses *A Tale of Two Cities* and presents a different reading of sympathy than I offer here, opposing it to 'sentiment'. She finds in Dickens's novel, and elsewhere in early nineteenth-century culture, that sympathy is formed via individual perception and judgement, while sentiment came to mean a more irrational, contagious and free-floating phenomenon that comes from without rather than within. Alongside rational sympathy, she claims, existed 'an older, though increasingly discredited model of contagious sentiment, a wash of feeling that overtopped the boundaries of judgment and perhaps even individuality' (165). She argues that while sympathy takes hold of the mid-Victorian imagination, this 'model of contagious, transpersonal emotion does remain in evidence even in the mid-nineteenth-century "realist" novel', where it is often associated with 'political threat – often specifically, the French Revolution' (167). I also find this contagious, transpersonal model of emotion in a range of texts from the period, but I do not find it so clearly distinct from 'sympathy'. In fact, rather than a separation of sympathy and sentiment, what I locate is a more flexible use of the term sympathy, as it retains a much more embodied and transpersonal meaning. While Gilbert's reading in many ways aligns with my own, an earlier version of this material appeared as an essay in Stephen Ahern's *Affect Theory and Literary Critical Practice* before Gilbert's *Victorian Skin* was published. I thus want to note that we came to our conclusions independently. I am grateful that I can acknowledge and build on her readings in this book.
21 See Allan (2015) and Ortiz-Robles (2010). Alisha Walters's (2020) recent work on affect and empire in Mary Seacole's *Wonderful Adventures of Mrs Seacole in Many Lands* (1857) is also worth noting. Walter's placement of affect within imperialist and racialised

contexts has exciting implications for future work on sensation novels.
22 Warhol details how sentimental fiction can make readers cry: a 'narratology of the techniques commonly employed in sentimental narratives' include narrative voices that employ poetic devices; suggestions that representation or language cannot express the depths of emotion; omniscient narration that emphasises the perspective of the sufferer; use of direct address; and frequent close calls and last-minute reversals (41–8). *East Lynne*, which borrows heavily from the sentimental mode, employs all of these techniques, as do many other sensation novels.

I

Immersive Reading and Sensational Emplotment

In Margaret Oliphant's 1862 essay 'Sensation Novels', she complains about the exaggeration and supposed speed of sensation fiction and other serial forms. By 1867, however, her vitriol was reserved for the genre's candid depictions of desire and its impact on young female readers (568). This later article, simply entitled, 'Novels', was part of a national conversation about women's reading, one prompted by the popularity of sensation fiction.[1] Oliphant worries that sensation fiction will disrupt the English practice of family reading and, instead, will lead young women to read and interpret sensation narratives in private (259). She is critical of both female sensation authors and readers:

> It is a shame to women so to write; and it is a shame to the women who read and accept as a true representation of themselves and their ways the equivocal talk and fleshly inclinations herein attributed to them. Their patronage of such books is in reality an adoption and acceptance of them. It may be done in carelessness, it may be done in that mere desire for something startling which the monotony of ordinary life is apt to produce; but it is debasing to everybody concerned. (275)

Oliphant makes two assumptions that were repeated by a range of reviewers in this period: that female readers understood these books to offer 'a true representation of themselves', and that this sensational realism was in opposition to 'the monotony of ordinary life'. In 1868, Francis Paget expressed unease about the 'kind of follies, scrapes, and difficulties' into which a girl might fall 'who should take the sensational novel as her guide in the commonplace events of everyday life' (308). A few years later, the author of 'The Vice of Reading' (1874) similarly argues that contemporary 'works of imagination' have 'a dangerous tendency: since they encourage hopes which are never fulfilled, nourish nothing but illusions, and ... engender a discontent with life as it exists' (253). This rhetoric offers little insight into the actual experiences of readers in this period, but the frequency of this kind of language indicates 'how much was imagined to be at stake in the ordinary act of picking up a novel to read' (Gettelman 112).

This act was clearly gendered, as women readers were understood to be more naive and more susceptible to what we might call fictional feelings. While Oliphant focuses primarily on inappropriate sexual desires, she also voices the concern that the genre encourages strong feelings of any kind, calling the sensation novel 'the narrative of many thrills of feeling' (259). Robyn Warhol's observation that in Western culture, 'textually induced tears' are associated with effeminacy, passivity and a susceptibility to manipulation is relevant here (31). Yet whether provoking tears or sexual excitement, the act of reading need not be understood as entirely passive or non-agential, as many sensation novels show. In this chapter, I discuss Amelia Edwards's *Hand and Glove* and *Barbara's History*, and Rhoda Broughton's *Cometh Up as a Flower*, all of which engage with the mid-century debate about women's reading and sensationalism. The novels feature young women whose absorbing reading lingers in their lived realities: the heroines understand and narrate the events of their lives as sensational as they form patterns of affect and expectation based on the narratives that they read. The female characters in these texts engage with pre-sensational modes – romance novels, gothic fiction and spasmodic poetry – but their arguments have explicit relevance for sensation fiction. Edwards and Broughton do suggest that there are risks to immersive reading, especially for young, unmarried women, but their depictions of women's reading practices and their theorisations of affect are more generous, playful and parodic than those offered by the reviewers above.

In representing the messy overlaps of fictional and real-world feelings, these novels explore the affective experience of emplotment, 'the way by which a sequence of events fashioned into a story is gradually revealed to be a story of a particular kind' (White 7).[2] David Herman explains that emplotment is 'the way events are, in being narrated, set out in a particular order that in turn implies a particular way of understanding causal-chronological relationships among them' (71). There are overlaps between emplotment and genre, especially if we understand genre, as Lauren Berlant does, to be 'an aesthetic structure of affective expectation' (4). Put simply, for these young women, sensational reading causes them to bring certain affective expectations into their lives. Yet it also permits these female character narrators to write themselves a life and formulate a meaningful affective language as they narrate the experience of inhabiting both a fictional world and a developing female body. Edwards and Broughton would agree with contemporary cognitive narratologists like Blakey Vermeule that fiction permits us to 'practice new emotional situations' (Vermeule xii). These novels thus provide models for ways in which women could engage with sensational narratives in safe, satisfying and even pleasurable ways.

Through such commentary on fictional reading, the novels revise what George Levine calls the 'disenchantment' plot, a common trope in the English *Bildungsroman*. This plot traces a hero or heroine 'who must learn to recognize and reject youthful fantasies (normally first learned from books) in order to accept a less than romantic and more tediously quotidian reality' (Levine 71). Nineteenth-century examples include Austen's *Northanger Abbey* (1817), Braddon's *The Doctor's Wife* and Dickens's *Great Expectations*. The heroines of Edwards and Broughton's fiction seem initially to follow this plot: Marguerite from *Hand and Glove*, captivated with romance novels, rejects her reliable fiancé and begins a new romance, only to realise that her new lover is a fraud. In *Barbara's History*, Barbara assumes that her husband is hiding his first wife in a secret room, à la *Jane Eyre* (1847). She later realises her mistake and reunites with her husband, after expressing remorse for her youthful fantasies. Finally, Broughton's Nell channels the tortured lover of Tennyson's *Maud* (1855) through her melodramatic excess, but she ultimately marries a boring older man and dies soon after. Despite the seeming endorsement of quiet marital life, the novels validate the women's so-called fantasies and, significantly, emphasise that a 'quotidian reality' has radically different stakes for men and women. Edwards and Broughton insist – if Broughton more firmly – that the sensational qualities of their characters' lives are worth telling. Additionally, the use of first-person character narration means that there is no condescending narrator observing a young woman's supposed missteps.[3]

In each novel, the sensational heroine is contrasted with a more pragmatic heroine who fits squarely in the realist mode and who presents an alternative reading model, though not always a positive one. The reader, too, must negotiate various narratives, as the texts are filled with quotations from a range of writers – both as chapter epigraphs and embedded within the novels – as well as references to other authors and works. These intertextual references show that Edwards and Broughton were demanding intelligent, critical readers who could assess and compare various narratives at once. Kate Flint has argued that Braddon and Broughton in particular encouraged their readers 'to enter into an active process of interpretation' (Flint 283). Karen M. Odden, who discusses Braddon's intertextuality in *John Marchmont's Legacy*, suggests that self-reflexive novels like these could 'teach a woman reader to sustain a balance between two modes of reading: one in which she empathically engages with the characters, and the other, in which she sustains self-awareness about herself as a reader' (23). Indeed, it is certainly possible to read in both modes. Warhol has questioned whether 'a critical awareness of formulaic effects is any defense against their power over audiences' (xvi). For instance, she discusses the 'mixed feelings' she has when engaging with the marriage plot as a contemporary feminist, what she refers to as 'the double experience of negative feminist political critique and positive physical readerly affect' (64). Discerning Victorian readers could similarly have mixed feelings when encountering sensation fiction. A state of affective dissonance, 'the unsettled state in which we experience more than one *feeling* at the same time', is often the situation of the sensational readers within these novels, as they are attracted to romantic and sensational plots but gradually become aware of the ways in which they can also be linked to their social subordination (Ladino 22).[4] While Braddon explores similar ideas in many of her novels, I focus on lesser-discussed novelists Edwards and Broughton, with the intention of broadening our understanding of sensation writing. Nonetheless, my claims about the ways in which these authors self-reflexively engage with sensationalism and narrative affects are relevant to a broad range of sensation writers.

In what follows, I first examine Edwards's *Hand and Glove*, an early sensation novel published in 1858: it details the young Marguerite's flirtation with a man who is not her fiancé, and this man's secret identity and dramatic suicide, but is simultaneously critical of such sensational contrivances through the narrator's disapproval of the heroine's scandalous reading material. Edwards further shows the results of women's uncritical reading in *Barbara's History* by juxtaposing the affective, fantasy-prone heroine Barbara with her more pragmatic aunt, who chides her for following gothic scripts. In its reference to, but simultaneous resistance from, the sensational device of the bigamy plot, Edwards complicates the novel's categorisation as sensation fiction.

In contrast to Edwards's vulnerable young women, Broughton's Nell LeStrange is a self-aware heroine who uses fictional forms, from Shakespeare to Victorian poetry, as a way to make sense of her affects and desires. The novel is ultimately more hopeful than Edwards's in showing how Nell builds upon the stories that she reads in her act of narrative self-construction. Nell tells the story of her past from a present in which she is dying and the man she loves has already died. Unlike Edwards's heroines, for whom entry into a sensational plotline poses social and bodily risks, Nell mourns the sensational plot that she will never have. Yet the overall tone of the novel is more playful than mournful, as Nell cites and references other literary texts with great pleasure. If Marguerite's primary influence is French fiction and Barbara's is *Jane Eyre*, Nell's is spasmodic poetry, a form of narrative poetry popular in England from the 1830s to the mid-1850s. The genre typically featured a dramatic poet-hero who seeks out strong sensations, and it was a physiological and affective form like sensation fiction, though spasmodic poems were typically written by working-class men. Nell appropriates the language of spasmodic poetry, in the process developing a vocabulary with which to articulate her own desire. The novel is an important example of the affective expression typical of sensation fiction, even if it also parodies that expression.

Feeling fiction in *Hand in Glove*

In her chapter on sensationalism in *A Literature of Their Own*, Elaine Showalter mentions a number of female sensationalists who 'valued passion and assertive action', including Braddon, Broughton, Marryat, Ouida and Amelia Edwards (154). Edwards, though recognised as an Egyptologist, is perhaps the least-known novelist of this group.[5] In the Victorian period, she was a popular literary figure who wrote eight novels and three travel narratives, contributed regularly to Charles Dickens's periodicals, and received honorary degrees for her work in Egyptology. All of Edwards's novels are characterised by sensational plotlines and an affective vocabulary. Her first novel, *My Brother's Wife* (1855), features an affair and a murder plot; *Half a Million of Money* (1865) features deceit and robbery; and her final novel, *Lord Brackenbury* (1880), begins with the main character's disappearance. Her novels articulate the female fantasies of escape and adventure that Showalter identifies as characteristic of the sensation genre, but they are also attentive to the ways in which such fantasies can lead to domestic discontentment.

Edwards's *Hand and Glove* is an important precursor to *Barbara's History*, and it helps to define what I see as her mix of realism and hyperrealism. While Edwards was not responding to the sensation debate in 1858 as explicitly as she would in *Barbara's History*, she was nonetheless writing a kind of popular fiction that would eventually be defined as sensation fiction, and was consciously reflecting on how such fiction could, or should, influence her readers. *Hand and Glove* is narrated by English governess Gartha Wylde, who is sent to the French countryside to work as a companion to the young, rich Marguerite Delahaye. The narrator, Gartha, is a stern realist, while Marguerite is a romantic young woman. The narrative recounts Marguerite's choice between her serious cousin, Charles Gautier, and the town's captivating new minister, Xavier Hamel, who initially wins the romantic rivalry. Just before Marguerite is to marry Hamel, however, secrets of his past emerge – including embezzlement and penal service – and he dies by suicide. This turn of events enables Marguerite to realise, with Gartha's assistance, that Charles is a more appropriate match for her after all. While Marguerite doesn't inhabit a pre-existing plot in the more literal manner of Barbara, the seductive Hamel comes to represent the most sensational element of the story: her romance with him effectively means entering a world of melodrama. Thus, though this early novel does not track emplotment in the explicit manner of Edwards and Broughton's later fiction, it sets up the association between sensational reading and romance that they explore.

Hamel seems to have stepped out of a novel into the quiet community of Montrocher. One of the villagers notes that 'there are plenty of young ladies who can see in him only a hero of romance' (123). His entry into Marguerite's life destabilises not only her plot but her identity. Like Isabel in Braddon's *The Doctor's Wife*, who imagines Lansdell to be 'the hero of a story-book' (214), and Laura in *Eleanor's Victory*, who wants her lover 'to be a little wicked; like the Giaour, or Manfred' (vol. 3, 98), Marguerite longs for a romantic hero to disrupt the monotony of her life. The word most often used to describe Hamel is 'fascinating': Gartha records that he possesses 'a something which was at the same time fascinating and repellent' and that his 'powers of fascination were almost magnetic' (64, 151). Natalie Rose has identified Dickens's repeated use of this word as related to anxieties about the will: 'The rhetoric of fascination in [Dickens's] works describes tenuously bounded selves whose volitional capabilities are too weak to withstand the psychic influence of other characters' (506). She cites a range of other mid-century thinkers, including Mill and Bain, who understand the will as 'fend[ing] off states of susceptibility, suggestibility, and fascination' (517). In the context of sensation fiction, fascinating characters not only influence others psychically but affectively. Rose explains that the power of fascination threatens discreet selfhood and 'lies in its anti-individualist traversing of borders', so that '[p]roperly regulated subjects' in Dickens's fiction 'must neither allow their vulnerable boundaries to be invaded, nor overstep those boundaries' (528).[6] Neither Hamel nor Marguerite are 'properly regulated subjects'; his physical presence causes Marguerite's body to betray her desire, as she blushes and stammers in his company. Yet Marguerite's reactions also show that there is a pleasure in such 'anti-individualist traversing of borders'. Indeed, borders are blurred as Hamel and Marguerite affect and are affected by one another's bodies.

Their first encounter occurs, scandalously, when Hamel gives his first sermon. This moment also sets up Marguerite's governess, Gartha, as a ready and willing body reader. Gartha notices that Hamel searches the audience but that his eyes eventually rest on Marguerite. Marguerite catches his gaze: she 'coloured crimson, strove to repress the faintest trembling of a smile, and fixed her eyes on her prayer book' (65). The blush, which Darwin calls 'the most peculiar and most human of all expressions', is a usefully ambiguous affect (*Expressions* 286). In *Victorian Skin*, Gilbert references Thomas Burgess's *Physiology or Mechanism of Blushing* (1839), the most substantial mid-century book on the blush, which notes that when blushing, one's face typically 'droops' and the eyes are averted (78). Marguerite's multifaceted reaction – her blushing, repression of a smile and averted eyes – registers her pleasure, self-consciousness and modesty all at once. While I read her affects as betraying these emotional states, Gartha never names them as such, allowing Marguerite's blush to highlight, in Gilbert's words, 'a process of bodily affect becoming, but not yet quite defined as, emotion' (65). The blush, like all affects, exists 'at the moment prior to the articulation of emotion that leads toward (or away from) knowledge, whether of the self of the object of observation' (65). In search of such knowledge, Gartha moves from observing Marguerite to watching Hamel: 'I could discern neither admiration nor disapproval in his face. It was the expression with which one would contemplate a picture, being more desirous to criticise than praise' (65). Hamel's intense look doesn't easily correlate to an existing emotion, hence Gartha's need for metaphor. Marguerite's affective dissonance in relation to Hamel continues when he more openly flirts with her in her home. This time, Gartha recognises and links Marguerite's affects with their associated emotions: as Hamel turns her piano pages and hangs over her 'like a lover', she is 'trembling, confused, happy and fearful at the same time' (150).

Edwards conflates courtship and reading when Hamel attempts to guide Marguerite's reading experiences. While skills employed in reading novels – specifically, Theory of Mind – could be translated to the courtship process, both reading and courtship risked exposing young women to behaviours and feelings of which they were meant to be ignorant. While Gartha attempts to extend Marguerite's reading interests to intellectual fare, Hamel offers her '*Indiana, Lelia, Mauprat*, and others of the early productions of George Sand' (112). She abandons the English reading Gartha recommends to her in favour of Sand's more risqué fiction. Gartha records, 'So fascinated was she by these extraordinary romances that, but for her English studies, she would have given up her whole time to them' (112). Victorian reviewers would later associate French novels with sensation novels: a reviewer of Collins's *No Name* (1862) called the sensation novel 'a plant of foreign growth', explaining, 'It comes to us from France, and it can only be imported in a mutilated condition' (*Reader* 14). Edwards travelled through France with a female friend before beginning *Hand and Glove*, and her biographer Joan Rees notes that the novel belongs to the time of Edwards's life when she visited artists' studios and smoked cigars, and 'when the writings and behaviour of George

Sand were part of the atmosphere of the circles she moved in' (71). Yet here Edwards employs the common practice of using the French novel as 'an instant signifier of immorality' (Flint 287).

Hamel, though, urges Marguerite to gain knowledge from Sand's novels, explaining that 'good novels are better than experience' (107). He furthermore encourages her by offering his own theory of reading:

> A novel should be read quickly, and without interruption – or left unread. Nay, I could almost go so far as to say that it is not worth reading if you can bear to lay it down at any moment, like a piece of needlework. The author should hold you captive, and the people of his book should become your own familiar friends. A novel is then an ideal world, which, while it lasts, seems no less real than our own. (107)

Hamel's idea that fictional worlds should be 'no less real than our own' suggests that truly immersive reading breaks down affective barriers between fictional and actual worlds. Both Gartha and Charles are unwilling that Hamel 'should mould [Marguerite's] character through the medium of a class of literature which, however admirable in its way, deals too largely with feeling to be quite healthy reading for the inexperienced and the young' (112). Sand's novels threaten, like Hamel himself, to overwhelm her, to awaken her body in a way that Gartha and Charles see as alarming. The novel makes clear the correlation between the plotting of Hamel and Sand's plots: both force Marguerite away from her arranged union with Charles and awaken her to other affective possibilities.

Yet Marguerite eventually abandons both her romantic reading and her sensational plot. Gartha records that after she leaves Hamel, she travels throughout Europe and the 'life of intellectual and bodily activity worked miracles upon her' (283). Her turn to Charles is a turn towards pragmatism and realism. Part of Marguerite's unhappiness in her initial engagement to Charles is that she was not permitted to choose her husband for herself. It is in her choice to marry him that Marguerite becomes a self-determining subject, one free to make her own decisions and to withstand the saturation of personal boundaries and affective plots. It is in this investment of free will over the wilful body that the novel ultimately departs from sensationalism. Yet even with its endorsement of conventionality and realism, the only period of her life and Marguerite's that Gartha narrates is the sensational part. Gartha and Marguerite's marriages are thus marked as nonnarratable, as incapable of generating a story and having a narrative future. In contrast, the sensational demands narration and is 'worthy of being told' (Prince 56). We can locate Edwards's sensationalism via this preoccupation with utilising sensational elements while simultaneously critiquing them.

Barbara's History rewrites the bigamy plot

Edwards's relationship to the sensation genre remained unstable: when she published *Barbara's History*, reviewers were unsure of how to classify the novel. The *Athenaeum* assumed that the sensational moments in the novel were simply evidence of Edwards pandering to a scandal-loving reading public, describing the novel as 'a compromise between [Edwards's] own sense of right and the depraved appetite of the public' (16). Three years later, when she published *Half a Million of Money*, the *Standard* labelled it 'improbable and sensational' but noted that it nonetheless remained 'far above the Miss Braddon school' (6). Without precisely articulating it, what these reviewers seem to express is the way in which Edwards's novels both exploit and condemn sensational techniques. Barbara begins the novel by explaining that her autobiography will only be the story of her youth, since 'the romance of life is mostly lived out before we reach middle age, and beyond that point the tale grows monotonous' (1). She thus sets up readerly expectations for a narrative that will be sensational. Just thinking back to her childhood and writing the phrase 'when I was young' causes her to break off and exclaim, '*When I was young!* They are but four words; and yet ... they have power to arrest my pen, and blind my eyes with unaccustomed tears' (1). Edwards opens the novel by foregrounding narrative affects, much like Walter's 'I tremble, now, when I write' (23). The very first page reveals Barbara's body as disruptive and wilful.

In contrast to the emotive Barbara is her Aunt Sandyshaft, a character so pragmatic and undemonstrative that she is comedic. For much of the novel, Barbara's aunt undercuts her niece's strong feeling with witty comments. The plot of *Barbara's History* borrows from Dickens's *David Copperfield* (1850), Charlotte Brontë's *Jane Eyre* and *Villette* (1853), and Wood's *East Lynne*, although the novel is most obviously indebted to *Jane Eyre*, as early reviewers noted.⁷ Barbara is rescued from an unfeeling father and negligent older sisters when her aunt, reminiscent of David Copperfield's Aunt Betsy, invites her to come live with her in the country. While there, Barbara develops a childish love for the adult Hugh Farquhar, a figure who himself recalls Brontë's Rochester. He encourages in Barbara a love of art, which she develops when she is sent by her father to a German boarding school. Hugh later finds her at the school, when she is now seventeen to his thirty-four, and Barbara accepts his offer of marriage, leaving her artistic career behind. Once living at Hugh's estate, however, Barbara appears to find herself beset by 'the traditional Victorian inconvenience of a previous wife still living', or what Maia McAleavey calls the 'spouse in the house' plot (Gilbert, *Disease* 10; McAleavey 47). She discovers a strange sitting room, hidden behind a secret library door, and sees a dark-haired woman wandering the property. Barbara flees and lives on the continent as a widow named Mrs Carylon, where she gives birth to Hugh's son and receives an offer of marriage, which she declines. Eventually, she learns from her aunt that Hugh is in fact not a bigamist, and she returns to her ailing husband in time to nurse him back to health.

While the novel flirts with a possible career in art for Barbara, her father teases her for thinking that painting could possibly be her 'profession' and tells her that she '*must* marry' (150). Although the professional plot is ultimately overturned for the romance plot, Barbara's capacity for deep feeling is linked to her artistic abilities and remains an important aspect of her identity. As a lonely, sensitive child who was 'quickly swayed to smiles or tears' (7), she finds salvation in a pile of boxes containing three or four dozen books, in a scene recalling David's discovery of his father's books in *David Copperfield*.⁸ She finds a 'second life in [her] books', relating, 'The personages of my fictitious world became as real to me as those by whom I was surrounded in my daily life' (7). Barbara demonstrates a similar blurring of reality and fiction later in the novel, when she sees the opera for the first time. In recalling the event, the older Barbara can remember no details of the performance, only her sensory experience: 'To this day I remember nothing but the bewilderment with which I gazed and listened. I can recall neither the names of the singers, nor the plot, nor the title of the piece, nor anything but the result produced upon myself' (219). She explains that the performance 'carried me out of myself' (219). Like the literary characters that young Barbara believes are 'real', when watching the opera, Barbara 'could hardly believe that all was not real – that these moving masses of soldiers, nobles, and priests were not actual characters, swayed by actual passion' (219). Edwards again shows how Barbara's narrative affects collapse the fictional and the real, so that such distinctions fail to matter for her.

Barbara's strong sensations are not always marked as harmful, but her imagination and keen sensory impressions become complicated when she learns of Hugh and creates a romantic image of him. Even as Barbara achieves her romantic fantasy in marrying Hugh, Edwards consistently deflates her heroine's imaginings. Like Hamel in *Hand and Glove*, Hugh's veiled past generates fascination and results in neighbourhood gossip: 'Tales of recklessness and profusion, of wild adventure, and of travels extended far beyond the beaten routes, were told of him throughout the county' (30). Barbara, though only a child, gets caught up in such gossip and associates Hugh's name 'with those of my favourite heroes', comparing him to Byron, as well as 'Sinbad and Don Quixote, Tom Jones, Prince Camaralzaman, and Robinson Crusoe' (31). Barbara's fantasies take a tangible form when she draws imaginary sketches of him in the flyleaves of her storybooks, integrating Hugh's likeness with the tales of adventure and romance that she enjoys reading. Though Barbara is not entirely disappointed when she finally meets her romantic idol, she admits that Hugh is not the 'brilliant hero with the Byronic collar whom I had been picturing to myself', as he is 'not handsome' and is older than she imagined (45). Yet when she meets him again, years later as a young woman capable of desire, she is so overcome that she faints: 'it was the sight of that one swarthy face, and the shock of those dark eyes shining into mine, that sent the room reeling' (160). Like Hamel, he is the primary source of sensation in the text and his influence encourages Barbara to read and narrate her own plot as sensational.

Hugh is both a figure of romance for Barbara and a character for whom the reader also has certain expectations, given his likeness to earlier Byronic heroes. His entrance into Barbara's life signals a shift in the narrative, as both Barbara and the reader anticipate sensational events. The wait is not long. Once in Hugh's family estate, Barbara discovers a secret room, hidden off from the library. As she enters the room, she relates her agitation via short, choppy phrases and questions: 'My heart beat violently. My forehead was bathed in a cold perspiration. I asked myself for the first time what it was that I was about to see when this door was opened? What chamber, long closed – what deed of mystery, long forgotten – what family secret, long buried, would be revealed to my eyes?' (349). Recalling Austen's Catherine from *Northanger Abbey*, Barbara becomes a melodramatic heroine in this moment, her body betraying the effects of her emplotment. She is prepared, and even hopeful, for the room to reveal a shameful secret or 'the sight of something strange and terrible' (349). Instead, she is disappointed not to find 'a floor stained, perchance, with blood, and furniture giving evidence in its disorder of some fearful struggle enacted long ago; [or] something, perhaps, even more ghastly still' (349). Instead of finding evidence of murder or domestic abuse, she finds only a 'pretty, cheerful, bright little sitting-room' (349). While Edwards foregrounds Barbara's fantasies, she does not, at least initially, permit her heroine to inhabit this sensational world.

Despite Barbara's disappointment upon discovering this rather banal backdrop for what she imagined might be a site of crime and passion, the sitting room does lead to the revelation of a secret. Hugh discovers Barbara in the room and in his convoluted confession he explains that he met a young Italian woman while on his grand tour of the continent years ago. She snuck her way onto his boat in order to run away from her husband, whom she had married only the day before. Though Hugh found in this situation 'an element of the ludicrous', he agreed to take responsibility for her protection (363). He allowed her to live in his home and offered her seclusion, and the woman remains 'haunted to this hour by a morbid fear of discovery' (364). Barbara takes her husband at his word and continues to live with Maddelena until she overhears Hugh call the woman 'sposia mia' (373). We learn later that Hugh conceded in calling Maddelena by her old pet name one final time out of pity. Again, Barbara's reaction is characteristically physical and sensational:

My head burned; my temples throbbed; fears, possibilities, retrospections, thronged and surged upon me, like the waves of a tumultuous sea. I could not think; for I had no power to arrest my thoughts. They racked me, tossed me to and fro, mastered and bewildered me. I could weigh nothing, compare nothing. I only felt that I was wrecked and heart-broken. (373–4)

Barbara has become a sensational body: she cannot 'arrest [her] thoughts', again like Collins's Walter, who is 'conscious of nothing but the confusion of my own thoughts' (27).

Believing that she is only Hugh's mistress and not his legal wife – and led by her wilful body rather than clear thoughts – Barbara decides to leave immediately for the continent with her maid. After months in Italy, Barbara, by a dramatic coincidence, encounters her aunt and learns the truth, that Hugh was never married to Maddelena. Aunt Sandyshaft's humour quickly deflates the drama of the last few months (and chapters). She is shocked to find that Barbara has given birth and exclaims, 'to run away was bad enough; but to commit the additional folly of a baby . . . Ugh!' (444). Aunt Sandyshaft's intrusion and the revelation that follows render sensational plotlines comical because of the raw realism she infuses into a plot that would otherwise stand as a sensational contrivance. She chastises her niece for letting her emotions overtake her: 'You "reasoned" about as much as a child that's frightened by a shadow. The consequence was that you acted like a fool, and ran away. I dare say you thought it very fine, and heroic, and dramatic, and all that sort of thing. Nobody else did' (448). With their opposing reactions, Barbara and Aunt Sandyshaft can be understood to embody two sides of a reader's mind or two very different readers: one who is consumed by the story, while the other critiques its very novelistic status.

Barbara's desertion of her husband can no longer be read as heroic or scandalous, but rather as the mistake of an impulsive and emotional woman – and the result of reading too many novels. The revelation that there is no scandalous secret propels Barbara and the reader away from a sensation plotline, though the surprise is not without its own set of awkward machinations. For instance, the *Athenaeum* insists that it 'break[s] down the entire framework of the story' (15). The reviewer explains that because the novel is a revision of *Jane Eyre*, the reader comes with the assumption that 'like Mr Rochester, Hugh Farquhar is already married' (15). Therefore, in order that Barbara

> may not be censured for pardoning the man who appears to have put upon her the worst affront husband can offer to wife, Miss Edwards covers her hero with so thick and complete a coating of whitewash that there is not enough darkness left to account for what has taken place in the story. It is shown that Hugh never married Maddelena –

the reader thereby learning that his indignation against Mr Farquhar as a bigamist had been misplaced, and that in addition to the pleasurable excitement of reading a good bigamy case, he has also the pleasure of discovering that the supposed criminal is innocent. (15)

Edwards thus delivers to her readers the best of both worlds: the 'pleasurable excitement' of reading sensation fiction complete with the 'pleasure' attached to the moral outcomes of domestic fiction. Mixed feelings, indeed. Though the reviewer initially seems critical of Edwards's novel, he admits, 'we like Miss Edwards all the better for her error. Consenting to humour the existing taste for bigamy stories, she was determined not to make too great a sacrifice of womanly dignity' (15). The reviewer implies that both the fictional Barbara's and the actual Edwards's dignity are preserved by this plot twist.[9] While Edwards's revelation that Hugh never attempted to commit bigamy mars the continuity of the story, he implies that she should be credited with this moral turn.

Yet rather than see Edwards's plot twist as simply 'whitewashing' in order to convey 'her own sense of right', we might imagine that Edwards was very consciously playing with sensational devices while simultaneously protecting herself from the kind of criticism that plagued female novelists like Charlotte Brontë or Braddon, as I explain in more detail in Chapter 2. Further, her intertextual references show Edwards demanding an intelligent reader involved in the act of assessing and comparing various narratives at once. Hyperrealism demands a reader not just attentive to (or hyperaware of) bodily descriptions but to intertextual references, since both offer clues to discerning readers. Contemporary reviewers did remark on the differences between *Jane Eyre* and *Barbara's History*: the *Morning Post* notes that Edwards 'has the strength, without the rudeness, which marked that memorable book *Jane Eyre*' (qtd in Rees 75), and *The Times* writes that *Barbara's History* 'moves along in a luminous atmosphere free from all taint of coarseness and crime' (6). Notably, Lucasta Miller explains that 'coarse' was a 'catch-all moralistic term' used by many reviewers of the Brontë sisters' work to identify their supposedly 'unfeminine and indecorous' writing (85). While reviewers positioned Edwards's work as less rude than *Jane Eyre*, similar to the manner in which she was thought to be 'far above the Miss Braddon school', her engagement with the plot of Brontë's novel points to an important continuity between the two texts (*The Standard* 6).

Specifically, in having Barbara believe that she was falling into the plot of Brontë's novel, and by representing this plot as inherently sensational, the novel proposes a genealogy of sensation fiction that begins with *Jane Eyre*. In fact, many critics – both Victorian and modern – have read *Jane Eyre* as an early sensation novel or as the novel that initiated the sensation craze. Oliphant writes that the origins of sensation fiction 'perhaps began at the time when Jane Eyre made what advanced critics call her "protest" against the conventionalities in which the world clothes itself' (258). And in 1867, George Augustus Sala reminds his readers that *Jane Eyre* 'was to all intents and purposes a "sensational" novel' (52). *Jane Eyre* thus figures as an important predecessor to the sensation genre, both because of the near-bigamy plot and because of Jane's wilfulness and her capacity for and attention to strong feeling.[10] In one of her 'protests', she notoriously claims, 'Women are supposed to be very calm generally: but women feel just as men feel' (109). *Jane Eyre* also opens with an intensely affective scene in which Jane battles with her cousin John: 'I felt a drop or two of blood from my head trickle down my neck, and was sensible of somewhat pungent suffering: these sensations for the time predominated over fear, and I received him in frantic sort' (11). The scene brilliantly establishes sympathy for young Jane and records her affects in ways that clearly anticipate sensation fiction.

Though conservative Victorian reviewers might have found Edwards's novel more acceptable than other stories of the sensational class, her lack of transgressive heroines has meant that she has been less enticing for critics looking back to the sensation novel in search of proto-feminism. The passionate Maddelena is certainly an intriguing female character, but her story is told primarily through Hugh's perspective – which is further mediated through Barbara's narration – and she only enters the novel near the end, in order to reunite Hugh and Barbara. Nonetheless, her story relates the limited possibilities for a woman in an unhappy marriage and is an example of the fantasy of escape that Showalter argues typifies the sensation novel. Her narrative bears similarities to the story of Barbara's sister Hilda, who marries a much older rich man, only to find that she is unhappy. Barbara believes that her sister sells herself for wealth and comfort: 'it was but a bartering of her youth and beauty! Money, dress, position, and the empty vanity of a title – these were her gods, and to these she offered herself as a sacrifice' (215). Edwards gives voice to

Hilda's unhappiness, and Barbara's sympathy tinged with disgust, but Hilda never contemplates leaving her husband. It is likely because of Edwards's concern with female vulnerability that she resists penning triumphant stories of escape and instead focuses on ridding her heroines of such fantasies. Though Edwards's sensation novels certainly indulge in fantasies about forging new identities,[11] Barbara's adoption of the persona Mrs Carylon is anything but liberating, much like the pain that Isabel Carlyle endures after she leaves her husband and impersonates a governess.[12] Indeed, only after Barbara no longer sees Hugh as a romantic hero, and after she recognises that the world she inhabits is not in fact a gothic or sensational plot, can she achieve a happy ending. As in *Hand and Glove*, though, the turn to realism is marked as nonnarratable. Barbara forecasts this on the first page when she says that after 'the romance of life ... the tale grows monotonous' (1).

Edwards does not offer morally didactic fiction – in fact, she once wrote that the didactic novelist was 'the most intolerable of literary bores' ('Art' 226) – but she encourages her reader to learn from the examples of her characters in their deciphering between fiction and reality. Her interest in rewriting the sensation plot and heroine seems to stem from her desire that women not become consumed by literary plots or beguiling men. In both body reading and romantic reading, Edwards's novels suggest, a degree of critical distance is desirable and necessary. Anna Maria Jones argues that sensationalism is 'about willing submission to the text, about agreeing to subject oneself to the "discipline" of reading', but for Edwards such submission can have its drawbacks (22). Nonetheless, Edwards contributed to sensationalism by rewriting other sensational narratives, and she further extended the boundaries of the genre by actively questioning its limits and asking her readers to question these limits with her.

Cometh Up as a Flower: writing the desiring and dying body

In contrast to Edwards, Broughton was associated with the aspect of sensationalism Oliphant found especially disturbing: women writers' increased candour about female pleasure and desire. This association has caused at least one contemporary critic to categorise her work as 'erotic sensationalism'.[13] *Cometh Up as a Flower*, with its frank heroine, whose blushes during an encounter with her would-be lover 'succeeded each other so rapidly that they almost made one continuous blush', certainly fits this categorisation (91). The so-called erotic effect of the novel is achieved through Nell's detailed first-person descriptions of her affects. The novel was initially serialised from 1866–7 in the *Dublin University Magazine* and then published anonymously as a two-volume novel by Bentley and Son in 1867. Broughton's first novel, *Not Wisely, but Too Well*, was serialised earlier, from 1865–6, but when she sent it to Bentley's for publication in volume form, Geraldine Jewsbury refused it, calling it 'the most thoroughly sensual tale I have read in English for a long time' (qtd in Heller, *Dead Secrets* 281). Broughton sent *Cometh Up* as a more respectable substitute, even though it too was considered scandalous when it appeared.[14] The *London Review* complained that the 'unmaidenly manner in which the heroine constantly dwells upon her lover's physical charms is not pleasant' and makes the book 'not one to be put into the hands of girls' (339). Nell's candidness is exactly the point, however: through her playful engagement with poetic verse, she finds a way to express her sensational and affective experience, appropriating it for her own unique needs and for a woman's developing voice. What Nell undergoes is not merely emplotment but a more agential process in which she can slip in and out of various literary forms and ultimately incorporate them into her own patchwork narrative.

Like *Barbara's History*, *Cometh Up* is a near-bigamy story: Nell LeStrange falls in love with an attractive young soldier, Richard M'Gregor, but is coerced by her money-hungry sister to marry an older man, whom she does not love, to save her family from financial ruin. Once married to Sir Hugh, she nearly elopes with her lover, who returns after a series of letters forged by Nell's sister have separated them. M'Gregor insists that they cannot run away together as it would tarnish her reputation, and they both eventually die: he due to an injury on the battlefield and she, later, from consumption. Her early death makes the novel an 'aborted *Bildungsroman*', since Nell matures but is denied social integration and happiness by the novel's end (Gilbert, 'Introduction' 19). Indeed, there is a tension throughout the novel between her youthful sensations and present diseased body, since we learn in the third chapter that Nell writes as she is dying of consumption. While Nell ultimately resists running away with M'Gregor, she is, like Jane Eyre, a figure of feminine revolt, perhaps most outspoken when she critiques contemporary marriage, referring to herself as her husband's 'property' (269). The *Spectator* noted that when *Cometh Up* first appeared, it 'fluttered women as *Jane Eyre* did' (343).

Nell is a voracious reader and playfully integrates the texts that she has read into her narrative. The novel's title is taken from the Bible and the first chapter alone mentions Shakespeare's *Hamlet*, theatre locations Drury Lane and Covent Garden, the Greek poet Pindar, epithalamiums (poems celebrating marriage), Gray's 'Elegy Written in a Country Churchyard', verses found on English gravestones, and popular piano music from the 1860s. Though Nell most often quotes from poetry, she also exhibits a self-consciousness about novelistic forms. For instance, when she first meets M'Gregor, while sitting alone in a graveyard, she records, 'There was nothing impudent in his gaze, none of the fervent admiration with which, at a first introduction, the hero in a novel regards the young lady' (39). In this moment, she resists the typical melodramatic plotting of a sensation novel, noting that M'Gregor's gaze 'simply expressed [a] moderate amount of curiosity' (39). Along the same lines, her romantic language is sometimes undercut by remarks from the older, dying Nell, who writes observations like, 'really I don't think that Englishwomen are given to flaming, and burning, and melting, and being generally combustible on ordinary occasions, as we are led by one or two novelists to suppose' (146). Remarks like this are a way for Broughton to poke fun at the affective language of sensationalism, while also calling attention to Nell's affective dissonance. Despite these wry asides, Nell clearly wishes that she had lived a life of sensation. After her unhappy marriage to Sir Hugh, and near the end of the novel, she writes, 'I am buried in an arm-chair in my boudoir, reading a novel. It interests me rather, for it is all about a married woman, who ran away from her husband and suffered the extremity of human ills in consequence' (313). Nell undercuts her novel's moral message, reflecting, 'I can hardly imagine that I should have been very miserable if Dick had taken me away with him' (313).[15] While Barbara is understood to be silly and, in Warhol's terms, 'effeminate' after impulsively entering a sensational plot, Nell, dismayed by her disappointing life, wishes she had done so.

While Broughton parodies or makes transparent sensational plotting, *Cometh Up* also betrays the investment in bodily materiality typical of the genre. Nell frequently describes her affects as wilfully betraying her emotions, often with a degree of humour.

During a meeting with M'Gregor, she complains, 'my detestable cheeks thought it necessary to hang out their ever ready flame signals again' (69). Later, 'my heart had taken to thumping loudly whenever I saw a man in the distance' (80). Her interactions with M'Gregor are notable for their sexual candour: while she does not precisely name her arousal, she records that he 'sent a sort of odd shiver – a shiver that had nothing to say to cold, through my frame' (58). Her struggle to name her affects – 'a sort of odd shiver' – of course only works to call attention to them. Furthermore, Nell's frequent use of present tense allows her to articulate her sensations with a sense of immediacy. When M'Gregor returns to surprise a now married Nell, her narration switches to present tense: 'We give each other no polite greeting; we stand by the crackling, cheery fire blaze, and say nothing for a while; only we look into each other's eyes, with passionate, desperate longing across the mighty chasm that yawns between us' (297).

While in these passages Nell seems to be able to articulate her desire quite clearly, she frequently borrows from the language of her favourite authors to express her feelings. Unlike Barbara, Nell's deepest pleasure seems to come from reading poetry rather than novels – and her engagement with Victorian poetry can offer a way in which to understand the novel's use of metafiction as a form of emplotment. Frequently, the story is interrupted by quotations from Romantic-era poets such as Lord Byron, Samuel Taylor Coleridge and William Wordsworth, as well as Victorian poets Robert Browning, Alexander Smith and Tennyson. Kate Flint has noted Broughton's propensity for quotation, suggesting that it may reflect a desire 'not to have [her] literary productions dismissed as utterly frivolous' (282). I would further add that Nell's reading and quoting is thematically important within the novel: rather than read these quotations as interruptions, poetry by Tennyson, Smith and others gives Nell an embodied vocabulary. In arguing so, I differ somewhat from Talia Schaffer, who questions Nell's agency. Schaffer stresses Nell's neglected education, her ignorance and her refusal to listen to her husband, sister and mother-in-law when they urge her to adapt to her marriage with Sir Hugh. Yet such a reading does not account for Nell's humour and literary playfulness throughout the text. I thus don't claim that 'Nell has no way of reading her own plot', but rather see her ability to switch in and out of a range of genres and forms as itself an agential process of identity formation (Schaffer, *Romance's Rival* 109).[16]

Tennyson is the most frequently cited writer in the novel: Nell quotes, misquotes or references his work over thirty times, often integrating lines of his poetry into her own sentences. While her integration is often unremarked, *Maud* receives a special mention. Nell makes a plan with M'Gregor for a clandestine evening encounter in her family's garden. She has no one to confide in, so, she says, 'I had to content myself with warbling "Come into the garden Maud", all over the house, and wondering whether the household did not guess at the personal application of the song' (145). Broughton, of course, anticipates a reader who will 'guess at the personal application' of Tennyson's words. This, the most famous line in Tennyson's poem, expresses the poet-speaker's wish that Maud would emerge from the ball that her brother has held for her. Maud does eventually leave, but so does her brother, resulting in a duel that ends with the speaker killing him. Thus, this line gestures to both the speaker's desire, with which Nell identifies, but also to the fact that his love could turn into maddening, jealous violence. Kristie Blair notes that *Maud* features 'a sensational plotline of suicide, murder, and doomed love, and unlike the mythical setting of *Idylls of the King*, this is placed against the contemporary backdrop of the Crimean War', likening it to sensation fiction (112). It also features affective language not dissimilar to Nell's own prose. When Maud blushes at the speaker, he records, 'And suddenly, sweetly, my heart beat stronger/And thicker, until I heard no longer' (308–9). *Maud*, with its nervous, mad and desiring hero, can also be situated within the genre of spasmodic poetry.

Nell's use of spasmodic poetry is particularly revealing, as the genre is an important predecessor to the sensation novel, despite the fact that the writers were primarily male. As Blair explains, using the language of 'convulsion, shock, spasm, and palpitation', the speakers in these poems are subject to intense sensation and are often carried away by their deviant passions, much like sensational heroes and heroines (113). In his oft-cited and critical 1863 review of the sensation genre, Henry Mansel distinguished between sensation fiction and spasmodic poetry: 'The sensation novel is the counterpart of the spasmodic poem. They represent "the selfsame interest with a different leaning". The one leans outward, the other leans inward; the one aims at convulsing the soul of the reader, the other professes to owe its birth to convulsive throes in the soul of the writer' (212). Mansel goes on to insist that commercially savvy sensation novelists only want to agitate their readers for the purposes of 'supply and demand', while the spasmodic poet is elevated by more inspired intentions as he 'writes to satisfy the unconquerable yearnings of his soul' (212). Spasmodic poems that Mansel might have had in mind were Smith's *A Life-Drama* (1853) or Sydney Dobell's *Balder* (1854). Elizabeth Barrett Browning, Robert Browning and Tennyson were also associated with the movement, both influenced by and influencing young spasmodic poets. Mansel's insistence on sensation's crass commercialism in contrast to the supposed authenticity of spasmodic poetry, not to mention the gendered implications of the male poet-genius, deserves to be challenged. While Mansel sees spasmodic poetry as leaning inward, Dobell's own poetic theory held that the uneven rhythm of spasmodic poetry allowed the reader to share the physical experiences of the poet and to 'forge intimate, affective links between poets and readers' (Rudy 79).

With its largely present-tense character narration, in which Nell muses about the parameters of her body and feeling, it is easy to see *Cometh Up* not as a break with the spasmodic school, as Mansel claims, but rather as an extension of such writing. These poets had an understanding of poetry as 'physiological and essentially noncognitive' in ways that are similar to sensation novels (Rudy 8). Yet Broughton does more than just revive spasmodic writing: she also has Nell quote directly from Alexander Smith's *A Life-Drama* at key moments in the novel. In contrast to Tennyson, Smith was a Glasgow poet with no formal training; his long dramatic poem is filled largely with soliloquies by his poet-hero Walter. Nell – and Broughton – finds in poetic verse and in the lyric 'I' a way to give voice to the immediacy of her emotional experience. Gilbert notes that sometimes Nell's reading can 'call attention to the inadequacy of existing literature to address her experiences' ('Introduction' 16). Similarly, Tamar Heller has suggested that Broughton places Nell 'at the intersection of tales of love rewarded and vice punished, competing stories of women's desire into neither of which Nell fits, and neither of which is appropriate to the more complex, unconventional narrative needed to "tell her experience as a body"' ('Introduction' xxxv). Poetry, however, offers Nell a way to tell this experience, to narrate what Victorian culture might deem unnarratable. To some extent, then, we might see Nell as actually relying on Mansel's distinctions, in particular his assumption that prose is more constructed, while poetry flows from 'convulsive throes in the soul of the writer' (212).

Specifically, Nell integrates poetry into her narrative in order to give her admittedly brief love story with M'Gregor greater meaning and weight. For instance, Nell opens chapter 13, having kissed her lover in the previous chapter, with a quotation from Smith's *A Life-Drama*: 'This world is very lovely; oh, my God, I thank thee that I live'. She continues:

> I could spout tomes of verse to-day; I cannot amble peaceably along the high road of prose; it is too level, too dusty, I must go cantering up the green slopes of poetry. I am craning my long young neck out of the morning-room window, which is barred, and there is only just room for my head to get egress between the bars; but the May air imperatively demands to be sniffed... 'I thank thee that I live', repeat I, piously, in recitative, while my round white chin rests on the knuckles of my two hands. (123)

Nell's supposedly 'pious' recitation is not biblical but poetic. Her sexual excitement in this moment is evident in her greedy breathing in of the spring air and her lingering over her own body: her 'long young neck' and 'round white chin'. Even with the limitations of first-person character narration, Nell manages to narrate her body from both within and without. Poetry, in this moment, allows Nell to express heightened emotions for which 'dusty' prose, even the prose of the sensation novel, seems unsuited. Ironically, many commentators on Smith's *A Life-Drama* pointed out that 'the poem seems to exist more for the sake of the images that constantly disrupt its narrative than for the story itself', a claim that might be made of Broughton's novel as well (Hughes 491).

This disruption via Smith allows Nell to linger in her moment of pleasure. It is an example of what Elisha Cohn has recently called a scene of 'still life', moments of reverie and trance that she locates in the fiction of Charlotte Brontë, George Eliot, George Meredith and Thomas Hardy. Cohn builds on Monique Morgan's understanding of the lyric as a 'suspended moment that stops the time of narrative and focuses instead on the "now" of composition and reception' (Morgan 4). Cohn argues that these novelists, all of whom were also poets, incorporated the lyric mode into their narratives as a way to suspend forward movement and progression: they 'privilege lyric as the genre of sensation, of the daydream, and of non-purposive

Immersive Reading and Sensational Emplotment 63

feeling or sensation' (Cohn 19). While Nell's use of the lyric mode, and her quoting from actual lyric poetry, are 'purposive' in that they develop the novel's love plot, Cohn's arguments nonetheless foreground the manner in which Nell's use of lyric is complementary to sensationalism. This moment also recalls Jameson's argument in *The Antinomies of Realism* that realism is distinguished by two competing impulses: the narrative impulse, which pushes the story forward and is defined by linear time, and affect, which resists both narrative and temporality. Jameson associates affect with a 'perpetual present', though one characterised by 'a "reduction to the body"' (28). While my focus on narrative affects underscores my resistance to entirely distinguish narrative from affect in this way, his claims nonetheless offer a compelling way to read the sensation novel. Specifically, the sensation novel's emphasis on bodily description is a way to challenge critics' insistence on its supposed speed, since such description can indeed pause the forward momentum of plot, if not to entirely resist it. What is especially striking about Nell's bodily description, though, is the way that it so often functions via citation, placing her own body in dialogue with other bodies and, again, her own narrative in dialogue with others.

Nell's citing from Smith adds a further metafictional element to the novel: the above phrase 'I thank Thee that I live!' is taken from a line of the speaker Walter's own poetry. Nell earlier cites Smith when she imagines that if M'Gregor were to die before her, she would fall on his body and herself die kissing him: 'As Hero gave her trembling sighs to find/Delicious death on wet Leander's lips' (112). In the context of *A Life-Drama*, this line about Greek lovers Hero and Leander is not about romance but poetry itself. Smith's long narrative poem begins with Walter '*Reading from a paper on which he has been writing*' (5) but he then tears it up, frustrated at his own incapacity to write, and paces the room, ranting:

> Poesy! Poesy! I'd give to thee,
> As passionately, my rich-laden years,
> My bubble pleasures, and my awful joys,
> As Hero gave her trembling sighs to find
> Delicious death on wet Leander's lips. (6)

Walter has 'a big heart and feeble hands' (6); while his heart beats intensely, his 'hands are weak' and cannot accurately record his feelings (7). Yet his own frustrations in articulating his feelings into written poetry – his inability to 'calm and tame the swelling of [his] heart' – actually gesture to his depth of feeling (7). As Warhol notes, it is characteristic of sentimentalism – and sensationalism – to imply that 'representation, in the form of mere language, is inadequate to convey the depths of emotion the characters and narrator are presented as feeling' (*Having a Good Cry* 44). Yet in claiming that his own emotions cannot be rendered in language – what Gerald Prince would call the 'unnarrated' – the reader must assist Walter by following his cues and taking 'an active part in co-creating the scene's affective power', just as Broughton's ideal reader does for Nell (Warhol 44). Furthermore, as Walter compares his love for poetry to that between Hero and Leander, Nell, in turn, compares her love for M'Gregor to the poetic frustrations of the spasmodic poet. For both Walter and Nell, such comparisons serve not just to elevate their feelings but to mark them as heroic figures and to situate them into pre-existing narratives. Though their romance is the central narrative, it is worth noting that Nell and M'Gregor in fact only meet a handful of times, but she nonetheless compares their story to myth, Shakespearean tragedy and pre-Raphaelite paintings.[17]

Again, while the moments in which Nell cites poetry from others could be read as disruptions – taking us away from her own story – they function, for Nell, as a way of immersing herself and the reader in the present moment and in her body. Critics have connected the urgency of time in the sensation novel to increased urbanisation and industrialisation, and even to the experience of riding the train, but in this case, an intensity of time and feeling is related not to technology but simply to the rhythm of poetry, which Blair has shown was linked by various Victorian poets to the rhythm of the heart. The brevity and measured rhythm of poetry ironically serve to represent Nell's deep feelings. The *Spectator* in fact compared the novel to poetry, noting that Broughton 'expresses through fiction an emotion, a doubt, a sentiment – call it what you will – which has rarely been expressed except in poetry, but which surges up now and again . . . a feeling not only that all is Vanity, but that all ought not to be, that there is some mistake, some misarrangement, some failure in the grand scheme' (343). This is a positive response to the novel but another instance in which a reviewer struggles to characterise the language of sensation fiction. As the reviewer implies, the sensational mystery of this text is not a conventional one in the sense of the disclosure of a dark secret or the revelation of a hidden identity, but the mystery of our bodies and souls. Volume 2 of the novel, for instance, opens with a passage from Wordsworth's 'Intimations of Immortality' (1807): 'Our birth is but a sleep and a forgetting' (199). Nell wonders, 'Is this life our beginning though we know it not to be our ending? Or is it only one of a series of existences through which we pass?' (199). The primary topic of this novel is, in fact, sensation: Nell struggles to articulate her own sensations and, as her body deteriorates, she imagines what the end of such sensations might mean, what world she will enter next.

Indeed, Nell's decaying body haunts the text as a reminder of what she will become. In the novel, desire is always linked to death, just as the fleshly body is always marked by its imminent absence. The title is taken from the Book of Job 14:1-2 and references life's suffering and brevity: 'Man that is born of a woman is of few days and full of misery. He cometh up as a flower, and is cut down' (*King James Version*, Job 14:1-2). The novel in fact begins with Nell sitting in a graveyard, contemplating death: 'When I die, I'll be buried under that big old ash tree over yonder – the one that Dolly and I cut our names on with my jagged old penknife nine, ten years ago now' (36). In this opening paragraph, Nell imagines, quite flippantly, her decaying corpse. By rejecting the family mausoleum, the tree that Nell and Dolly playfully marked their names on as children ironically becomes a gravestone, their jagged names an epitaph. What is striking about this opening scene is not only the way in which Nell breezily imagines her own death, and of course foreshadows it, but that this gravesite serves as the space in which she and M'Gregor first meet. The entire scene, much like the novel itself, presents an odd mixture of elegiac and romantic impulses.

Nell's process of borrowing from other narratives thus permits her to write herself into the love plot that she was unable to experience fully. Yet Nell's act of narrative resistance is only necessary because she is forced to live a plot written by another woman, her sister Dolly. Dolly writes to M'Gregor posing as Nell and insists that he not reply to her letter. Dolly also intercepts M'Gregor's letters, making Nell think that he has forgotten her and thus freeing her up to marry Sir Hugh. Nell admits, 'I have fallen into the trap she laid for me!' (298). Meanwhile, and ironically, Dolly achieves her happy ending. While the realistic readers in Edwards's fiction are to be lauded for their intelligence and critical awareness, Dolly, Broughton's realistic reader, is too critical and too willing to work within the flawed Victorian marriage market. She might have been the protagonist of another sensation novel, and, indeed, her mercantile interests rival Lucy Audley's. She tells Nell that there is no 'old lord between the three seas, so old, so mumbling, so wicked, that I would not joyfully throw myself into his horrid palsied old arms, if he had but money; money! money!' (204). In contrast, Nell describes her own marriage as a funeral, and records her wealthy husband's unwanted caresses with great attention to her physical sensations: 'His arm is round my waist, and he is brushing my eyes and cheeks and brow with his somewhat bristly moustache as often as he feels inclined – for am I not his property?' (269). Notably, she uses the present tense here, making her disgust for her husband as visceral as her desire for M'Gregor. That Dolly is not punished in the manner of a sensational heroine comes much to Nell's surprise: 'Here is a young woman who has told lies, has forged, has wrecked the happiness of her sister's whole life, and she is punished, how? – why by marrying a lord with £80,000 a year. Truly poetic justice is confined to poetry indeed; and comes down never to the prose dealings of everyday life' (315). Poetry is thus overturned for prose, just as romance is overturned for 'everyday life'. Yet the novel also challenges Victorian realist convention, so reliant as it was on idealism and the notion of a moral universe.

Cometh Up ends with Nell's dying words. The final chapter in the two-volume edition is broken up into two diary entries. Nell opens her final entry by announcing, 'These are the last words I shall ever write' (333). In what follows, Nell paraphrases the Bible, specifically Isaiah 33:24, as she dreams of 'A land where the inhabitant shall no more say I am sick' (333). She admits, 'That text never struck me particularly when I was well. I suppose now that I am so full of aches and pains it comes home to me more' (334). As Nell prepares to leave her material body, she abandons spasmodic poetry for the lessons of the Bible, thinking, 'Perhaps that text has something to say to me' (334). These final lines gesture to a version of poetic justice – perhaps one that would have satisfied some Victorian readers – in that Nell seems to find peace in this brief religious awakening. The final lines of the novel are a call to Christ: 'O Lord Jesus Christ! let me be in that city by this time to-morrow night! Grant me entrance there! Open to me when in fear and trembling I knock' (334). For this reader, Nell's final lines recall the final lines of *Jane Eyre*, in which Jane receives a letter from the dying St John Rivers. Jane explains, 'I know that a stranger's hand will write to me next, to say that the good and faithful servant has been called at length into the joy of his Lord' (452). Jane ends the story of her own life with St John's words, in which he proclaims his readiness for death: 'Amen; even so come, Lord Jesus!' (452). While Nell's 'Open to me when in fear and trembling I knock' may betray less certainty than St John's final call, her apostrophe nonetheless evokes his dying words, aligning her not with the happily married Jane, but with her disappointed lover. The original serialised version of *Cometh Up* included an additional epilogue, written by 'a stronger hand' – recalling 'a stranger's hand' – that sums up Nell's final moments (336). Yet Broughton's abrupt novel ending seems somehow more fitting, as it ends not with the closure provided by an unnamed narrator but literally by Nell's body, by her final heartbeat. While throughout the novel, the dying Nell used novels and poems to tell the brief story of her life, her narrative finally ends with the dominance and inescapability of the material body.

Nell's final request for entry into heaven is also a request for at least a limited form of poetic justice. As I have argued throughout, Nell, like Edwards's heroines, must negotiate her fictional and actual worlds by reassessing her expectations for romance and a just world. Like an actual reader who must 'sustain a balance between two modes' of engagement, one in which she gives way to feeling and another in which she recalls that she is reading a fiction, the heroines in Edwards and Broughton's fiction struggle to understand their own emplotment (Odden 23). In so doing, they highlight a key aspect of all sensation novels: that giving way to the agency of the body is both thrilling and frightening. It is worth emphasising that such self-conscious engagements with sensational plotting do not always imply an ambivalent relationship with sensationalism. For instance, in Braddon's *Eleanor's Victory*, Eleanor determines to find her father's killer, but she has inherited her theatrical father's 'notions of justice and honour', which are drawn from the 'flimsy ideas of a stage play, [rather] than the commonsense views of real life' (vol. 1, 281). Her friend Richard warns her, 'The future is not a blank sheet of paper, for us to write any story we please upon; but a wonderful chart mapped out by a divine and unerring hand' (vol. 2, 90). In fact, though, all of these novels suggest that the truth is somewhere in between: Barbara and Nell both write and are written into sensational plots. And such metafictional playfulness was a consistent aspect of sensationalism, not merely a way to challenge it.

These novels demonstrate the ways in which fictional stories and their associated affects become rooted in the identities and material lives of their characters, and they model possibilities for reading both critically and with pleasure. They furthermore encourage actual readers to reflect on our own expectations and affects as we read.

Notes

1. Cvetkovich, Flint, Gilbert and Phegley have all discussed the anxieties associated with women's reading in this period. The emergence of sensation fiction was also related to the growth in periodical publications, and thus in serial fiction more broadly. The mid-century saw a huge rise in the number of periodicals publishing serial novels. Additionally, the price of both periodicals and novels dropped, allowing for a larger and more diverse readership (Cvetkovich, *Mixed Feelings* 16).
2. Narrative theorists who use the term tend to draw from White or Paul Ricoeur, who frames it as the act of configuring events, actions and desires into plot. Ricoeur discusses emplotment in *Time and Narrative*, especially volumes 1 and 2. Drawing on Aristotle, he explains that narrative is distinguished from ordinary life because of emplotment: rather than events that take place in a possibly meaningless succession, emplotment provides a structure. He likens emplotment to Aristotle's *muthos*, which means 'the organization of the events' (33).
3. Singular character narration is relatively rare for the sensation genre, which tends to feature either numerous character narrators or so-called omniscient narrators. Yet it is typical for the *Bildungsroman*. In an examination of Braddon's early fiction, Anne-Marie Beller argues that a narrative of female development is 'embedded within the sensation plot' as the heroine is exposed to events and experiences that lie outside of conventional respectability ('Sensational Bildung?' 115). The novels that I discuss in this chapter can all be classified as sensational *Bildungsromans*.
4. Jennifer Ladino explains that affective dissonance is a 'counterpart to what psychologists term cognitive dissonance' (23). Sianne Ngai's 'affective disorientation' is similar. She calls this an ambiguous affect,

or 'what we might think of as a state of feeling vaguely "unsettled" or "confused"' (14).

5 Most of the research on Edwards, nearly all of which has been written in the past ten years, focuses on her travel writing, which she completed near the end of her life. An exception is Anne-Marie Beller's excellent chapter on Edwards in *A Companion to Sensation Fiction*.

6 I have argued elsewhere that a range of Victorian authors depict 'fascinating' characters in similar ways, especially in the context of male characters that risk invading the physical boundaries of the women they captivate. See my *The New Man, Masculinity, and Marriage in the Victorian Novel* for a further discussion of fascinating men in the context of homoeroticism in Dickens's fiction and the Byronic hero in Brontë and Eliot's fiction.

7 *The Times* noted the novel's likeness to *Jane Eyre*, and the *Athenaeum* observes that Edwards is indebted to *David Copperfield*, *Villette* and *Jane Eyre*.

8 Young David stumbles across novels such as *Roderick Random*, *Tom Jones* and *Robinson Crusoe*, and finds 'constant comfort' in his solitary reading (67). The novels serve as a distraction from his stepfather's cruelty: 'They kept alive my fancy, and my hope of something beyond that place and time' (66).

9 In terms of the novel's morality, Beller makes the point that 'Not only was a checkered past on the man's part far more acceptable to Victorian sensibilities, so too was the non-Englishness and peasant status of the fallen woman, Maddalena' ('Amelia B. Edwards' 357).

10 In another example linking *Jane Eyre* to sensationalism, H. L. Mansel, in his oft-quoted 1863 diatribe against the genre, writes that he is 'thrilled with horror' by the thought that the 'man who shook our hand with a hearty English grasp half an hour ago . . . may have a mysterious female, immured in a solitary tower or a private lunatic asylum, destined to come forth hereafter to menace the name and position of the excellent lady whom the world acknowledges as his wife' (575–6). Though the bigamy plot would come to be a cornerstone of the sensation genre, Mansel's reference to the mysterious woman in 'a solitary tower' is clearly indebted to *Jane Eyre*.

11 Edwards's final novel, *Lord Brackenbury*, is an escapist fantasy. In the novel, the rightful Lord Brackenbury flees to Italy and lives under an assumed identity, while his younger brother, unaware that his older sibling is still alive, reluctantly pronounces his brother dead, taking his title and riches. We only discover at the end of the novel that the older brother lives, and that he has enacted this elaborate

plot so that he could escape his responsibilities as a lord and live a simple life as an Italian sailor. The rightful Lord never tells his English brother (or his Italian wife or father-in-law) his secret, and the novel ends with him continuing life as an Italian sailor.

12 *Barbara's History* draws from the plot of Wood's *East Lynne* in other ways: Barbara's little room in Italy is reminiscent of Isabel's room in France, and the name that Barbara adopts, Mrs Carylon, is suggestive of Mrs Carlyle, the name that Isabel loses when she abandons her husband. Also, both women run away rashly, without full knowledge of their situations. But again, Edwards offers a corrective in that Barbara runs away from – and not towards – a supposedly immoral man, and, even more importantly, the child she delivers is her husband's, not her lover's.

13 Andrew Maunder classifies *Cometh Up* as erotic sensationalism in his *Varieties of Women's Sensation Fiction* series.

14 *Not Wisely* was originally serialised in the *Dublin University Magazine*, which was edited by Broughton's uncle, Sheridan Le Fanu. *Not Wisely* appeared as a triple-decker in autumn 1867 after significant editing. In what follows, I cite from the edited, two-volume novel of *Cometh Up*. As Gilbert explains in her excellent Broadview edition, the novel version adds chapters on Dolly's marriage and Nell learning of Richard's death.

15 Gilbert remarks that Nell is likely reading Anne Marsh-Caldwell's *The Admiral's Daughter* (1834). The plot also bears similarities to Wood's *East Lynne*, as others have noted.

16 In *Victorian Metafiction*, Tabitha Sparks focuses on Nell's self-conscious use of fiction (rather than poetry), and she makes the persuasive argument that fiction serves Nell better than the autobiographical mode.

17 Nell also crafts herself as a romantic heroine through references to art, especially Victorian paintings: on a walk with M'Gregor, she records, 'we pose ourselves in the attitude of the famous "Huguenot" picture' (155), presumably referring to John Everett Millais's popular painting *A Huguenot, on St Bartholomew's Day Refusing to Shield Himself from Danger by Wearing the Roman Catholic Badge* (1852). Nell also imagines dying by suicide in a manner reminiscent of Millais's *Ophelia* (1851–2), asking the reader, 'should I practise some picturesque form of suicide? should I drown myself in the garden pool, and be found with my long red hair inextricably entangled among the duckweed?' (159).

2

Morbidity and Sensational Authorship

This chapter explores the effects of sensational narratives on the body of the author rather than the reader. In the previous chapter, I discussed Henry Mansel's depiction of the sensation writer as mechanical and profit-driven. He claimed that the spasmodic poet writes to gratify 'the unconquerable yearnings of his soul', while the sensation novelist writes for the purposes of 'supply and demand' (212). This more mechanical model of authorship was widespread across reviews of sensation fiction. For instance, the *Saturday Review* said that Collins had only 'Mechanical talent' and compared him to a cabinet-maker (249). Braddon was similarly accused of being 'a novel-producing machine' ('Literature: Miss Braddon's New Novel' 2). Another model of authorship plagued Braddon and other female sensation writers, one that was arguably even more damning. In contrast to the mechanical model was what we might call the knowledge model of authorship, which understood female authors' work as the products of their dubious knowledge and experience. It can be summed up by Henry James's notorious assessment of Braddon: 'She knows much that ladies are not accustomed to know' (594). Oliphant also comments on Braddon's 'bad' knowledge, claiming that she must not know 'how young women of good blood and good training feel' ('Novels' 260). Implicit in this model is that the sensation author – and the female author especially – can only write through personal experience; her characters' immorality therefore must reflect her own lived experience or, at the very least, her understanding of the world. Braddon, whose name was 'a byword for all that was lauded and loathed about the female "sensation novelist"', was particularly vulnerable to such criticism because her scandalous past as an actress and her relationship with her married publisher, John Maxwell, were well known to the public (Beller, 'Popularity' 245).

Yet Braddon responded to these models in creative ways. In *The Doctor's Wife*, she cannily pokes fun at the mechanical understanding of authorship via Sigismund Smith. Smith must write four stories a week for a public demanding 'a continuous flow of incident', so he writes what he calls 'combination' stories, stories that are combined, or stolen, from other writers (45). He explains that the best thing to do 'if you haven't got ideas of your own, is to steal other people's ideas in an impartial manner' (45). Poking fun at the knowledge model of authorship was not as easy. In 1864, John Maxwell attempted to mitigate the problem of Braddon's reputation – and the ways in which her sensational life and novels were interconnected – by leaking to the press that they were legally married. (In fact, they wouldn't be until 1874, by which time his estranged wife had died and they could finally marry after living together for years and having six children.) Maxwell's plan backfired when his brother-in-law informed the press that his wife was still living (Phegley 114). More successful was Braddon's effort in 1866 to shift not the public perception of her past but the perception of sensation fiction through the creation of her own monthly periodical, *Belgravia: A London Magazine*. With *Belgravia*, she could publish and edit her own work and thus not rely as heavily on reviewers' assessments.[1] Given Braddon's interest in defending sensation fiction as a legitimate form and her tendency towards self-reflexivity, it is surprising, as Anne-Marie Beller notes, 'that among Braddon's characters there are not more figures of the woman writer' ('Popularity' 253). Others, however, did write such characters.[2] In this chapter, I explore depictions of sensational female authorship as they relate to knowledge and feeling, focusing largely on a little-known novel, Florence Wilford's *Nigel Bartram's Ideal*.

Why female authors? As with sensation readers, sensation authorship was frequently gendered female – this despite the evidence that many of the most popular writers were men, such as Collins, Dickens, Reade and Edmund Yates. A reviewer of Wilford's novel in fact calls sensation 'the lady's peculiar field' (*Saturday Review* 59). Further, even though many sensation authors had scandalous or at least unorthodox domestic arrangements (Braddon, Collins, Dickens, Marryat and Reade all had relationships outside of marriage), female authors clearly bore the brunt of criticism that conflated their private lives with their fictional characters. Thus, in a period that tended to believe the axiom 'That which is in bad taste is usually bad in morals', not only was their popular fiction ripe for critique but their ethics, feelings and bodies were too (Rae 181). Wilford's *Nigel Bartram's Ideal* takes on these topics in 1869, when debates about sensational authorship and the role of the vindictive reviewer were well known to the reading public. The novel employs, as one reviewer put it, 'the only too commonplace plot of the wife's secret' (*Saturday Review* 59). Yet the heroine, Marion, does not have a secret child or abandoned husband: Marion's dark secret is that she penned a wildly popular sensation novel, one that her husband Nigel reviewed severely upon its publication. He admits, 'it is an odd chance which brought together an authoress and her harshest reviewer' (221). My central claim in this chapter is that the female author's body and its associated affects, in both Wilford's novel and in contemporary reviews, becomes a kind of barometer by which her work and morals are judged. Somewhat ironically, Wilford uses one of the tools of sensationalism – reading the affective body – to critique the effects of the genre on Marion's 'morbid' body.

This chapter doesn't take established sensation novels as its focus, as later chapters do, but instead reads texts and reviews that engaged with and even condemned sensationalism. Despite the parallels to sensation fiction evident in Wilford's novel – an intense focus on characters' wilful bodies and a flawed and (near) sinning woman at its centre – it attempts, like Braddon's *Doctor's Wife*, to distance itself from the genre. Wilford's narrator states, 'If this were a sensation novel I might try to make an exciting scene out of this meeting' (289), and Nigel insists, 'I am not the model husband of a sensation novel, a poor blind tool in the hands of less scrupulous people' (208). More to the point, though, is that the novel is pointedly critical of sensation fiction, showing how Marion moves from such perverse influences to supposedly loftier ideals upon her marriage. Marion abandons sensational writing and reading by the novel's end, and she attempts to conform to her husband's conventional ideal of femininity, 'a quiet, gentle little soul who should be entirely womanly, and yet intelligent enough to sympathize with his intellectual tastes' (27). That said, in her focus on women's restricted social roles and the difficulty of conforming to such roles, Wilford betrays concerns that preoccupied sensational novelists. Specifically, the novel explores just what a conventional or ideal woman might be.

The novel furthermore interrogates what a conventional woman should feel. Again, as Sara Ahmed claims, scholars interested in affect and emotion 'need to consider how emotions operate to "make" and "shape" bodies' (*Cultural Politics* 4). Wilford suggests that for Marion the process of writing a sensation novel is not cathartic but, rather, sensational affects stick to her and make her 'morbid'. The term 'morbid' signals Marion's unhealthy state when she writes her novel, and this word was frequently used in reviews of sensation fiction. *East Lynne* was seen as 'morbid', with Wood herself criticised for being 'led far astray from the ordinary current of human life' (Hutton 1068–9). Pamela Gilbert has shown how the language of disease and contamination was used extensively in relationship to sensation novels, and the recurring use of the word 'morbid' in these reviews can certainly be associated with this tendency. Yet the term came to be a stand-in not just for fiction but also for people who were in any way considered a threat to social order, who were 'led far astray from the ordinary current of human life', such as childless adults, effeminate men and queer women.[3] In 1855, one writer noted that 'morbid' 'has acquired a perfectly new meaning of late years, and is made to include . . . all views of life that are coloured by other than comfortable feelings' (qtd in Meadows 6). The use of the term, then, became shorthand for socially unacceptable behaviours, feelings and people in the mid-century. The morbid woman, with her misdirected feelings, is what Ahmed calls an 'affect alien', someone who does not experience the so-called right feelings from the right things. Affect aliens are 'those who are alienated by virtue of how they are affected by the world or how they affect others in the world' (*Promise* 164). Marion is an affect alien at the beginning of the novel, but the plot is that of a morbid woman reformed – not an unknown trajectory in the sensation genre, even if the more familiar narrative might be the morbid woman extricated from society.

In this novel, the author's plot is an affective plot, and Wilford's use of metafiction reveals the narrative's judgement of both 'good' fiction and feelings, much like the novels that I discussed in Chapter 1. Yet this tidy trajectory is destabilised by the flashes of feminist critique that appear throughout the novel, primarily through the narrator's criticisms of Nigel's 'harshness and prejudice' and the depictions of Marion's struggle to conform (246).

While Marion's wifely submission is ultimately celebrated, Wilford nonetheless shows the challenges inherent in being a clever and unconventional woman writer in the mid-century. In addition to later New Women fiction, the novel bears similarities to two other novels about female authorship from this time period: American Louisa May Alcott's *Little Women* and Charlotte Mary Yonge's *The Clever Woman of the Family*. As I explain below, Jo's sensation fiction similarly worries her eventual husband, who finds it 'full of morbid fancies' (297). In these novels, the body of the woman writer becomes a source of interest and concern: in Wilford's novel, Nigel and Marion spend much of the novel misreading one another's bodies. With its intense focus on Marion's affects, the novel exemplifies the threat and dissonance exhibited by the body of the female sensation author. While Wilford is critical of sensationalism, she is also critical of the tendency for conservative reviewers to unthinkingly conflate authors with their sensational female characters. The novel thus revises the knowledge model of authorship, as well as Nigel's ideal, showing how Marion's identity and body exceed these limiting models of both authorship and femininity.

Body reading, writing and *Nigel Bartram's Ideal*

Little is known today of Florence Wilford. She was a friend of Charlotte Yonge's and a member of Yonge's Gosling Society. Yonge, along with her cousin, Mary Coleridge, started an essay society for young girls in 1859. The young women called Yonge Mother Goose and they were her Goslings. Each girl adopted a unique pen name such as Ladybird or Shamrock; Wilford's was Turk's Cap. They wrote two essays a month for her, and the strongest essays were circulated among the women, so as to offer them an alternative educational and intellectual community. Wilford was one of three older women recruited during the 1860s; she joined in 1865 when she was twenty-nine.[4] A number of Wilford's works were published in Yonge's *The Monthly Packet*, an Anglican-sponsored magazine for younger members of the English church that Yonge founded in 1851, and her short stories were often chosen for the special Christmas numbers. In a letter from Yonge to Wilford in 1886, Yonge complains that the 'general run' of young women are 'deteriorated', and she specifically mentions a girl 'who could hardly get out of reading bad sensation novels because of the talk about them' (27 January 1886). Wilford's relationship to Yonge is helpful in situating her conservative beliefs and resistance to sensation fiction, coupled with her concern for women's intellectual outlets. In her focus on the difficulties inherent in being a clever woman, Wilford is clearly indebted to her mentor's *The Clever Woman of the Family*. Wilford's uneven feminist politics and her difficult-to-classify writing are perhaps why she has not been of great interest to contemporary critics or those who undertook important feminist recovery work in the 1980s. Yet *Nigel Bartram's Ideal* deserves to be part of this ongoing project.

Wilford's novel opens with the protagonist, Marion, leading a seemingly quiet existence with her sister and brother-in-law, and caring for their children. When Nigel begins to court Marion, he explains that he recently reviewed an anonymous novel called *Mark's Dream* whose author he judges to be a man of 'most decided genius, but perhaps not of very high principle' (17). Marion and Nigel soon marry, and she attempts to mould herself to match his very specific ideals. When Marion takes a fever, she admits to Nigel that she in fact wrote *Mark's Dream*. He assumes that she is delirious, and it is not until later in the novel that he realises she was telling the truth. He asks, 'I am to understand, then, that you are a sensation novelist; that you wrote the book which I scarcely thought fit for you to read?' (206). Nigel insists that she not publish further work and Marion agrees. Later, when Nigel realises Marion's real talent, and when they financially require her to work, he permits her to publish again. Not only does she publish a second novel, though not one of the sensational variety, but she steps in for her husband when he is too ill to pen his periodical reviews. By the end of the novel, Nigel must come to terms not only with his initial, misplaced ideal of womanhood but he must also accept that his wife's intellectual talents are greater than his own.

Marion comes to write a sensation novel not because she has led a sensational life, but because of her educational influences. The absence of a mother as a guiding force and a rather irresponsible father means that young Marion read books by 'free-thinking authors, and some ... French novels', and that her companions were her father's dissolute friends (108). The novel that she writes, *Mark's Dream*, centres on a morally ambiguous mother. It opens with Mark, a young boy, believing that he has witnessed his father's murder. His mother insists that it was only a dream and assures him that his father died a natural death. Mark's mother remarries and when he grows up, he discovers that his stepfather in fact murdered his father. Even after he accuses his stepfather, his mother remains loyal to her new husband and flees with him to the continent. After his stepfather's death, Mark visits his mother on her deathbed in a scene that Nigel describes as 'beautiful and touching' but 'rather a Pagan ending' (21). The mother, Nigel thinks, is the most remarkable figure in the novel. She is 'the most *real* character I have ever met with in fiction; one can't help admiring her above all things, though she is in a measure guilty; and it is just that which makes the book harmful' (20–1). A pained but guilty mother is of course reminiscent of *East Lynne* and part of the critical outrage surrounding Wood's novel was her sympathetic – or at the very least ambiguous – portrayal of Isabel Carlyle. Marion's sister Blanche betrays the novel's actual source material when she says that it 'reminds me of rather an old tale our nurse used to tell us, about what happened in a family where her mother was housekeeper' (23); the narrative, then, is based on local gossip, not Marion's history.

Despite the fact that Marion keeps her authorship a secret from Nigel, she is not portrayed as a deceiving sensational heroine in the manner of Lucy Audley. When Nigel first meets her, she 'bowed quietly, and looked a little anxious and thoughtful' (2). This initiates the novel's, and Nigel's, close observation of Marion for signs of authentic feeling: she is not able to fully hide her feelings from others, as her 'anxious and thoughtful' affects reveal (3). Her inability to dissemble is shown to be an important attribute of her character, such that her body's honesty trumps her actual dishonesty. The novel is filled with scenes of characters reading and reacting to one another's bodies in order to access their emotional states. As I explained in the introduction, Theory of Mind or mind reading, 'our ability to explain people's behavior in terms of their thoughts, feelings, beliefs, and desires', is often made explicit in the sensation genre as characters' motives are constantly under question (Zunshine, *Why We Read* 6). Mind reading, which can occur via verbal or nonverbal cues, happens largely via the body in this genre. Alan Richardson has noted of nineteenth-century novels that the reticence required by society meant that observing others' body language, or using 'nonverbal' evidence, is vital for characters and readers who attempt to read one another's minds (86). In addition, though, Richardson explains that evidence that is 'verbal but nonsemantic (vocal tones that may tell more than the words themselves)' is also important in these texts (86). For instance, when Nigel asks Marion whether she enjoys living with her sister's family, she 'absently' responds, 'I suppose so' (6). 'Then, as if she had become aware that this answer must have sounded odd, she continued with more animation, "Yes; I have learnt to like it very much"' (6). This admission of possible unhappiness, coupled with her accidental betrayal of her feelings, causes Nigel to become intrigued by Marion and to watch her for further missteps.

Yet in an example of misreading that is typical of both mind reading and sensational plotting, he does not understand her reaction to his review of *Mark's Dream*. Zunshine would remind us that misreading another's intentions is still mind reading and is, after all, 'just what a good story needs' (*Getting Inside* 72). As Nigel discusses the novel, he 'scanned critically the half-averted face at the far end of the room. It was dropping over the [needle] work again, but it was crimson even to the brow, and somehow or other Mr Bartram came to the conclusion that she had read the book, and read it by stealth' (17). Marion's blushing 'crimson' reveals her agitation and recalls O'Farrell's understanding of the blush as a form of 'somatic confession' (5). Additionally, her 'half-averted face' shows that she is attempting to resist others' efforts at interpretation; it also might reveal her shame. Nigel's 'somehow or other' shows his Theory of Mind at work, but without the proper context he cannot read her accurately. Marion's body tells a story and affects others in the room, but the reasons for her blush remain unclear. The narrator also attempts to throw off readers' efforts: when Nigel mentions that *Mark's Dream* demonstrates talent but that he finds 'fault with its *morale*, which I think decidedly bad and calculated to do mischief', Marion 'raised a startled face from her work a moment, perhaps surprised to hear him speak so seriously' (16). The narrator's 'perhaps' leads readers astray: this alarmed look is not due to his serious tone, as we will later learn, but to her own authorship.

Marion's 'startled' look is also an example of what Zunshine calls 'embodied transparency'. She identifies a narrative tradition of 'putting protagonists in situations in which their bodies spontaneously reveal their true feelings, sometimes against their wills' ('Theory of Mind' 72). We see this when Mr Darcy's paleness betrays his anger in Austen's *Pride and Prejudice* (1813): 'His complexion became pale with anger, and the disturbance of his mind was visible in every feature' (ibid.). Zunshine provides three 'rules' for depicting moments of 'embodied transparency':

> The first rule is *contrasts*: an author has to build up a context in which the character's transparency stands out sharply against the relative lack of transparency of other characters or of the same character a moment ago or a moment after. The second rule is *transience*: to be believable, instances of transparency must be brief. The third rule is *restraint*: more often than not, characters struggle to conceal their feelings and by doing so become transparent. (*Getting Inside* 30)

Marion is much like Marguerite, Barbara and Nell in that she is generally transparent and emotive. She differs from Darcy in this way, but she does stand out against other characters' relative lack of transparency in the novel. In fact, keynote of the sensational body is transparency: many sensational plotlines are initiated by a wilful body, only to be followed by impulsive actions or words.

A knowing reader might catch on to Marion's comments about *Mark's Dream* as well as the reasons for her affects, but Wilford takes great pains to show that Nigel's preconceived ideas about women prevent him from seeing the truth. In other words, it's not only that he doesn't realise that Marion authored the novel, but that Nigel's worldview prevents him from even imagining that possibility and thus correctly reading her embodied transparency. In a lengthy passage, the narrator explains:

> He did not *mis*interpret [Marion's reactions], but the true interpretation he never guessed. He was ridiculously blind, you will say. Yes, I grant it; but so has many a one been before and since. We fancy that we can gauge each other's natures, and we complacently assign certain qualities to certain faces, and our own conception of our neighbour's character is so present with us, that it comes between us and the reality, and prevents our reading it aright. First impressions have with most of us all the force of tradition, if not of historic truth, and, strong in our preconceived ideas, we miss the knowledge which further acquaintance might have given us; we pass over facts, and warnings, and surprises, which might, one would think, have had significance for any one not resolutely obtuse.
>
> Marion had the outward characteristics of Mr Bartram's ideal, *therefore* she had, no doubt, the inward too . . . .. It was very illogical and absurd, but it made him very comfortable. (52–3)

The narrator stresses that preconceptions can prevent 'our reading' others' bodies and minds 'aright'. This passage contains lessons typical of sensation novels: do not assume that one's physical appearance tells us everything about their character, and, relatedly, pay attention not just to 'outward characteristics' but, rather, to unconscious or uncontrolled bodily affects, the body's 'warnings, and surprises' (53). Sensationalism, indeed, works to train readers in close reading and body reading. This passage can also be read as a diatribe against nostalgic masculinity; throughout the novel, Nigel is made uncomfortable by Marion's genius. Thus, while the novel explores the impact of authorship on the young female body, it also maps Nigel's affects.

Part of the challenge in reading Marion properly comes from the conflation of her publication of *Mark's Dream* and her relationship with Fabian Ord, a childhood friend and potential love interest. When he arrives to visit Marion and Nigel after their marriage, he stuns Nigel by suggesting that Marion is 'cleverer than any of us' (156):

> If one of his auditors looked more surprised than another at this reference to Marion – Marion, of all people! – it was her husband. He raised his eyes to her with a smile of amusement, but could not comprehend the glance of almost agonized appeal which she turned upon Fabian. Her lips unclosed, but she said nothing, and it was Nigel who made for her the disclaimer which he supposed her modesty desired.
>
> 'Mrs Bartram is the last person to think she can cut a Gordian knot', – mentally adding, 'or to wish to be thought clever either'. (156)

This scene serves as a clue of Marion's authorship and, significantly, is another moment in which Nigel cannot understand his wife's affects: he cannot imagine what the glance of 'agonized appeal' that she sends to Fabian might signal (156). Moments later, Marion catches Fabian alone and warns him that '*He* does not know' (157). Nigel's precocious sister, Ada, overhears and worries that there is a 'strange mystery, and perhaps not quite a credible mystery either' between Marion and Fabian (157). In conflating Marion's authorship and her friendship with a man who is not her husband, Wilford implies that both activities are morally questionable.

While Ada is mistaken in believing that Marion and Fabian might be carrying on a covert affair, the very fact that Fabian knows Marion in a way that Nigel does not presents a challenge to their marriage. The plot clearly implicates Fabian in Marion's authorship, since he helped her to get her first book published and begins to help her a second time when she hopes to assist Nigel's brother-in-law financially. When Nigel finally discovers that Marion published *Mark's Dream* and that she desires to publish a second novel, the men clash, Nigel insisting that Marion refrain from publishing and Fabian believing that to do so would be to hide her talent from the world. Nigel later admits to Marion, 'there was a dangerous contrast ... between his admiration and longings for fame for you, and my contemptuous crushing of your powers' (366). Yet their clash is not merely about literary authorship but about their love for Marion. Fabian finally confesses to Marion that he loves her, and the narrator characteristically lets Marion's body respond: 'Was she very wicked or very innocent, that the colour did not mantle even for an instant on her cheek?' (239). In a typically sensational move, the narrator asks the reader to explicitly judge and read Marion's body (and mind) for herself. We never learn to what extent Marion knew of Fabian's desire, but her decision to send him away and refuse to see him because she 'can have no friend who is not my husband's friend also' signals her loyalty to Nigel (239). The fact that Marion decides not to publish her second novel and refuses to see Fabian – both in the hopes of making Nigel happy – again links these potentially sensational activities. While neither her authorship nor friendship explicitly paints Marion as 'wicked', both influence her reputation in serious ways.

Fabian's relationship to sensationalism, though, is made most explicit in the conclusion to his role in Marion's plot: on a visit to a monastery, Nigel and Marion are confronted with 'Brother Jerome of the Benedictines', who is also Fabian Ord (288). His desire for Marion is made clear given that sexual denial is the outcome of her refusal. The narrator insists that 'If this were a sensation novel', she might make 'an exciting scene' out of their reunion (289). Instead, recalling Henry's lecture to Catherine in Austen's *Northanger Abbey* – 'Remember the country and the age in which we live' (186) – the narrator notes that 'scenes seldom occur in real life, especially among English people, and in this nineteenth century' (289). Instead of melodramatically displaying their emotions, they (supposedly more realistically) refrain from expressing them, even though the narrator insists that they struggle internally: 'love, hate, jealousy, pity, regret, remorse – passions enough for a whole drama were within their breasts; but they spoke, looked, acted, as if nothing of all this had existed. It was very commonplace' (289). While presenting her own theory for what is realistic or 'commonplace', Wilford also provides a good definition of sensationalism. The complete internalisation of feeling here is indeed anomalous of sensation fiction; yet this is ironic in that it is uncharacteristic of much of Wilford's novel. This scene is Ord's last appearance and, like the abandonment of her career as a sensation novelist, Marion's abandonment of Ord represents a step towards Nigel and domestic contentment and away from her youthful morbidity.

Morbidity and sensationalism

As I noted in the introduction to this chapter, Wilford is critical of sensation fiction but also of the tendency for reviewers to unthinkingly conflate female authors with their characters, what I call the knowledge model of authorship. In taking on the topic of literary reviews, Wilford opens up the novel's self-reflexive discussion of sensation fiction to include not just the roles of readers and writers but the cultural impact of reviews. In *Wilkie Collins and Other Sensation Novelists*, Nicholas Rance suggests that *Nigel Bartram's Ideal* is 'about a female sensation novelist whose career obviously is modelled on that of Mary Elizabeth Braddon' (72). Yet the fact that Marion only writes one sensation novel, coupled with her conventional domestic existence, marks her as radically different from Braddon. Nonetheless, Rance is right to point out that, like Braddon, critics imply that Marion's past must be as questionable as that of her characters. In Nigel's own review, he writes, 'the writer of "Mark's Dream," if a woman, must be one who had a strange and sad acquaintance with the darker side of life, who understood but too well the black secrets of the human heart; who had herself sinned and suffered, and had written out of the depths of her own miserable experience' (49). When Marion reads this, she responds physically, 'with a shudder of strong distaste' (49). Nigel's notion that Marion must have 'a strange and sad acquaintance with the darker side of life' is indeed reminiscent of many reviewers' responses to Braddon's work. W. Fraser Rae wrote, in response to Aurora Floyd's whipping of Hargraves, 'An authoress who could make one of her sex play the chief part in such a scene, is evidently acquainted with a very low type of female character' (98). Later in the novel, Nigel admits that he 'made the old mistake of identifying the writer with the book, and thinking that because Marion has described an erring woman . . . therefore she herself could not be innocent' (334). Wilford shows that not all female sensation writers were themselves sinning and suffering, and the novel thus critiques the limitations of the knowledge model of authorship.

Despite this criticism of the easy movement between character and author, the novel does associate the writing of sensation fiction with morbidness. In the narrator's words, Marion 'had had a very miserable youth, [and] a very undesirable education: she had grown morbid, and her morbidness has worked itself off in a strange unhealthy book, to which her genius had lent a rare attractiveness' (245). The word 'morbid' appears a number of times throughout the book, and it is significant as what history of emotions scholar Barbara Rosenwein would call an 'emotion word' (13). Marion's sister confesses that when their old nurse told them stories, 'a deliciously morbid feeling crept over [them]' (23); Marion calls her younger self a 'horrid, morbid, wretched little self' (112); and she calls her book 'that morbid novel' (213).[5] One of the reviewers of *Nigel Bartram's Ideal* even picks up on this term, noting that *Mark's Dream* 'is a sort of exhalation of a mind in a morbid state, thrown out like a disease clearing the constitution' (*Saturday Review* 59). While Marion doesn't live the scandalous life of her heroine, the novel is nonetheless at pains to link sensational authorship to an unhealthy mental state and body. Indeed, one of the implications in both the novel and its reviews is that for a female writer, writing is not merely an intellectual exercise, but one rooted in the body.

In the previous Chapter, I suggested that *Jane Eyre* figured as a proto-sensation novel; the Brontë sisters also figure as predecessors for 'morbid' sensation authors. Their writing was frequently described as morbid and one reviewer of *Nigel Bartram's Ideal* suggests that the model for Marion was Charlotte Brontë.[6] Their supposed morbidity was not only evident in their writing but in their lives, where it seemed to stem from their social isolation and overwrought feeling. Deirdre D'Albertis argues that Elizabeth Gaskell's *Life of Charlotte Brontë* 'establishes, however unwittingly, Brontë's morbidity as the authoritative model for women writers' (20). Gaskell writes that Brontë was liable 'to morbid and acute mental suffering' (185).[7] To be morbid meant not only displaying inappropriate feelings but spending too much time reflecting on those feelings. Gaskell calls attention to 'Brontë's morbid preoccupation with her own health' and 'the relentless nature of [her] self-absorption' (D'Albertis 23). In Brontë's biographical notice of her sisters, she notes that the 'morbid' Anne witnessed disturbing things and 'what she saw sank very deeply into her mind; it did her harm. She brooded over it till she believed it to be a duty to reproduce every detail' (xlvii). Anne's morbidity, like Charlotte's, stems from a self-absorbing turn inward. The link between morbidity and sensationalism is thus clear: the emotional state and the genre are both too absorbed in feelings, both one's own and those of others.

Sara Ahmed's concept of the affect alien helps to place the Victorian morbid woman in context. Ahmed explains that 'you can be affectively alien because you affect others in the wrong way: your proximity gets in the way of other people's enjoyment of the right things, functioning as an unwanted reminder of histories that are disturbing, that disturb an atmosphere' (*Promise* 67). Put simply, Marion's morbidity disturbs Nigel. The narrator notes that Nigel's assumption that Marion is 'a quiet, gentle little soul' is 'very illogical and absurd, but it made him very comfortable' (27, 53). To be affectively alien does not only mean that Marion makes others uncomfortable; it also makes her uncomfortable when she does not experience the so-called right feelings from the right things. Ahmed notes that the right feelings are aligned with certain 'objects' that circulate as social goods – so that happiness is aligned with marriage or a family in heteronormative culture, for instance (41). Ahmed continues, 'When we feel pleasure from such objects, we are aligned; we are facing the right way. We become alienated – out of line with an affective community – when we do not experience pleasure from proximity to objects that are attributed as being good' (41). Sensational writing and publishing are not 'attributed as being good' for women by Nigel and conservative Victorian culture. Oliphant's reviews of sensation reading and writing are one such example of the way in which affect aliens threatened the culture at large and were seen as disturbing. Even the sensation heroine, as characters like Lady Audley, Isabel Carlyle and Nell LeStrange exemplify, is herself a threatening affect alien, questioning Victorian marriage and the possibility of happiness in quiet domesticity.

This association between female morbidity and sensational authorship is visible in other novels of this period: in the same year that *Nigel Bartram's Ideal* was published in England, Louisa May Alcott released the second volume of *Little Women*, which similarly features a clever young woman who publishes sensation novels that are labelled 'morbid' (297) and the subsequent rejection of such 'trash' as she receives the education required from an older, intelligent man (385). The tomboyish Jo is certainly an affect alien in her culture, even if she amuses others more often than she disturbs them. Readers' perceptions of *Little Women* and Alcott herself were altered by the discovery of Alcott's sensation fiction in the 1970s; of note is Madeline Stern's re-publication of *Behind a Mask: or, A Woman's Power*, originally published in 1866 under the pseudonym A. M. Barnard.[8] Wary of the knowledge model of authorship, I will not assume that all of Jo's experiences can be mapped onto Alcott's own, but I do argue that sensation fiction features as a key intertext for *Little Women*. As Judith Fetterley puts it, 'To read *Little Women* without benefit of *Behind a Mask* is to misread it' (2–3). Like Marion, young Jo writes not about her own life but instead draws from her reading influences: 'Her theatrical experience and miscellaneous reading were of service now, for they gave her some idea of dramatic effect, and supplied plot, language, and costumes. Her story was as full of desperation and despair as her limited acquaintance with those uncomfortable emotions enabled her to make it' (294). Note the recurring links between morbidity, sensationalism and 'uncomfortable emotions'. The reviews of Jo's first book are mixed: while one reviewer praises its 'truth, beauty, and earnestness', another finds that it is 'full of morbid fancies . . . and unnatural characters' (297). And while Alcott suggests that young Jo is simply naive, when Jo later lives apart from her family, the very process of writing sensation fiction makes her morbid.

Like the characters that I discussed in Chapter 1, Jo begins to experience emplotment such that she inhabits a sensational world: while in New York, she immerses herself in sensationalism in order to research her own books. Her publisher, Mr Dashwood, requests books from her that are 'short and spicy, and never mind the moral' (377). In turn, Jo imitates the work of 'Mrs S. L. A. N. G. Northbury' (293), an allusion to American sensationalist E. D. E. N. Southward. She obsessively searches newspapers for accidents and crimes, reads about poisonings and studies 'faces in the street' (378). In focusing only on perversity and strong feeling, and in experiencing the world as though she herself is a sensational character, the narrator warns that she 'was beginning to desecrate some of the womanliest attributes' of her character (378):

> She was living in bad society, and imaginary though it was, its influence affected her, for she was feeding heart and fancy on dangerous and unsubstantial food. . ..
>
> She was beginning to feel rather than see this, for much describing of other people's passions and feelings set her to studying and speculating about her own, a morbid amusement in which healthy young minds do not voluntarily indulge. (378)

Jo's sensational reading and writing turns inward and makes her morbid. Jo is too attentive to the 'passions and feelings' of both herself and others, and the implication here is not that her writing is cathartic but, rather, that it is non-cathartic or sticky. Yet while she 'rashly took a plunge into the frothy sea of sensational literature . . . thanks to the life-preserver thrown her by a friend, she came up again, not much the worse for her ducking' (377). Her 'friend' is the soft-hearted German professor whom she eventually marries, Mr Bhaer. As with Marion, Jo's love interest, who is also her intellectual guide, functions to curb her morbidity.

Like Nigel, Bhaer judges sensationalism harshly. Bhaer finds a sensational periodical in his schoolroom and criticises its contents as 'not for children to see, nor young people to read', mimicking Oliphant's criticisms of the genre. In turn, Jo 'betrayed herself . . . by a look and a blush' (383). As with Marion, Jo's authorship is exposed by her blush, suggesting that she is aware of the inappropriateness of her writing. The narrator notes that 'the Professor saw a good deal more than people fancied . . . it occurred to him that she was doing what she was ashamed to own, and it troubled him' (384). More adept at mind reading than Nigel, Bhaer decides to not outwardly accuse Jo but to criticise the genre. When he calls it 'bad trash', Jo defends the publication of such stories by insisting, 'Many very respectable people make an honest living out of what are called sensation stories' (384). Providing a common metaphor for sensationalism, he replies, 'There is a demand for whiskey, but I think you and I do not care to sell it. If the respectable people knew what harm they did, they would not feel that the living *was* honest' (384). Again, Jo's shame is registered via her blushing face as 'her cheeks burned' (385). Gilbert argues that the metaphor of reading 'as eating or ingestion has a special significance in this era of preoccupation with the boundaries of the body and their violation' (21). Addiction and ingestion were dominant metaphors for sensational reading, which was thought to have 'a degenerative effect' upon the body (22). Alcott shows how sensational writing has similar bodily and mental effects on Jo. Jo thus resolves, as Marion nearly does with her second book, to burn her work. Like *Nigel Bartram's Ideal*, *Little Women* takes a harsh stance on the morbid genre, with Jo writing 'no more sensation stories, deciding that the money did not pay for her share of the sensation' (386). Yet also like Wilford's novel, Alcott's narrative cannot help but playfully reference sensationalism; on just the next page, the narrator records that 'while her pen lay idle', Jo was 'laying a foundation for the sensation story of her own life' (387).

Clever women as affect aliens

While, like Jo, Marion ultimately rejects her morbidness and becomes a good wife (*Good Wives* was in fact the title of the second volume of *Little Women* in the UK), *Nigel Bartram's Ideal* also offers a critique of women's pressure to conform to a limited ideal of womanhood, one shown to be restrictive for both the mind and body. In this way Wilford aligns herself with sensation writers like Braddon and Collins, who showcase and critique women's restricted roles in mid-Victorian society. Sensation authors were of course not the only mid-century writers to address 'the woman question', but the novel's metafictional engagement with sensation fiction seems to encourage such specific comparisons. In *The 'Improper' Feminine*, Lyn Pykett argues that the sensation heroine embodies 'an uncertainty about the definition of the feminine, or of "woman." Woman ... whether as heroine or as villainess (or, as is usual in sensation fiction, as a combination of these two roles), is almost always at the center of the sensation novel' (81–2). Again, the very title of Wilford's novel calls attention to Nigel's traditional ideal of femininity. While the movement from morbid author to good wife might suggest a clear path towards conventionality, attending to Marion's rich and often conflicting emotional life allows for a more complicated reading of this novel. The 'morbid' woman, with her affective and emotional life correctly channelled, becomes not just a good wife, but a clever woman. Yet the clever woman, too, must contend with affective alienation.

Nigel's ideal is far from a clever woman: he admits to a 'horror of strong-minded women' (30). The problem for Marion is that in denying her cleverness, she must act falsely and self-consciously. As I noted in the introduction, Rebecca Stern has linked rhetoric from both conduct manuals and texts on industrialisation to show the range of mid-century authors who criticised mechanical, rehearsed or self-conscious behaviour as inauthentic and unnatural. Referencing the work of Thomas Carlyle and John Stuart Mill, she notes that by 'making visible the performative components of identity, self-consciousness threatens to produce the "mechanical character" against which these writers expostulate' (441). While we might be tempted to equate unconsciousness with mechanical behaviour, Marion shows how in trying to self-consciously match Nigel's ideal, she risks becoming mechanical. On their honeymoon when they 'saw beautiful things or spoke on high and noble subjects, she said so exactly what he wanted said, and no more', her self-censorship here in contrast to her body's inability to censor (118). She learns of her new husband that 'like most well-bred people, he could only tolerate unconventionality up to a certain point; that, in fact, to please him she must not be mechanical or commonplace, and yet never original enough to make any one stare' (119). Wilford, in exploring what it means to be 'mechanical', articulates similar problems of identity that Mill spends much of *On Liberty* exploring. He claims, 'No one's idea of excellence in conduct is that people should do absolutely nothing but copy one another' (59). The irony is that at the beginning of the novel, caring for her nieces and nephews, and not engaging in a full intellectual life, Marion was, in the narrator's words, 'too much reduced to the state of a machine' (69). Her life as a domestic caregiver and her later life as a wife risk making her into 'a mere domestic machine' (120). If sensational writing is associated with an excess of feeling and morbidity, then life as a machine-like housewife seems to demand self-censorship and a suppression of feeling.

Despite Marion's self-censorship, many of the other characters in the novel see through her. Indeed, her unconventionality and cleverness are evaluated much as her body is. Nigel's friend Hugh sees that Marion is 'far from being conventional' (138) and Nigel's sister, Ada, implores him later in the novel, 'Don't keep taming her down into [an] intelligent appreciative creature just clever enough . . . to enjoy other people's cleverness' (340). While Marion assures Ada that publishing *Mark's Dream* was the greatest mistake of her life, she is quite ready to take up writing a few pages later, when Nigel encourages her to return to it. Nigel's change of heart is twofold. In pragmatic terms, he is recovering from an illness that leaves him unable to work steadily and they thus need the income that her writing can bring. In addition, though, he recognises his own culpability in stifling Marion's talents, admitting to his brother, 'I am not sure that we men ever *quite* like to feel ourselves inferior to our wives in anything but goodness. We believe, and we like to believe, that they are purer and better than we are, but I don't think we altogether wish them to be cleverer' (331). Nigel's realisation seems to critique the ideal of the angel in the house, since he exposes the limits to which men will idealise women. Yet Marion is 'clever' and all of these conversations about her cleverness – much like the discourse about morbidity – situate her within a recognised model of identity and behaviour (if not with the affective community of women that Wilford herself had). The *Saturday Review* called the novel 'a clever woman's plea for clever women' (59).

The term of course recalls Yonge's *The Clever Woman of the Family*, which appeared in print just before Wilford's novel. Like Edwards, Yonge's relationship to sensation fiction can be described as ambivalent. June Sturrock refers to Yonge's 'quasi-sensation novels' such as *The Trial* (1864), and Clare Walker Gore finds that traces of the '"sensation" craze ... can be seen in Yonge's own novels of the period' (74, para 4). In addition, Tamara Wagner and others have remarked on Yonge's self-reflexiveness and the ways in which her work is concerned with novel reading and writing; indeed, *Clever Woman* is an example of such work.[9] The so-called clever woman of Yonge's novel is Rachel Curtis, who rebels against the limitations of domestic womanhood, but just as significant and perhaps cleverer is Ermine Williams, an invalid who is also an author. The novel reveals Yonge's 'concern with the potential of fiction to reach a wide readership and either to educate it or to lead it astray through mere sensational stimulation' (Wagner 306). For instance, although Rachel is not a voracious reader, simply a discussion of George Eliot's *Silas Marner* (1861) is curative, providing her with 'no excitement of nerve, no morbid fancy to trouble' her sleep (442).

Like *Nigel Bartram's Ideal*, the novel vacillates between arguing for women's intellectual outlets and reasserting patriarchal hierarchies. For instance, when Rachel asks the sympathetic Colonel Keith 'his opinion of female authorship', she is surprised to hear him insist that it is 'often highly useful and valuable' (174, 175). She is taken aback, she says, since 'Men generally grudge whatever they think their own privilege' (175). Yet his model of female authorship, perhaps like Yonge's own, accommodates traditional femininity. He praises authors who scorn publicity: 'Much of the best and most wide-spread writing emanates from the most quiet, unsuspecting quarters' (175). In claiming that there is a difference 'between being known to write, and setting up for an authoress', Colonel Keith praises the model of unconscious selfhood that Stern emphasises as so vital to Victorian femininity and Victorian personhood more broadly (175). The novel, too, stresses the way in which women are moulded by men: 'unwilling as she would have been to own it, a woman's tone of thought is commonly moulded by the masculine intellect, which, under one form or another, becomes the master of her soul' (506). In Yonge's novel, the clever woman can only exist because of a man.

The problem of the 'clever woman' – and her need to exhibit both intelligence and femininity – was clearly a topic of great interest in Yonge's circle. In 1868, Anne Mozley, a friend of Yonge's and a regular periodical contributor, penned an article in *Blackwood's* called 'Clever Women', in which she identifies the marital problems that arise when a wife is a clever woman:

> Superior intellect can scarcely be what is called attractive. A man is wise to desire to remain intellectual head of his own home, nor do things go quite as they should do where the disproportion of intellect is conspicuously on the wife's side. In the view of two making a complete whole, the woman is not a better complement to the man for being very much above, or for having an intellectual side apart from him, clamouring for expression. (594)

This problem of intellectual superiority is of course precisely what Wilford would fictionalise a year later in *Nigel Bartram's Ideal*, though with more sympathy for the clever woman. Nigel initially seems to mimic Mozley, saying, 'I think it is generally best in married life that when any decided superiority of this kind exists it should be on the man's side; but there is no use in trying to make facts fit into our theories of what is desirable' (264). Marion, with a 'faint smile', agrees: 'There must always be a certain superiority in a man's mind to a woman's, let the "women's right" people say what they will' (264). Nigel, though, 'impatiently' calls her response an 'ingenious evasion' and forces her to admit that she is 'much cleverer for a woman than I for man' (264). While Nigel still maintains a gendered hierarchy even in his humble admission, the novel pushes beyond Yonge and Mozley's idealisation of masculine intellect.

While Nigel must revise his feminine ideal, the novel also details Marion's growing self-acceptance and confidence. The narrator laments that Marion continues to hide her genius 'in shrinking self-distrust and misplaced humility' (246). The narrator's notion of her humility as 'misplaced' tells us something of her judgement, as does her comment that by not publishing her second book, Marion's 'genius . . . was henceforth to be crushed out as a useless, unworthy gift' (209). It is useful to recall the affect alien's relationship to happiness. Ahmed explains, 'To be alienated from happiness is to recognize not only that you are the one who is out of place but also that you cannot make yourself be in place' (156). Hyper-aware of her own unbelonging, Marion wishes that she were like other women. She says to Nigel, 'I want to be the sort of woman that you once thought me – that you can love' (270). Yet Nigel admits that he wants her to be her 'true self' and 'to have done with acting altogether', setting up the impossible situation that she be either cleverer than him or a false version of herself (270). For much of the novel, Marion vacillates between these two equally alienating states and tries to find a middle ground, what she calls that *'via media* which is always so difficult to walk in, that golden mean which is always so hard to strike' (119–20). What Marion describes is affective dissonance, which I discussed briefly in the last chapter. Jennifer Ladino explains that affective dissonance is a conflicted or unsettled state, 'characterized by an ironic doubleness, or even multiplicity' (23). Marion desires to express her genius but also to please her husband, and she finds happiness in both efforts. Yet she can only reconcile her mixed feelings after Nigel has done so. Significantly, both come to realisations after periods of illness and fever from which they reawaken and are eventually reconciled, their new affects and identities emerging out of states of bodily trauma.

If the novel doesn't find a place for the morbid woman, it does find a place for the clever woman, showing Marion working alongside her husband, in an unusual ending that anticipates New

Women writing of the later century. Wilford thus modifies the knowledge model of authorship, as Nigel is able to finally forgive Marion for her first novel because he acknowledges that clever people need not experience things in order to write about them. He admits that 'genius has its dark inspirations as well as its bright ones; that lofty and steadfast souls so dowered can read and interpret mysteries which to others only become plain through actual personal experience' (334). Marion not only returns to writing fiction, eventually publishing that second novel which contains 'a plot that is full of interest, and yet [is] not sensational', but she also replaces her husband in the criticism line, taking over his periodical assignments (352). Before he finally concedes to her abilities and allows her to write, Nigel first asks her to merely copy his newspaper articles for him. She does so without remark, but when he asks for her opinion and she candidly offers it up, he is insulted: 'I beg your pardon for setting you to copy my trash; it does not do to have an amanuensis so much cleverer than one's self' (263). And of course, he is right. The unconventional writer cannot simply copy another's words. Ultimately, it is Marion who suggests that she take over for Nigel when he falls ill, her affective dissonance registered in her face: Nigel 'saw how the quick colour flamed in her cheek, and how there was a bashful trouble in her eyes, though she was smiling' (352). Her first assignment is, of course, an article on sensation novels. While Nigel is shocked that Marion would take it, she assures him, 'I think I could say some right and true things about sensation novels; I think I do see in a measure both the good and the bad in them' (352).

The novel ends with Marion coming to some acceptance over her identity as both a writer and a wife. No longer an affect alien, she is able to experience both the 'happiness of being allowed to serve' Nigel and the 'artist's pleasure in her work' (213). She understands her role as 'bread-winner for a time' as a way to help her husband, whom she still maintains is 'her superior, her king' (347, 362). The novel also implies that Marion's movement into periodical reviews and novel writing is a healthy outlet for her cleverness. Her second novel is lauded by reviewers, who praise 'the vein of deep original thought which ran through the light tissue of clever fiction' (358). Morbidity is replaced by cleverness, just as sensation fiction is replaced by 'clever fiction'. The metaphors in Wilford's imagined review ('vein', 'tissue') demonstrate that both the textual body and authorial body are finally deemed healthy.

One of the reasons that critics considered the sensational female author to be alarming was her likeness to the sensational (anti-) heroine – and Marion figures as both. Two aspects associated with the mechanical model of authorship that I discussed at the beginning of this chapter were an emphasis on plot and audience manipulation. The sensational heroine, too, was frightening for her ability to plot and manipulate others; she was criticised for being morbid, unnatural and overly self-conscious. Beth Palmer, who argues that Braddon, Wood and Florence Marryat saw their authorship as 'a performative activity', also calls Lucy Audley 'a self-conscious actress who re-packages and performs her own life story' (55). By way of conclusion, I want to note how Alcott's *Behind a Mask*, in its self-conscious adoption of sensation techniques, offers a similarly parodic example of the sensation heroine/author. In *Behind a Mask*, the plotting Jean Muir hopes to marry a wealthy man. She succeeds when she enters the Coventry home as a governess and charms all three of the Coventry men, marrying the wealthiest of them all. Alcott shows how she constantly stages scenes for the men to witness, expertly employing her Theory of Mind: she makes sure that one catches her crying in her room and another sees her gazing at his portrait. Only in her own room does she stop performing:

> Still sitting on the floor she unbound and removed the long abundant braids from her head, wiped the pink from her face, took out several pearly teeth, and slipping off her dress appeared herself indeed, a haggard, worn, and moody woman of thirty at least. The metamorphosis was wonderful, but the disguise was more in the expression she assumed than in any art of costume or false adornment. Now she was alone, and her mobile features settled into their natural expression, weary, hard, bitter. (11–12)

Jean's 'metamorphosis' reveals her ability to manipulate others with her body. Her extensive plotting is not fully revealed until the end of the novel when the other characters discover her letters, written to (and sold by) a fellow scheming woman. They show that they have all fallen into her preconceived plots. In this way, Jean, like other sensational anti-heroines such as Lydia Gwilt who use the written word to detail their own machinations, resembles a sensational author.

Yet Jean's body and her 'weary, hard, [and] bitter' expression also reveal how exhausting her performance is. Despite Marion's happy ending, the actual example of Wilford's life shows how difficult it could be for the female writer in Victorian England. In 1889, Charlotte Yonge wrote to the Royal Literary Fund, requesting that they consider Wilford's application for assistance. She writes, 'I have known her for nearly thirty years as a person of great merit, personally, and considerable talent and industry ... there can scarcely be a case more worthy of consideration'. She explains that 'More than ordinary troubles in her family' have left Wilford in 'very reduced means, and have tried her health and spirits most severely ... attacks of insanity have, during the last few years, rendered mental exertions more difficult, or rather, impossible' (19 June 1889). While Marion gets pleasure in both writing and caring for her husband, Wilford's heartbreaking case shows that the pressures of caring for her family and writing took its toll on her body. While the periodical press and Wilford herself overwhelmed the female sensation author with a weight of ideological baggage, Wilford's own story is a reminder of the vulnerability of the female author's body. In the next chapter, I explore examples of metaphorical reading and authorship, attending in greater detail to the social vulnerability of the female body.

Notes

1 For more on Braddon's role as editor of *Belgravia*, see the chapter on Braddon in Beth Palmer's *Women's Authorship and Editorship in Victorian Culture: Sensational Strategies*.
2 In addition to the examples cited in this chapter, it is worth noting that Dora Russell's *The Drift of Fate* (1895) offers a humorous depiction of a female sensation writer. The protagonist, Nell, who has run away from her older husband and is working under an assumed name, discovers that her employer is a sensation author. Mrs Wilmont struggles to find a plot for her next novel and realises that Nell is 'the very thing for a heroine' (243). Not only does Nell's life story give her a plot, but Mrs Wilmont starts to interfere in Nell's life. When Nell is ultimately reunited with the man she loves, Mrs Wilmont is delighted and the novel ends with her letter to the happy couple, in which she proclaims, 'It's a charming end to a romance' (316). For more on Russell, see Janice Allan's entry in *A Companion to Sensation Fiction*.
3 For instance, a late-century lecture on 'Family Life' refers to 'childless and unencumbered adults' as 'unnatural' and 'morbid' (qtd in Walther 66). Eliza Lynn Linton, in *Sowing the Wind* (1867), calls the

effeminate Sir John Aylott a 'morbid' husband (98). Martha Vicinus notes in *Intimate Friends* that it was one of the code words used to describe 'women who seemed too interested in a particular friend' (xxii). She refers to late-century debates about whether homosexuality was morbid or the *repression* of homosexual tendencies was morbid (206). Elizabeth Meadows argues that at the same time that the meaning of 'morbid' was a 'contested term in literary criticism', it 'expanded from physical pathology to include states of mind characterized by an obsessive preoccupation with unpleasant topics' (5).

4 For these details I have consulted the useful website of the Charlotte Mary Yonge Fellowship, which has a section on the Gosling Society, including a list of known members.
5 It is no surprise that Broughton's Nell admits at one point to having a 'morbid longing to do something startling, something that would break the gelid monotony of my existence' (159).
6 The reviewer comments that Marion's 'powers and success find full example and justification in the example of Charlotte Brontë' (60).
7 Gaskell 'stresses again and again how this very lack of external engagement beyond the confines of the self is at the foundation of Charlotte Brontë's character' (D'Albertis 24). Brontë's Lucy Snowe from *Villette* was frequently called morbid. In a letter to her publishers, Brontë addressed this complaint. Her reply, reprinted in Gaskell's *Life*, serves as both a rebuttal and a validation: 'You say that she may be thought morbid and weak, unless the history of her life be more fully given. I consider that she is both morbid and weak; her character sets up no pretensions to unmixed strength, and anybody living her life would necessarily become morbid' (392).
8 For more on *Behind a Mask* in the context of transatlantic sensation fiction, see Phegley et al., *Transatlantic Sensations*, which features several essays on Alcott's work.
9 Wagner locates in Yonge's fiction 'a self-critical reflection' (305) and Karen Bourrier suggests that *The Heir of Redclyffe* has an 'awareness of its own genre' (126).

3

Privacy and 'Public Feeling' in *Salem Chapel* and *Armadale*

While I have discussed Margaret Oliphant's role as a critical reviewer of sensation novels, this chapter explores her surprising foray into sensationalism, *Salem Chapel*. I read *Salem Chapel* alongside Wilkie Collins's *Armadale*, focusing on their depictions of public and private feelings. Characters in each novel fantasise about the idea of a private body, immune to social forces and community gossip, yet these texts consistently collapse the public and private, showing that the body, like the home, is leaky and permeable to the eyes and affects of others. For instance, town gossips are often humorous characters in Victorian fiction, but in *Salem Chapel*, Oliphant depicts the local gossip, the young, disabled Adelaide Tufton, as frightening in her ability to pry information out of vulnerable townspeople. When Mrs Vincent insists on making her usual house calls despite the fact that her daughter, Susan, is assumed to have scandalously run away with an older man, she knows that she must face Adelaide. She tells her maid, 'I must go out, Mary. . . . I must do my duty if the world were all breaking up' (250). When she arrives at the Tuftons' home, she is confronted with Adelaide's discerning eyes:

> 'Indeed it is a pity when people have anything to conceal,' said poor Mrs Vincent, thinking, with a sensation of deadly sickness at her heart, of the awful secret which was in Mary's keeping, and faltering, in spite of all her self-command. She rose up hurriedly, when she met once more the glance of those sharp eyes: she could not bear that investigation; all her dreadful suspense and excitement seemed to ooze out unawares, and betray themselves; her only safety seemed in flight. (253–4)

This moment sets up the various conflicts that I trace throughout this chapter. Sensation fiction relied upon a kind of voyeuristic pleasure, associated as it was with the 'satisfaction or thrill of seeing' (Cvetkovich, *Mixed Feelings* 24). In the case of Mrs Vincent, as with many sensational heroines, her body risks revealing these secrets, as her 'suspense and excitement seemed to ooze out unawares', a compelling description of the ways in which affects can be unwillingly transmitted. Yet Oliphant constructs this scene from the perspective of Mrs Vincent rather than Adelaide, and so what might have been an exciting moment of disclosure is instead written as one of anxiety and vulnerability.

Oliphant thus overturns a conventional sensational device and its associated affects. I see her and Collins as explicitly responding to the notion, explored by Cvetkovich, that sensation novels like *Lady Audley's Secret* and *The Woman in White* rely on 'the figure of the mysterious woman and the affective power of secrets' (8). Cvetkovich questions whether the mystery woman can ever be a figure of resistance, and Oliphant and Collins ask this question as well. Typically, in sensation fiction, the villain demands privacy more than any other character, closely guarding his or her dark secret. But in Oliphant's novel, virtually everyone is terrified by the threat of exposure as a range of characters attempt to conceal Mildmay's shooting and the Vincent family's connections to the soiled affair. These concerns with privacy gesture to Oliphant's reluctance to engage fully in the thrills of exposure. While communal surveillance is not an unusual theme in Victorian fiction, the thrills that Oliphant explores are explicitly linked with sensational modes of reading. Adelaide's 'sharp eyes' are related to the 'watchful eyes of "the flock,"' which 'were all around spying upon the dreadful calamity which had overwhelmed' Mrs Vincent and her son, Arthur (201). The spying community, like the gossipy Adelaide, stands in for a group of voracious, sensational readers. Just as Adelaide reads the living, breathing world around her as though it is a fiction, Arthur Vincent later finds his family's tragedy printed in the 'newspaper of the day' and 'made into a romance of real life' (291). While previous chapters examined solitary reading or writing, this chapter explores reading publics and affective communities in the context of sensationalism.

In Collins's novel, town gossips and nosy reporters are similarly threatening. My reading of *Armadale* is structured around a phrase that Collins uses to describe the collective feeling of both a small town and the nation: 'public feeling' (426). Like Oliphant's 'flock', Collins's 'public' can be equated with a group of readers. The 1860s saw a growing number of articles about a devouring reading public, and while Collins certainly benefited from that very public, *Armadale* betrays an anxiety – mixed with a degree of humour – about the role of this consuming mass of readers. In this novel, it is Lydia Gwilt, the scheming anti-hero, whose story is printed for all to read in the newspaper: first, when she is tried for murder and, second, when she is held up as a wronged woman in the local paper of Thorpe-Ambrose. Collins compares Lydia's murder trial to the actual trial of Madeleine Smith, a young Scottish woman who was accused of poisoning her lover, and whose appearance underwent heavy scrutiny.[1] Lydia exemplifies the idea that Victorian women must be skilled in the art of disguise and performance: she is a lady's maid turned forger turned murderess turned governess turned (possibly reformed) wife. Her ability to mould both her own narrative and her body places her in the public's favour, but she is also made vulnerable by that very public. Collins's depiction of Lydia anticipates Cvetkovich's later work exploring 'the role of feelings in public life'. Part of the 'Public Feelings' project founded in 2001, this work questions, among other things, 'how to give feminism greater impact in the public sphere' ('Public Feelings' 459). While Collins's 'public feeling' refers to public opinion that is affectively driven rather than a clear political project, he is nevertheless explicit about the ways in which public feeling impacts men and women differently.[2] The historical examples that I discuss in this chapter – both fictional and non-fictional – are capable of telling us much about 'the role of feelings in public life' and how such feelings intersect with gender expectations and performances.

This desire to locate the truth of one's character through the body was of course a phenomenon widespread across Victorian culture, evinced by the interest in phrenology, physiognomy and degeneracy. The correlation between outer appearance and inner character was also a recognised characterological trope within Victorian fiction. The bodily exposure that I am describing here is different, however, because it is fleeting and unpredictable: the court reporters watching Lydia and the actual Madeleine Smith are looking for the body to betray its affects, if only for a moment. The notion that there is a kind of truth to such bodily exposure recalls Emily Dickinson's 'I like a look of agony,/Because I know it's true' (1–4), as well as Zunshine's embodied transparency. As I explained in the previous chapter, Zunshine provides three 'rules' for depicting a moment of embodied transparency: it must stand out from other moments, it must be brief, and it must be accompanied by the character's attempt to hide their feelings (*Getting Inside* 30). In the scene from *Salem Chapel*, Mrs Vincent runs off before a true moment of transparency can be realised, but it nonetheless focuses on her restraint as she falters, 'in spite of all her self-command' (253). As I explore in this chapter, moments of embodied transparency result in a form of social pleasure, 'a titillating illusion of superior social discernment and power' ('Theory of Mind' 72). Adelaide clearly represents that mix of pleasure and power, and this is also the position of the sensation reader. Oliphant and Collins attend to the pleasures of such moments of truth but also to their sadistic tendencies and the vulnerabilities of the bodies that are under scrutiny. While I focus most explicitly on gender in what follows, categories of race, class and age all influence the stakes of what it means to have one's body give way to feeling. In sensation novels, moments of embodied transparency are most common for heroines, who are depicted as more skilled in the art of performance but also desperate to hide their secrets. Thus, while these novels do rely on scenes of desperate concealment, they are also attentive to the fact that 'bodies that leak feelings are socially vulnerable' (*Getting Inside* 33).

Issues of privacy and exposure are not only related to the body (or to the home, which often stands in for the body), but also to printed texts throughout these narratives and within sensation novels more generally. In both *Salem Chapel* and *Armadale*, personal information circulates via newspapers, sermons, letters, telegraphic messages and diary entries. These are non-fiction narratives, but they are often read and written as fictions. While Arthur is horrified by the fact that his sister's story is made into a melodramatic narrative in the local newspaper, Lydia anticipates such a reaction and knows that the local townspeople of Thorpe-Ambrose will regard her as a kind of character. When Lydia publicly shares a letter of reference in an attempt to vindicate herself, the narrator notes wryly that the public now 'considered [her] to be quite a heroine' (427). She also creates her own sensational narratives: as she narrates her life story, she admits that it is drawn from 'the commonplace rubbish of the circulating libraries' (594). Lydia's acceptance of her own fictionality may make her a villain but it also affords her a kind of freedom. In what follows, I explore the ways in which Oliphant and Collins use their characters – Arthur and Adelaide in *Salem Chapel* and Allan and Lydia in *Armadale* – to reflect on the ethics of sensationalism. The earnest men contrast with the (seemingly) unfeeling women, but all become absorbed by sensational plots and must make sense of their own roles as consumers of, characters in, and authors of sensation narratives.

Sensational scripts and vulnerable bodies in *Salem Chapel*

Salem Chapel has become the benchmark text in discussions of the boundaries or overlaps between sensationalism and domestic realism. Tamara Wagner notes, 'Given Oliphant's well-known hostility toward the genre, it is perhaps not surprising that her venture into sensationalism has become a classic example of the peculiar self-consciousness that could accompany a seemingly forced adoption of its most popular paradigms' (215–16). The novel appears in Oliphant's *The Chronicles of Carlingford*, a series tracing the quiet provincial life of Carlingford, and it charts the entry of the town's new Dissenting minister, Arthur Vincent. Initially disappointed by the lacklustre town, Vincent soon meets the mysterious Rachel Hilyard (actually Rachel Mildmay) and discovers that she is in hiding from her abusive husband and living under an assumed name. She also keeps her daughter hidden in a neighbouring town. Rachel is the primary sensational force in the novel: soon after meeting her, Vincent learns that his sister has run off with an older man, who is, coincidentally, Rachel's estranged husband. Susan Vincent turns up days later, stunned, hysterical and accused of shooting Colonel Mildmay, while Rachel is in fact the culprit. Rachel Mildmay and Mrs Vincent are both mothers who must hide their feelings and the stories of their lives in order to protect their children. Oliphant thus replaces the sexual passion typical of sensational heroines with the more respectable maternal passion (Jones 239).[3]

Salem Chapel was hugely popular and became a financial success for Oliphant. 'The story was successful', Oliphant writes in her autobiography, 'and my fortune, comparatively speaking, was made' (91). However, this critical success was tempered by reviewers who disliked the melodramatic plotline. While the *Spectator* thought that the novel would 'take a permanent place in English literature', they also recommended that the 'Mildmay melodrama' be 'skilfully removed from the book, by some neat surgical operation' (1639). Similarly, the *National Review* was confused by the 'two different and incongruous parts, – the plot of a sensation novel, and a series of descriptions of the inner life of a dissenting congregation' (350). Such criticisms continued into the twentieth century.[4] A handful of critics, including Shirley Jones, Tamar Heller and Marlene Tromp, have foregrounded the novel's very hybridity as worthy of examination, suggesting that the novel can tell us something about sensation's relation to realism. Such readings have focused primarily on the three main female characters, Mrs Vincent, Susan Vincent and Rachel Hilyard, and their relationships to female passion and voice.[5] My reading, by contrast, focuses primarily on Arthur Vincent and the minor character Adelaide Tufton, and their roles as sensational readers and authors.

In one of the novel's most self-reflexive moments, Oliphant seems to guide the reader away from indulging in sensationalism while she is in engaged in the very act of writing it. Just after his sister has arrived at his lodgings, delirious and followed by a policeman, Vincent stumbles upon the local newspaper at his lawyer's office, which has printed her story. He notices that the clerks in the office are 'talking over the newspaper, full of lively interest and excitement' (291). He finds with disgust that '[i]t was Susan's story that interested them; the compiler had heightened with romantic details those hideous bare facts which had changed all his life, and made the entire world a chaos . . . and all over the country by this time, newspaper readers were waking up into excitement about this new tale of love, revenge, and crime' (291). Vincent responds like a sensational reader, 'wiping the heavy dew from his forehead, half frantic with rage and despair' and 'tingling in every nerve' (291). Jessica Valdez has recently argued that sensation authors commented on 'novelistic discourses in their fictionalisation of news and newspapers' since 'devices commonly seen as particular to sensation and melodrama are also an integral part of the newspaper and its practice of community building' (95). Tamar Heller similarly calls attention to this moment as self-reflexive, suggesting that it emphasises Oliphant's conflicted relationship to sensation since she, 'like the tabloid papers that hawk Susan's story . . . uses scandal to sell her fiction' (103). Indeed, the exposure of Susan Vincent's story in the local newspaper may be the novel's most self-reflective moment, but the narrative engages consistently with issues of privacy and the public sphere in a manner that questions the ideological functions of sensationalism – specifically the genre's reliance on the exposure of women's vulnerable bodies. Rather than consider *Salem Chapel* as an anti-sensation novel, I instead see it as an example of the flexibility of the form as Oliphant uses sensational modes in order to critique women's social and domestic vulnerability, much like Broughton, Edwards and even Wilford. The novel thus provides another instance of how sensationalism can be traced across a range of Victorian fiction.

Despite his aversion to his sister's story being enjoyed by newspaper readers, Vincent is attracted to sensation. What Oliphant calls Vincent's penchant for 'fancy', coupled with his 'ignorance of the real world', makes him seem more like a vulnerable Victorian heroine than a Dissenting minister (6). Vincent is disappointed by the dull tradespeople with whom he finds himself surrounded and for whom he is spiritually responsible: 'Greengrocers, dealers in cheese and bacon, milkmen, with some dress-makers of inferior pretensions, and teachers of dayschools of similar humble character, formed the *élite* of the congregation' (2). The novel maps Arthur Vincent's progression from a man invested in romance and melodrama, to a manipulator of sensation, to, finally, a mature man who has endured emotional suffering. Through his growth, Oliphant directs her readers to be cautious in their sensational investments, and the novel equates public exposure not with voyeuristic excitement but with anxiety. Mrs Vincent plays a significant role in moulding Vincent's narrative affects.

Vincent complains late in the novel that the women around him – his sister, his mother, Rachel and Rachel's daughter Alice – fill his life with sensation: 'His life was invaded by these women, with their mysteries and agonies' (411). Yet before his ailing sister invades his life, Vincent actively seeks out mysterious women. His plot, in fact, bears some similarity to that of Barbara and Nell. In his search for sensation, he becomes attracted to two very different women – the beautiful young widow Lady Western and the isolated, bitter Rachel Hilyard – and they each affect his ability to minister. If Lady Western provokes dreams of 'fairy visitants and unreal scenes' (69), Rachel offers Vincent a picture of 'the dark world of her own experience' (22). In a moment that recalls the opening of *The Woman in White*, Vincent encounters Rachel on an empty Carlingford street close to midnight, following an evening sermon. Initially, Rachel attempts to demystify her odd meeting with Vincent: 'If anybody saw you talking to an equivocal female figure at eleven o'clock in George Street, think what the butterman would say' (89). Her mention of 'equivocal female figure[s]' and 'the butterman' in the same sentence shows how such mystery fits awkwardly in the world of Carlingford. And when Vincent asks dramatically, looking into the home that houses Lady Western and her half-brother, 'what is there in the dark-veiled house yonder that draws your steps and mine to it?', Rachel chastises him for 'talking romance and nonsense' (89). This is an example of what Laurie Langbauer has identified as a motif in Oliphant's work, whereby she includes 'sensational elements in her realism but constantly calls attention to them as overly conventionalized moments' (68). Yet this is also typical of hyperrealism and of sensation fiction, as I have been arguing. Despite Rachel's self-aware comments, she nonetheless indulges in sensational reflections: 'Misfortune seems to lie in wait about these black corners. I think of women wandering along dismal solitary roads with babies in their shameful arms – and of dreadful messengers of evil approaching unconscious houses, and looking in at peaceful windows upon the comfort they are about to destroy' (91). For Rachel, such thoughts of misfortune stem from her own hardships. Vincent, however, has led a sheltered life and these melodramatic notions remain separated from real ramifications, much like Adelaide's emotional disconnection from the world around her.

Vincent spreads such melodramatic sentiments to his flock the following day, mirroring how sensation was seen to be a 'virus . . . spreading in all directions' ('Belles Lettres' 270). Earlier in the novel, when he is frustrated at how beholden he is to his parishioners, Vincent imagines his pulpit to be 'a preaching shop, where his success was to be measured by the seat-letting, and his soul decanted out into periodical issue under the seal of Tozer & Co.' (48). This metaphor of the periodical writer is fitting, not only because Arthur ends the novel by becoming an author and because of the wordplay implied in *author/Arthur*, but because the young minister employs fictional conventions in his sermons. He uses sensational techniques at the most innocuous of affairs, a church tea meeting:

> He told them he had been gazing at them this hour past, studying the scene before him; how strangely they appeared to him, standing on

this little bright gaslighted perch amid the dark sea of life that surged round them; that now he and they were face to face with each other, it was not their social pleasure he was thinking of, but that dark unknown existence that throbbed and echoed around: he bade them remember the dark night which enclosed that town of Carlingford, without betraying the secret of its existence even to the nearest village; of those dark streets and houses which hid so many lives and hearts and tragic histories[.] (102)

Vincent's speech, the narrator states with some humour, is the 'strangest that ever was listened to at a tea-party' (102). Yet unlike Rachel, who is moved to consider the 'dark streets and houses' because of her own tragic life, Vincent recognises his detachment from his own speech. He sees his flock's alarmed reactions and feels 'how unreal was the sentiment in his own breast which had produced this genuine feeling in others' (103). Rather than stop or bring them into his confidence, Vincent plays with the terrified audience, 'deepen[ing] his colours and mak[ing] bolder strokes of effect' (103). He is, as Shirley Jones has noted, a successful sensation author in this moment (243).

Recalling Mansel's notion that 'a tale which aims at electrifying the nerves of the readers is never thoroughly effective unless the scene be laid in our own days and among the people we are in the habit of meeting', Vincent's technique of setting his 'tragic histories' in Carlingford could not be more effective (575). Oliphant's description of the townspeople aligns them explicitly with sensation readers: 'If they had been witnessing a melodrama, they scarcely could have been more excited' (103). The narrator describes their affects and emotions in detail: they experience 'shivers of restrained emotion', 'the faces grew pale and the eyes bright', and they are 'startled, frightened, [and] enchanted' (102, 103). After shifting the atmosphere in such a dramatic way, Vincent feels 'mingled self-reproach and amusement' (103). The narrator explains, 'Somehow, even when one disapproves of one's self for doing it, one has a certain enjoyment in bewildering the world' (103). It is difficult not to think of Oliphant-as-author here, writing in a genre that she both condemns and enjoys. Yet this passage also contains a subtle criticism of the churchgoers, who are so easily bewildered. Vincent quite effortlessly puts 'the most dreadful suggestions in their minds', and Oliphant seems to imply that the reader would not fall into the same trap as the gullible readers/listeners within the novel (103). That is, she both criticises Vincent's exploitation of sensational techniques, and also suggests that the people of Carlingford could be more discerning readers. Vincent's enjoyment is short-lived: in the very next scene he overhears the Mildmays arguing, and his performative sensationalism confronts genuine human suffering.

Vincent soon moves from being a sensation author to a character caught up in a sensational plot over which he has no control. Immediately following his speech, he eavesdrops on a conversation between Rachel and her estranged husband, which takes place outside his window. In this moment, in which Vincent unthinkingly intrudes upon a private, domestic argument – though one that admittedly takes place in a public space – he shifts from being a detached author of sensation to a figure immersed in world of sensation. Jones argues that 'Oliphant's relocation of Vincent in relation to the sensational, from distanced manipulator of his seemingly vulnerable audience to an engaged subject of sensational experience, outlines [her] own conflicts with the sensational form' (243). Indeed, Vincent's subsequent immersion into the Mildmays' life alerts him to the dangers of melodrama. What Vincent overhears is a heated conversation in which Rachel warns Mildmay to stay away from their daughter and threatens to kill him: 'If I had a knife, I could find it in my heart to put an end to your horrid career' (106). It is Mildmay, however, who nearly strikes his wife with his walking stick, but finally resists. Vincent becomes complicit in their family affair: Rachel finds him afterwards and asks if she can send her daughter to live with his mother for protection. Vincent, now a sensation hero, agrees and races off to dispatch a telegram to his mother. The arrival of Alice Mildmay, as well as her father, into the Vincent home interweaves the narratives of these two families, so that they become 'companions in misfortune' (160).

Throughout the novel, Oliphant emphasises how the home, like the body, is vulnerable to foreign influences and affects. Rachel warns Vincent that his mother is too 'generous in [her] reception of strangers' (95). She confesses her uneasiness about his mother and sister living alone in Lonsdale, explaining, 'it does not do for women to be as magnanimous and generous in their reception of strangers as you are' (95). It is, in fact, Mrs Vincent's misplaced hospitality that causes Mildmay to enter the family home in the first instance. She admits, 'It was very foolish ... but he came to make inquiries, you know. I answered him civilly the first time, and he came again and again. It looked so natural' (159). This is an excellent example of the way in which sensation fiction calls attention to so-called natural behaviour: Mildmay's body language is so rehearsed that Mrs Vincent misses observing his machinations. As she comes to recognise the association between the sanctity of her home and her daughter's body, however, Mrs Vincent becomes obsessed with the family's privacy. She attempts to make up for her lapse in judgement by maintaining an obsessive hold on the flow of information within Arthur's lodgings. Anxieties about the permeability of the family home become indistinguishable from anxieties about Susan's vulnerable body; indeed, Susan's body becomes 'representative of that home's sanctities' (Trodd 12). Mrs Vincent more than once cautions her son, 'Susan must not be spoken of through our anxiety' (201). When Arthur suggests that they might confide in their servants, Mrs Vincent replies, 'you are only a man, and don't understand. . . . Nobody must have anything to say about my child' (203). She implies that mothers – and women in general – understand the vital importance of keeping family secrets, and she works obsessively to maintain a hold on the family's information.

Despite her desire to present a calm front, her bodily affects risk betraying her anxiety, as the example with which I began this chapter demonstrates. Yet her struggle for composure does not compare to the spectacle that is Susan's delirious body. Susan returns to Mrs Vincent not so much a young woman as a thing. Oliphant borrows from the language of Mary Shelley's *Frankenstein* (1818) in describing Susan as a nearly inhuman creature. The sensationalism of the scene is increased through Oliphant's use of free indirect discourse, employed to express Mrs Vincent's horror:

> What was it? rising darkly, rising slowly, out of the shadows in which it had been crouching, a huddled indistinct figure. Oh God! not Susan! not her child! As it rose slowly facing her, the widow cried aloud once more, and put her hand over her eyes to shut out the dreadful vision. Ghastly white, with fixed dilated eyes – with a figure dilated and grandiose – like a statue stricken into marble, raised to grandeur – could it be Susan who stood there, without a word, without a movement, only with a blank dark gaze at the horrified woman, who dared not meet those dreadful eyes? When life rallied in Mrs Vincent's

horror-stricken heart, she went to the ghastly creature, and put warm arms round it, and called it Susan! Susan! Had it any consciousness at all, this dreadful ghost? had it come from another world? The mother kissed it with lips that woke no answer – held it motionless in her trembling arms. She cried again aloud – a great outcry – no longer fearing anything. What were appearances now? (262)

The shock of Susan's traumatised body forces Mrs Vincent to give way to feeling and abandon 'appearances' altogether (262). This scene, more than any other, represents the maternal melodrama that Jones identifies as characteristic of the novel. Increasing Mrs Vincent's horror, Susan does not recognise her mother and struggles to access language: 'It began to shiver with dreadful trembling fits – to be convulsed with long gasping sobs' (263). Mrs Vincent is alarmed by 'the dreadful vision' that is Susan's body, 'lying in the interstices between virginity and fallenness, speech and secrecy, private and public realms' (Heller 96). As the narrator notes, the 'sight of her daughter in this frightful condition, coming after all her fatigue and strain of excitement, unnerved Mrs Vincent completely' (263). Yet when the doctor and the detective visit, Mrs Vincent attempts to contain the visual spectacle that is Susan.

The reader's voyeuristic witnessing of Susan's 'frightful condition' is constantly tempered by Oliphant's insistence on narrating the mother's frightened response (263). As Heller notes, and Mrs Vincent seems to recognise, 'What Susan is really on trial for ... is not so much attempted murder as sexual desire' (96). When the detective storms into the apartment, announcing that Susan is to be arrested for attempted murder, Mrs Vincent shocks him by pushing him out of the room and locking the door. It is not simply his accusation that disturbs Mrs Vincent, but his intrusion into her private rooms and his gazing on Susan's 'half-insensible form', which she interprets as a kind of violation (267). She sees him not as a policeman but as a 'stranger, who had put himself so horribly in possession of Susan's sick-room' (266). This scene reads like an extended, horrifying period of embodied transparency as Mrs Vincent struggles to control her feelings. Zunshine notes that moments of embodied transparency in fiction and film frequently occur in the space of the theatre, since it is 'a place where [characters] can catch a glimpse of unguarded body language and thus learn something important about other characters' feelings' (*Getting Inside* 55). This is certainly true in Victorian fiction, but the sickroom is also one such place, as Mrs Vincent recognises. Mrs Vincent allows the doctor to remain, but even he reads Susan's hysterical abandon not as the result of an innocent girl confronted with violence but, incorrectly, as evidence that she has sinned sexually. The doctor finds her to be 'a grand form as she lay there upon that bed – might have loved to desperation – fallen – killed' (267). He reads her body not informed by medical knowledge but by sensational scripts.

The doctor's assessment shows that Mrs Vincent ultimately cannot control the narrative of her child's body, but she nonetheless continues to try. When Vincent returns, she insists that he not speak so freely in front of Dr Rider about their family. Yet Vincent, who has seen the town newspaper but has shielded it from his mother, explains, 'there is nothing private now in our family affairs' (325). His mother is unaware of the 'vulgar publicity to which poor Susan's story had come', and such ignorance allows her to maintain her strength (327). When a second story is printed and Tozer, the church deacon, congratulates Mrs Vincent on the good news – that Susan has been exonerated of the charges and her reputation recovered – Mrs Vincent assumes naively that the newspaper has printed news of Susan's recovery from her fever. Mrs Vincent, though adept at dealing with Arthur's flock, is unable to compete with the 'vulgar publicity' of the newspapers and the public flow of personal information.

Gossip and Adelaide's 'sharp eyes'

Surprisingly, one of the most menacing characters in the novel comes in the form of the young invalid Adelaide, the inquisitive daughter of the former minister. Adelaide's 'sharp eyes' represent an invasion of privacy that is alarming but unavoidable. Her insatiable desire for drama and local gossip makes her a model of depraved readership, but in her ability to interlace the tales she hears, she further becomes a sensation author, much like Arthur. She enters the novel at three key points: when Arthur first arrives in Carlingford, when the Vincent family is in the midst of their domestic trial, and just after the affair has been resolved. Despite her invalidism, Adelaide is a dominant force, overpowering her elderly parents and even Arthur, who feels defenceless in her presence. She is a fascinating example of a female character who exceeds the limitations of her own potential physical vulnerability, and she thus presents a model radically at odds with that of Mrs Vincent or her daughter.

Adelaide's 'affliction' confines her to a cushioned chair that the narrator describes as 'her shell and habitation' (25), and in this chair she sits and knits all day. She is a

> very pale, emaciated, eager-looking woman, not much above thirty, but looking, after half a lifetime spent in that chair, any age that imagination might suggest; a creature altogether separated from the world – separated from life, it would be more proper to say – for nobody more interested in the world and other people's share of it than Adelaide Tufton existed in Carlingford. (25)

It is hard to read Adelaide's body, since she lives in her 'shell' and is 'any age that imagination might suggest', and her illegibility seems to afford her a degree of power (25). Despite her confinement, Adelaide's 'sharp tongue' and piercing eyes make her far from a helpless victim (26). Her severe demeanour means that the townspeople are not accustomed to offering her pity or sympathy, as her circumstances might encourage. Instead, 'Few people could afford to be sorry for so quick-sighted and all-remembering an observer; and the consequence was, that Adelaide, almost without knowing it, had managed to neutralise her own disabilities' (28).

It is both her store of knowledge and her ability to draw information from new victims that gives Adelaide her power. Mrs Tufton explains, 'Dear Adelaide does love to hear what's going on. It is almost the only pleasure she has' (28). Because of her separation from life, she receives a kind of perverse pleasure in discovering other people's secrets. When Vincent arrives, Adelaide is already aware that he has been to visit Rachel Hilyard: 'I'll tell you who you've been to see. That woman in Back Grove Street – there!' (28). Despite never having met her, Adelaide tells him that Rachel 'married somebody who turned out badly' and is currently in hiding (28). When Vincent expresses his surprise that Adelaide knows so much about someone she has never met, she explains, 'I put things together, you see; and it is astonishing the number of scraps of news I get. I shake them down, and then the broken pieces come together; and I never forget anything, Mr Vincent' (29). Adelaide is thus not a passive listener: when she puts 'the broken pieces' together in an attempt to construct a coherent narrative from the stories she hears, she becomes an author. The danger in her authorship is that the stories remain just that; in her detached mind they are separated from any real-world ramifications.

Her detachment, coupled with her desire for sensational thrills, makes Adelaide a dangerous metaphorical reader and author, and she quickly emerges as a threat to the Vincent family. As I have noted, Mrs Vincent, with her obsessive concern with propriety, visits the Tuftons' home late in the novel in a desperate effort to reassure them (falsely) of the family's domestic contentment. Adelaide explains her insatiable craving for gossip to her new victim: 'I have no share in life myself ... and so, instead of comforting myself that it's all for the best, as papa says, I interfere with my fellow-creatures. Oh, pray, don't be sorry for me. I get on as well as most people. Nobody in this place ever succeeds in concealing anything from me' (253). For a woman like Mrs Vincent, who is at that very moment obsessively guarding the fact that her daughter has disappeared, Adelaide's admission reads like a threat. While Oliphant worried about the affective attachment that female readers might experience when reading sensation novels, as I detailed in Chapter 1, here she is critical of Adelaide's disengagement. Instead of reading novels as though they were real, Adelaide reads the world around her as though it is fiction. When Vincent leaves after his first visit, she sits knitting 'with the zest of a spectator at the commencement of an exciting drama' (32).

Adelaide is an adept body reader, and her eyes come to represent her ability to invade the private feelings of others. They are described as having 'a vindictive feline gleam' and as revealing 'a certain mischievous and pleased satisfaction' when she makes others uncomfortable (29, 31). When Mrs Vincent visits Adelaide, she becomes 'aware that to confront those eyes was a more dangerous process than any which she had yet been subjected to in Carlingford' (251). Adelaide's prying eyes are thus evidence of the widespread collapse of public and private in Carlingford and the anxieties that ensue when the domestic cannot offer protection from public exposure. Coupled with her piercing stare is her constant knitting. By rendering knitting – an innocuous, feminine domestic activity – dangerous, Oliphant further emphasises a lack of security within the home. While Adelaide's eyes allow her to penetrate others' secrets, her knitting comes to represent the outpouring of their stories as Adelaide, with her simultaneous listening and putting together, is at once parasitic sensation reader and writer. Oliphant's biographer Elisabeth Jay finds that sewing frequently represents a metaphor for women's writing in Oliphant's work (34). And Adelaide's relentless knitting represents the flood of other people's stories and her ability to imaginatively interweave them. She seems to knit/write Vincent's fate when she proclaims, 'This one will *not* hold out two years' (32).

Ultimately, Adelaide leaves the novel as a strange, almost inhuman object of pity and disgust. She represents, to Vincent, a kind of 'life in death' (443), and her immobility and monotony, after he has endured so much in Carlingford, strike him as pitiable: 'When he thought of that helpless woman, with her lively thoughts and curious eyes, always busy and speculating about the life from which she was utterly shut out, a strange sensation of thankfulness stole over the young man; though he was miserable, he was alive' (443). Oliphant wrote that the novel 'is one of the chief amusements of all secluded and most suffering people' ('Novels' 257). Adelaide's creation of a fantasy world, Oliphant's comment implies, is not unusual for a person with such a disability, but her effects on those around her amount to a rather brutal and morbid form of amusement. Though, because of her isolation, the damage Adelaide can enact is limited, she nonetheless emerges as a threatening figure to both Arthur and Mrs Vincent in their struggle to keep their family secrets protected. Further, Adelaide's voracious desire for scandal figures as a warning for Oliphant's readers to evade such models of readership. Her seemingly invulnerable body thus does not offer a corrective to Susan's vulnerability.

For Vincent, the sensational world by which he is consumed not only forces him to reconsider his attraction to melodrama but further prompts him to question his faith and vocation. While Victorian and twentieth-century critics disapproved of Oliphant's unusual merging of the sensation plot and that of the parish, it is precisely this contrast of the sensational and the spiritual that informs Vincent's crisis. As he travels around the country, searching for clues of Susan's whereabouts, he hears a church bell and is reminded that the day is Sunday, a day when he should be preaching. This prompts him to feel that life is 'all disordered, incoherent, desperate – all its usages set at nought and duties left behind' (225). Vincent is overwhelmed by the chaos he now sees and imagines in the world. When, in the midst of their suffering, Tozer encourages Vincent to write his sermon and save souls, Vincent is alarmed at this responsibility in light of his new, troubled view of mankind: 'Saving souls! – which was the criminal? which was the innocent? A wild confusion of sin and sorrow, of dreadful human complications, misconceptions, of all incomprehensible, intolerable thoughts, surged round and round him as he wrote' (305). Vincent eventually decides to leave the ministry and go into literature. No longer interested in the sensation genre, he becomes the founder of the 'Philosophical Review' (457). Though, by the end of the novel, he still wears his clerical coat and calls himself a minister, he has stopped preaching. His confrontation with the sensational is thus life-altering.

Vincent's troubled experience with his family teaches him about the dangers of indulging in public melodrama and the need for privacy, which becomes, for the Vincent family, the very crux of the domestic ideal. When he learns that his sister will not be charged for the shooting of Mildmay, Vincent is relieved that Susan is finally '[d]elivered from this dreadful accusation – allowed to drop back at least with her broken heart into the deep silences of privacy and uninvadable domestic life' (321). Although Vincent achieves a kind of domestic fantasy at the end of the novel, living like 'an enchanted prince in a fairy tale', this idealised ending cannot compete with the overarching narrative of the novel (460). Despite Oliphant's glorification of domestic isolation, itself a result of the trauma the family has endured, the novel as a whole troubles the notion that domestic life and the domestic body can be truly 'uninvadable'. Susan's body and her 'broken heart' bear the brunt of this invasion, but Rachel's adoption of a false identity and Mrs Vincent's cautions to Arthur – 'you are only a man, and don't understand' (203) – reveal the range of ways in which women in the novel must contend with the sensational exposure of affects that they wish to remain hidden.

'Public feeling' and gendered performance in *Armadale*

Although Collins's relationship to sensationalism was radically different from Oliphant's, he too was anxious about a growing, devouring reading public. A good example of this vision of the Victorian reading public comes from an 1863 article in Dickens's *All the Year Round* entitled 'Not a New "Sensation"', likely authored by Dickens himself:

> It is much the fashion now to dwell with severity on certain morbid failings and cravings of the grand outside Public – the universal customer,

the splendid bespeaker, who goes round every market, purse in hand, and orders plays, poems, novels, pictures, concerts, and operas . . . . [B]ecause this faithful patron chooses to have his meats highly spiced and flavoured, the cry is, an unnatural appetite for sensation! (517)

And yet the author insists that this greedy public, which demands sensational stories in a range of mediums, is not new in English history: 'this taste for fiery sauces, and strongly-seasoned meats and drinks, is of very ancient date; nay, with the public – so long as it has been a public – it has been a constant taste' (517). Setting up claims later repeated by George Augustus Sala in 'On the "Sensational" in Literature and Art', the author suggests that a public desire for sensationalism in fact began not with Braddon or Collins but with Shakespeare.[6] Yet the author does not just trace a history of sensational media in English culture but, rather, a long history of the English public as formed through their shared consumption of sensationalism: 'the public – so long as it has been a public' has had a sensational appetite (517).

Collins too constructs the English public as formed through their shared consumption of sensational tales. In a letter to his mother, while he was writing the wreck episode from *Armadale*, Collins writes that he hopes that the 'public' will respond positively to his novel: 'I am making my own flesh creep with what I am writing just now of the new book. Whether the public flesh will follow my example remains to be seen' (September 1864). In 'The Unknown Public', originally published in *Household Words* in 1858 but included in *My Miscellanies* (1863), Collins refers to the 'public to be counted by millions; the mysterious, the unfathomable, the universal public of the penny-novel-Journals' (159). This *'public of three millions'* is united through their shared taste and reading material (160). Collins is critical of the 'average intelligence' of this group after reading through some of the poorly written serialised stories himself, but he notes that the 'future of English fiction may rest with this Unknown Public, which is now waiting to be taught the difference between a good book and a bad' (162, 177). Collins himself certainly had the capacity to help shape this emerging public as they developed an understanding of literary taste, but his very notion that they must be taught such taste implies that 'the public' is not very discerning. Indeed, in *Armadale* 'public feeling' is capricious and demanding. What becomes clear from his references to the 'public' is that Collins equated this term with a group of readers, readers who may have read privately and felt their flesh creep, but who then spoke to others and gossiped about characters. Public feeling, in this context, is synonymous with group feeling, but it is also feeling for public figures and fictional characters, about the ways in which we feel strongly for those we do not know. This novel, like *Salem Chapel*, is deeply invested in reading publics and their affective responses to the fictions that they consume. My reading of *Armadale* is structured around two uses of the phrase 'public feeling' as employed by the incisive lawyer, Pedgift Senior.

Armadale features a lengthy and notoriously convoluted plot that includes the stories of four men named Allan Armadale. The first generation of Allans compete for the same woman and same fortune. When one murders the other by permitting his death by drowning, their sons – Allan and the renamed Ozias Midwinter – must live with the results. Yet the two younger men possess an instant and intuitive sympathetic attachment towards one another, as I discuss in Chapter 5. When Allan inherits a large fortune and property in Norfolk, Ozias seems to possess no feelings of jealousy whatsoever. Enter Lydia Gwilt. Lydia, a scheming, intelligent and beautiful woman of thirty-five, captivates both younger men. She arrives as a governess to a young woman whose family rents property from Allan, but her chequered past involves murder and forgery. She first intends to marry Allan, then Ozias, and then to murder Allan, solely to gain a fortune as the widow of Allan Armadale. Her plan is challenged when she falls in love with Ozias, and the narrative ends with her sacrificing herself for him when he enters the murderous trap that she had laid out for his brother.

The first use of the phrase 'public feeling' relates to Allan's inappropriate treatment of Lydia, as felt by the town of Thorpe-Ambrose. Allan's new role as a gentleman of property comes with an obligation that he does not anticipate, that of appeasing his nosy community, and his supposed mistreatment of Lydia is an early stumbling block. The second instance of 'public feeling' that I discuss refers to the public's response to Lydia, and it is connected to the actual trial of Scottish socialite Madeleine Smith, who was accused of poisoning her lover in 1857. As Jessica Valdez notes, Collins 'transforms the wealthy socialite into a marginalized 35-year-old adventuress of misleadingly youthful appearance' (106). Collins refers to the London public's sympathy for a beautiful young woman accused of murder, so that the 'public' specifically refers to those Londoners attending criminal trials and reading salacious newspapers, a public drawn to sensation. As I show, these publics react to Allan and Lydia very differently, such that 'public feeling' works to assess and regulate bodies and their social performances, much as it does in Oliphant's *Salem Chapel*.

Allan Armadale is initially pleased with his new role as heir to the estate at Thorpe-Ambrose, which comes with eight thousand a year: a fortune, as Lydia well knows. What the earnest Allan does not yet realise is that his position, much like Arthur Vincent's role as the local minister, comes with a performative element. When Allan first inherits the estate, he is meant to enter the town via a public procession. His dislike of decorum and showmanship causes him to decline such a production. Yet he must appease the insulted townspeople when he does arrive. His servant Richard

> found his master the subject of public discussion. The opinion of Allan's conduct among the leading townspeople, the resident gentry of the neighborhood, and the principal tenants on the estate was unanimously unfavorable. Only the day before, the committee for managing the public reception of the new squire had sketched the progress of the procession; had settled the serious question of the triumphal arches; and had appointed a competent person to solicit subscriptions for the flags, the flowers, the feasting, the fireworks, and the band . . .. And now, by Allan's own act, the public welcome waiting to honor him had been cast back contemptuously in the public teeth! (227–8)

While Allan's rejection of the procession may only betray his modesty, it also signals his lack of understanding regarding local custom and the public role that he must now play. He furthermore underestimates the vehemence of the 'public teeth', a metonymic image that is even more alarming than the 'public flesh'.

One of the qualities that separates Allan and Lydia is that she is savvy in the ways of public performance, while Allan is not. It is both a flaw and part of his charm that he is utterly uncertain of how to act around others. His primary character trait might be his impulsiveness: the narrator writes that he is '[a]ccustomed to let his impulses direct him' (416), a trait in stark contrast to Lydia's premeditated plotting. This difference also betrays the fact that Allan, as a wealthy white man, simply has not had to be as cautious as Lydia. We might recall Mrs Vincent's rebuke to Arthur, 'you are only a man, and don't understand' (203). While Allan finds the townspeople's disappointment rather amusing, he agrees to pay them calls to apologise, an act that quickly backfires as candidness does not sit well with the local gentry. He explains to them:

> I wanted to escape the speechifying – my getting up, you know, and telling you to your face you're the best of men, and I beg to propose your health; and your getting up and telling me to my face I'm the best of men, and you beg to thank me; and so on, man after man, praising each other and pestering each other all round the table. (240)

His account – which exposes the falsity belying their local customs – only serves to annoy the townspeople. The reader, who has a greater understanding of Allan and knows that he is a harmless, if naive, young man, is unlikely to side with the townspeople. The 'public' is thus rendered quick to judge and harsh in their opinions. The notion of parading Allan around as the town squire, even though it has radically different gendered and classed associations, does bear some similarity to Lydia's early life as an advertisement. While she is more willing to play the game of public performance – or rather, does not have as much of a choice in it – Allan's very reluctance to perform betrays his sincerity.

But again, what Collins consistently shows is that this sincere man is misread and judged by the public. His next public scandal results from his attempt to protect his young lover, Neelie, by looking into the references provided by Lydia, her governess. Lydia, who certainly has a past worthy of investigation, has a dramatic and strategic response to Allan's attempt at detection. Lydia 'could not condescend – in justice to herself, and in justice to her highly respectable reference – to defend her reputation against undefined imputations cast on it' (427). She quits her position as Eleanor Milroy's governess but stays in Thorpe-Ambrose so as to reject the notion that she was guilty of any wrong, a move calculated to appeal to the townspeople. While Allan is oblivious of the fallout of his actions, Pedgift Senior, his lawyer, writes to him while he is away from his property, urging the young man to return to town to address the gossip circulating about him. He explains, in a letter marked 'Private and confidential', 'I cannot reconcile it with my sense of duty to your interests to leave you any longer in ignorance of reports current in this town and its neighborhood, which, I regret to say, are reports affecting yourself' (426). He elaborates, in a passage that tracks the circulation of local gossip:

> The first intimation of anything unpleasant reached me on Monday last. It was widely rumored in the town that something had gone wrong at Major Milroy's with the new governess, and that Mr Armadale was mixed up in it. I paid no heed to this, believing it to be one of the many trumpery pieces of scandal perpetually set going here, and as necessary as the air they breathe to the comfort of the inhabitants of this highly respectable place.
>
> Tuesday, however, put the matter in a new light. The most interesting particulars were circulated on the highest authority. On Wednesday, the gentry in the neighborhood took the matter up, and universally sanctioned the view adopted by the town. Today the public feeling has reached its climax, and I find myself under the necessity of making you acquainted with what has happened. (426)

The gossip about Allan's supposed mistreatment of Lydia starts with a vague rumour circulating in the town, then moves to specifics 'circulated on the highest authority', then to the gentry solidifying the view of Allan as the oppressor, to 'public feeling' finally reaching its climax across all classes. Allan's private actions have become public knowledge. Note the similarity between the town of Thorpe-Ambrose and the sensational reading public: scandals are 'as necessary as the air they breathe' to the town's inhabitants (426). Despite Allan's central role here, this is ultimately a story about a vulnerable woman and her past behaviour, like the stories that circulate about Susan in *Salem Chapel*.

Lydia's awareness about embodied transparency and gendered performance marks her as distinct from Allan. She cannily reorients what could have been an exposure about her past into a narrative in which she emerges as the wronged heroine. Pedgift explains, in the same letter to Allan:

> [Lydia's] letter has been shown publicly, and has immensely strengthened Miss Gwilt's position. She is now considered to be quite a heroine. The *Thorpe-Ambrose Mercury* has got a leading article about her, comparing her to Joan of Arc. It is considered probable that she will be referred to in the sermon next Sunday. We reckon five strong-minded single ladies in this neighborhood – and all five have called on her. (427)

Lydia has called in the assistance of the town and has transformed herself into a public figure, with printed and spoken word coming to her aid, not to mention the 'strong-minded' spinsters of the town. While Oliphant details the way in which Susan's narrative is taken away from her, Collins shows how Lydia uses the local townspeople and media for her own ends. Lydia has become a sensational 'heroine' to the people of Thorpe-Ambrose. Yet why does the public care about her?

In *Why Do We Care about Literary Characters?* Blakey Vermeule argues that fictional characters have a social function in that they 'are the greatest practical-reasoning schemes ever invented. We use them to sort out basic moral problems or to practice new emotional situations' (xii). In answer to her book's question, we care about literary characters because we care about gossip: 'we need to know what other people are like, not in the aggregate, but in the particular' (xii). Our brains, she insists, are hardwired to desire such information. In fact, similarities between reading novels and listening to gossip came to the fore in the 1860s. Francis Palgrave, in his attempt to identify 'the wrong' in English reading practices of 1860, complained that novels were becoming indistinguishable from 'living gossip' (488): 'The root of the wrong appears to be, that people, unless profession or scientific interest influences them, go to books for something almost similar to what they find in social conversation. Reading tends to become only another kind of gossip' (488). Sensation fiction in particular was associated with gossip, and Collins was likely not naive about such comparisons. His depictions of town gossipers and the voracious circulation of private information, however, suggest a scepticism about such forms of communication. And while portrayals of gossip are not unusual in Victorian fiction, novels like *Armadale* self-consciously link gossip to sensationalism since both demand the close reading of bodily affects and how they circulate, as well as the close reading of affective narratives.

Lydia uses the townspeople when she shows her supposedly private letter 'publicly', but they are also using her for their own entertainment and to make themselves appear morally superior. Public feeling is in her favour now, but such feelings are fickle. What is striking about this example from *Armadale* is its reliance not just on conversation but on printed text: people become characters when they are written about in the papers. Pedgift warns Allan that the town's other lawyer, whom Allan alienated when he passed him over as a potential lodger, 'has been showing everywhere a somewhat rashly expressed letter you wrote to him on the subject of letting the cottage to Major Milroy instead of to himself, and it has helped to exasperate the feeling against you' (428). In response to all of this, Pedgift Junior suggests that they telegraph a message back to Pedgift Senior as it is 'the quickest way of expressing your feelings, and the cheapest' (429). Yet rather than write a personal message back to Pedgift Senior, they take advantage of the exchange of print already occurring and send back a message that reads, 'Spread it all over the place that Mr Armadale is coming down by the next train', a private telegraph intended to be distributed publicly (430). Pedgift Junior, savvy in the ways of small-town gossip, insists, 'If you want to upset the whole town, one line will do it. With five shillings' worth of human labour and electric fluid, sir ... we'll explode a bombshell in Thorpe-Ambrose!' (429). Yet any potential 'bombshell' resulting from Allan's re-entry into the community is overshadowed by Lydia's pre-emptive moves.

Lydia Gwilt, Madeleine Smith and 'outward effect'

In fact, the second instance of 'public feeling' also concerns these three characters, Allan, Lydia and Pedgift Senior. Pedgift tells Allan that Lydia came to visit him in his office and that she was performing the role of the demure, forgiving woman, insisting that she didn't blame Allan for what happened. When he sees her, Pedgift is reminded of the criminals that he saw at Newgate, who similarly performed their piety. He notes that the female criminals who were genuinely 'wicked and unquestionably guilty' all appeared to have a 'self-possession that nothing could shake' (443). But, once you determined the weak spot in their story, the tears would stop abruptly, and 'out came the genuine woman, in full possession of all her resources, with a neat little lie that exactly suited the circumstances of the case' (443). Such a moment of transparency occurs with Lydia in his office: when he finds the weak point in her story, 'Down dropped her pocket-handkerchief from her beautiful blue eyes, and out came the genuine woman' (443). Even Lydia has her brief moments of embodied transparency. When Allan is shocked by this comparison and exclaims, 'The next thing you'll say, Mr Pedgift ... is that Miss Gwilt has been in prison!' (443), Pedgift responds, 'She may have richly deserved to see the inside of a prison, Mr Armadale; but, in the age we live in, that is one excellent reason for her never having been near any place of the kind. A prison, in the present tender state of public feeling, for a charming woman like Miss Gwilt!' (443–4).

I will discuss Lydia's own experience in the courtroom and prison below, but Pedgift's reference to the 'present tender state of public feeling' likely refers to the trial of Madeleine Smith. Collins alludes to the trial in 'The Poisoned Meal' (1858) and *The Law and the Lady*, but the link between Lydia and Smith demands further attention. Smith's trial in fact brings together the various concerns of this chapter: the collapse of public and private affects, the social performance of gender and class, and the gendered implications of embodied transparency. Smith, a twenty-one-year-old Scottish socialite, was accused of murdering her former lover, Pierre Emile L'Angelier, by poisoning him with arsenic. Her trial began in Edinburgh on 30 June 1857 and ended with the verdict 'not proven', unique to Scottish law. Part of what made the affair so notorious was that L'Angelier and Smith had exchanged passionate, detailed love letters to one another. Like characters in a sensation novel, they used one of Smith's servants and a female friend of L'Angelier as go-betweens in their exchange (Hartman 53). She burned most of his letters but he kept hers, even after she became engaged to another man and demanded them back. L'Angelier refused to return the letters and even threatened to show them to her father; he was murdered soon after. Yet the letters were exposed in a far more dramatic fashion when they were found by police and used as evidence, read at the trial and even reprinted for curious Victorian readers. Smith's letters, typically signed 'thy ever-loving and ever-devoted Mimi, thy own wife', were extremely candid (Jacobson 286). She records their first sexual encounter without any sense of shame or embarrassment. The presiding judge was 'astonished by Madeleine's "licentious" letters and hyperbolically declared that one passage, in particular, was written "in terms which I will not read, for perhaps they were never previously committed to paper as having passed between a man and a woman"' (Hartman 71). It is not difficult to see a link between Madeleine's candid letters and Lydia's. The first half of *Armadale* is written in third-person narration and focuses on the men, while the second half includes Lydia's letters and diary entries (101). Although Lydia's letters are addressed to her adoptive mother, Mother Oldershaw, they record her attempts to seduce both Allan and Ozias.

Yet the even more significant link between the historical Smith and the fictional Lydia is that Madeleine, like Lydia, influenced 'public feeling' because of her appearance. The Victorian public was obsessed with this scandalous story of a young, wealthy woman put on trial for murder, but their interest was further piqued by Smith's beauty and poise at the trial itself. A volume called *Glasgow Poisoning Case: Unabridged Report of the Evidence in this Extraordinary Trial, with all the Passionate Love Letters by the Prisoner to the Deceased, and Numerous Illustrations, including Portrait of Madeleine Smith*, which was published the same year as the trial itself, includes a huge fold-out illustration of the trial, with Smith seated in the prisoner's box. The author records in detail the events of each day in court. The report for the first day, 30 June, records that 'a considerable crowd' assembled outside the court and when the clock struck eight, 'a rush was made for admission' (6). The author then provides a description of Smith's arrival in court:

> when all eyes were turned in the direction of the bar, a very young lady of short stature and slight form, with features sharp and prominent, and restless and sparkling eye, was seen to ascend the trap-stair, and step into the dock with all the buoyancy with which she might have entered the box of a theatre. This was the prisoner Madeleine Hamilton Smith, who took her seat with perfect composure[.] (6)

Immediately following the report is a section entitled 'PERSONAL APPEARANCE OF THE PRISONER', which offers detailed records of her appearance by different writers: 'One writer describes her personal appearance as more than ordinarily prepossessing. Her features, he says, express great intelligence and energy of character' (6). Another notes that her 'complexion, in spite of prison life, is clear and fresh – indeed, blooming' (7). When the 'not proven' verdict was read aloud and there was a 'loud burst of applause from all sides', Smith demonstrated her characteristic 'calmness and composure, although there were occasional evidences in her veiled countenance how great her effort was so to sustain herself' (76).

This emphasis on Smith's appearance, via both description and illustration, is due to the fact that the audience and reporters could not understand how a young, beautiful, middle-class woman could have committed such a crime. Karin Jacobson goes so far as to suggest that the jury's verdict of 'not proven' was a result of their 'inability to reconcile her ladylike appearance with the cunning and cruelty necessary for murder' (300).[7] Yet what is notable about the assessments provided by the court writers is not simply that Smith was an attractive woman, but that she presented 'perfect composure' 'in spite of prison life'. This performance of poise – whether she really felt such calm or not – was consistently remarked upon. Another volume, entitled simply *The Trial of Madeleine Smith*, notes that she presented a 'firm and unmoved appearance' and that she entered the second day of the trial with 'self-possession' (13). When the writers comment on her effort 'to sustain herself', they are looking for moments of embodied transparency that might reveal Smith's true feelings. While the sickroom is one such place where the body might betray one's feelings, the courtroom is clearly another.

While I discussed Zunshine's notion of embodied transparency in the context of the innocent Mrs Vincent and Susan above, sensation authors most often employ this technique in relation to sensational villainesses. This bears out the assumption that these devious women are more skilled in social performance or falsity, but also that their supposedly more tender, womanly affects must at some point betray themselves through their bodies. The comforting notion is that behind every villainess is a hysterical woman waiting to come out – an assumption in line with Cvetkovich's insistence that 'the figure of the mysterious or criminal woman has just as often been mobilized in order to control femininity as to undermine it' (*Mixed Feelings* 51). Criminal sensation heroines like Lady Audley exemplify Zunshine's claim that '[b]ecause we are drawn to each other's bodies in our quest to figure out each other's thoughts and intentions, we end up *performing* our bodies (not always consciously or successfully) to shape other people's perceptions of our mental states' ('Theory of Mind' 69–70). Furthermore, characters that consciously perform in this manner are typically more engaging to readers, especially to readers of sensation and detective fiction. Indeed, many sensation novels achieve their affective tension through the forced performances of the female anti-heroines, women like Isabel Carlyle and Lucy Audley.

Lucy Audley may in fact be the prototype for such depictions, as throughout *Lady Audley's Secret* Braddon makes clear her heroine's need to perform. When Lucy is alone in her chambers, she is startled by a knock at the door: 'She rose, and threw herself into a low chair near the fire. She flung her beautiful head back upon the soft cushions, and took a book from the table near her' (254). The narrator then calls attention to this response:

> Insignificant as this action was, it spoke very plainly. It spoke very plainly of ever-recurring fears – of fatal necessities for concealment – of a mind that in its silent agonies was ever alive to the importance of outward effect. It told more plainly than anything else could have told how complete an actress my lady had been made by the awful necessity of her life. (254)

Lucy's attention to 'outward effect' dictates how she moves around the world and, as Braddon notes, this performance is necessary if she is to maintain her social position. Scenes of embodied transparency with Lucy are rare and therefore significant. For instance, early in the novel, when her mistress hints that Sir Michael Audley will likely propose marriage, Lucy 'dropped the brush upon the picture [that she was painting], and flushed scarlet to the roots of her fair hair; and then grew pale again, far paler than Mrs Dawson had ever seen her before' (13). Pamela Gilbert notes there is an important distinction between the self-aware and (supposedly) modest blush and the more mechanical flush (78). The blush involves, in Darwin's words, 'the thinking about what others think of us' (300). In contrast, the 'flush' was seen as an 'animalistic response resulting from emotion that is not combined with aware "self attention"' (Gilbert 78). Lucy's flush is important here: 'Lady Audley never blushes, because she has no shame, only fear of being caught' (102).

In *Armadale*, Lydia's appearance demands a similar scrutiny. Part of the horror associated with her appearance in the novel is that Lydia's history is not actually visible on her body. A notorious review by the *Spectator* focused on the crime of Lydia's age, calling her 'a woman fouler than the refuse of the streets, who has lived to the ripe age of thirty-five, and through the horrors of forgery, murder, theft, bigamy, gaol, and attempted suicide, without any trace being left on her beauty' (638–9). Like Lucy, she hides a nervous interior through a performance of self-possession. Sensation fiction frequently detailed women's gifts for imposture via their familiarity with clothing and cosmetics. For instance, Lucy tells her maid, Phoebe, 'with a bottle of hair-dye, such as we see advertised in the papers, and a pot of rouge, you'd be as good-looking as I, any day' (58). And Collins's *The Law and the Lady* focuses on Victorian women's use of arsenic to improve their complexion, even as it becomes a deadly weapon in that novel. Madeleine Smith in fact claimed that she purchased arsenic to lighten her skin, as she had seen advertised in the papers (*Glasgow* 22). Lydia's mentor in all things devious, Mother Oldershaw, is a cosmetics expert with 'twenty years experience among our charming sex in making up battered old faces and wornout old figures to look like new' (191). When Oldershaw tells Lydia to use her applications to look even younger, Lydia scoffs at the need for make-up to disguise her age: 'Keep your odious powders and paints and washes for the spotted shoulders of your customers' (193–4). Indeed, part of what is so threatening about Lydia is that she has no need of cosmetics and clothing to improve her appearance and make her attractive to the younger Allan and Ozias.

Yet there are moments when her façade comes close to cracking. One of the few moments of embodied transparency related by the novel's omniscient narrator comes after Midwinter has left Lydia's apartments, a scene in which she has pleaded her case against Allan. While she expertly works her narrative skills, her body too works upon Midwinter as he yields 'to the magnetic fascination of her touch' (465). Yet once he leaves, Lydia transitions from seductress to isolated woman: 'A change came over her the instant she was alone. The colour faded out of her cheeks; the beauty died out of her eyes; her face hardened horribly with a silent despair. "It's even baser work than I bargained for," she said, "to deceive *him*"' (468). The narrator tells us that her fading colour and hardened expression signal her 'despair' at realising that duping Midwinter is not as pleasurable as duping the hapless Allan. Collins does not end the scene there, however. Rather than have only the narrator and reader observe Lydia's moment of transparency, he also shows how Lydia watches herself. In an attempt to reconcile her affective dissonance, Lydia stops and 'address[es] the reflection of herself in the glass' (468):

'Have you got any conscience left? And has that man roused it?'

The reflection of her face changed slowly. The color returned to her cheeks, the delicious languor began to suffuse her eyes again. Her lips parted gently, and her quickening breath began to dim the surface of the glass. She drew back from it, after a moment's absorption in her own thoughts, with a start of terror. 'What am I doing?' she asked

Privacy and 'Public Feeling' 125

herself, in a sudden panic of astonishment. 'Am I mad enough to be thinking of him in *that* way?' (468)

This is a surprisingly candid description of a woman's sexual desire in mid-Victorian fiction. It is telling that Lydia reads her desire for Midwinter not as the natural outcome between two sympathetic people but as madness. Lydia then exhibits a kind of emotional distance from herself, bursting into a 'mocking laugh' at the woman in the mirror, who is a kind of second self (468). This is in fact what she terms her diary, another instance of her multiplicity. She writes, 'My misery is a woman's misery, and it *will* speak – here, rather than nowhere; to my second self, in this book, if I have no one else to hear me' (659). In fact, more often than having readers witness moments of embodied transparency, Collins has Lydia pen confessions to Mother Oldershaw or write them in her diary.

This formal choice allows Collins to avoid the potentially sadistic scene of female bodily exposure – and the scene above also partially does so by having no one to witness Lydia's changing complexion. Instead, Lydia's diary becomes the place in which she meditates on her social performances and her private feelings. For instance, she admits that as she tries to seduce that 'fool' Allan Armadale, the only challenge is 'the difficulty of concealing my own feelings', specifically her dislike of him (343). Later, when talking with Allan on the train, it becomes harder for Lydia to conceal her own plotting:

> As the time wore on, I began to feel a terrible excitement; the position was, I think, a little too much for me. There I was, alone with him, talking in the most innocent, easy, familiar manner, and having it in my mind all the time to brush his life out of my way, when the moment comes, as I might brush a stain off my gown. It made my blood leap, and my cheeks flush. I caught myself laughing once or twice much louder than I ought; and long before we got to London I thought it desirable to put my face in hiding by pulling down my veil. (589)

Like Lucy, Lydia is a flusher not a blusher. Her comments above reflect her hyper-awareness of the need to control her physical impulses and to resist any outpouring of nervous excitement. Her act of pulling down her veil reveals her knowledge of the ways in which her body can be read by others and her desire to control the narrative of her life.

The report of Lydia's own trial for poisoning her husband comes later in *Armadale*, delivered by the unfeeling private investigator James Bashwood to his father, who is infatuated with Lydia. Though the public interest in the trial and the beautiful young murderess suggests that Collins is clearly borrowing from Smith's case, unlike in Smith's trial, the verdict in Lydia's case is guilty. When the judge reads the verdict aloud, the young Bashwood reports, the 'female part of the audience was in hysterics; and the male part was not much better. The judge sobbed, and the bar shuddered. She was sentenced to death in such a scene as had never been previously witnessed in an English Court of Justice' (644). The embodied reaction of the courtroom is similar to that of the churchgoers in Oliphant's novel and offers another example of collective affects. Yet Lydia is saved from a life in jail by adept authors, who transform her into a sympathetic character:

> On the evening of the trial, two or three of the young buccaneers of literature went down to two or three newspaper offices, and wrote two or three heart-rending leading articles on the subject of the proceedings in court. The next morning the public caught light like tinder; and the prisoner was tried over again, before an amateur court of justice, in the columns of the newspapers. (644)

He explains that because of the public outcry, the Home Secretary reversed the verdict and instead 'the verdict of the newspapers carried the day' (645). What is striking about this reaction is that the public responds as though they know Lydia because of the fictional narratives that circulate about her. While Lydia's own performance at the trial captivates those in attendance, once she is created into a literary character, public feeling is further stimulated (11). Lydia's story, however, doesn't end there. James Bashwood tells his father, 'You know what happened when the people found themselves with the pet object of their sympathy suddenly cast loose on their hands? A general impression prevailed directly that she was not quite innocent enough, after all, to be let out of prison then and there! Punish her a little – that was the state of the popular feeling' (645). Again, public feeling is fickle and demanding as Lydia is marked as 'not quite innocent enough'.

Lydia is then jailed only briefly for robbery, rather than murder, and is able to reinvent herself once she is freed.

Lydia is not only a character for others to write about, but, as a number of critics have noted, she is herself a kind of author, adept at sensational plotting and manipulating narrative affects. Michael Tondre calls her an 'authorial figure ... who works to usurp the plot through the manipulations of melodramatic conventions', and she embraces this role (691).[8] Her letters and entries show that she is candid about constructing her life like a fiction. When she writes an anonymous letter to Major Milroy to warn him about his daughter's flirtations with Allan, she notes, 'If I had been a professed novelist, I could hardly have written more naturally in the character of a servant than that!' (559). After she tells Midwinter her life story, she admits in her diary that it is a pastiche of sensational tropes: 'There was nothing new in what I told him: it was the common-place rubbish of the circulating libraries. A dead father; a lost fortune; vagabond brothers, whom I dread ever seeing again; a bed-ridden mother dependent on my exertions' (594). And, finally, when she is a bored married woman, instead of reading a novel, she picks up her own diary for entertainment, recording, 'what a life it was, at Thorpe-Ambrose! I wonder I kept my senses. It makes my heart beat, it makes my face flush, only to read about it now!' (662). Lydia has become a character, even to herself. In a moment that we might describe as a fictional character questioning her own fictionality, she later asks, 'Why am I not always on my guard and never inconsistent with myself, like a wicked character in a novel?' (677).

It is easy to forget that she is initially mixed up in the affair of the first generation of Armadales because she is a forger, appropriating someone else's identity, someone else's plot. Additionally, her life story begins not with her birth but with her entrance into Thorpe-Ambrose as an advertisement. Foregrounding her ability to transform and commodify her appearance, she works as an advertisement for a 'traveling quack doctor' who exhibits her as 'a living example of the excellence of his washes and hair-oils' (632). As with Broughton's Nell, writing thus emerges as an important way for Lydia to understand herself and negotiate her various personas. It furthermore gives readers privileged access to her private thoughts: we learn, for instance, that she is addicted to opium and grinds her teeth, signs that her anxiety is taking shape physically. Deborah Wynne notes that through Lydia's letters and diary, 'Collins reveals the usually hidden aspects of the private self' (153). The March 1865 instalment of *Armadale* began with the chapter 'Lurking Mischief', which includes the first letters between Lydia and Mother Oldershaw with no commentary or framing from the omniscient narrator. Wynne writes, 'At the very moment when readers need to know how to 'place' these two women and gain more details about their mercenary plot, Collins withdraws his third-person narrator, offering only the women's letters and a suggestive chapter title' (159). She argues that the inclusion of Lydia's diary and letters in this manner 'amounts to a collusion with the culture of spying and secrecy which pervades the novel' and much sensation fiction (153). The shocking moment in Collins's *The Woman in White* when Fosco reads Marian's diary without her permission and records his own response is a good example of such spying. Consider, too, the voyeuristic impulses behind Robert and George's sneaking into Lady Audley's rooms in Braddon's novel. Yet there are conflicting impulses at work in Collins's inclusion of Lydia's diary. Often, her candid diary entries fill in gaps that she leaves purposefully absent from her letters to Oldershaw or others. Thus, while readers do occupy a privileged position in reading them, the entries also reveal a far more multifaceted picture of this woman and of the exhausting performance that she undergoes.

Lydia's final letter, written solely to her husband, Midwinter, is important in this regard. Lydia's final scenes, perhaps fittingly, take place at a sanatorium. Run by Dr Downward, an associate of Mother Oldershaw's, an abortionist and a hack psychologist, the sanatorium is the place where Lydia plans to entrap and murder Allan by pumping poisonous gases into his room. Yet when he and Midwinter switch places, Lydia pulls out her unconscious husband, pens a final letter, and enters the deathly room herself. She ends her letter by saying,

> Forget me, my darling, in the love of a better woman than I am. I might, perhaps, have been that better woman myself, if I had not lived a miserable life before you met with me. It matters little now. The one atonement I can make for all the wrong I have done you is the atonement of my death. It is not hard for me to die, now I know you will live. Even my wickedness has one merit – it has not prospered. I have never been a happy woman. (806)

Even if Lydia gets the final word on the narrative of her life, it is difficult not to read the letter and her final actions as feminising Lydia through her feelings of atonement, and as a fitting punishment for her sins. In this way, her ending is radically different from Mother Oldershaw's. In a letter from Pedgift Senior to Pedgift Junior that serves as part of the novel's epilogue, we learn that Oldershaw has become a 'public amusement' (812). Pedgift Senior finds himself at a performance in London entitled 'Sunday Evening Discourses on the Pomps and Vanities of the World, by a Sinner Who Has Served Them' (812). The 'eloquent' performer is Mother Oldershaw, and Pedgift describes her 'sermon' as 'a narrative of Mrs Oldershaw's experience among dilapidated women, profusely illustrated in the pious and penitential style' (812). Oldershaw thus adapts her narrative for a new crowd and remains in the public sphere, while Lydia's last letter, a private one, ends her unhappy life.

Near the end of the novel, Lydia writes in her diary, 'I deserve to suffer; I deserve neither love nor pity from anybody. – Good heavens, what a fool I am! And how unnatural all this would be, if it was written in a book!' (683–4). Comments like this lead me to believe that Collins was using these characters and the discussion of public and private feelings to work through the effects of sensationalism. Affects leak out of bodies and into spaces like the sickroom, the courtroom and the home, and this transpersonal quality of affects consistently challenges the notion of private versus public feelings. While *Salem Chapel* and *Armadale* do expose women's secrets and affects in a sensational manner, that sensationalism is tempered by Oliphant and Collins's thoughtful meditations on privacy, gendered performance and the social regulation of women's bodies. In the following chapter, I attend to transpersonal affects in greater detail, focusing on theories of crowd and mob behaviour in sensation narratives.

Notes

1 Smith's entrance into the courtroom was likened to her entrance onto a stage. As one observer noted, during the first day's proceedings, 'the prisoner maintained a firm and unmoved appearance, her keen and animated expression and healthful complexion evincing how little, outwardly at least, she had suffered by the period of her imprisonment and the horror of her situation' (7).

2 Within affect theory, 'public feeling' is often synonymous with political feelings.
3 In her reading of *Salem Chapel*, Jones borrows from E. Ann Kaplan and Lyn Pykett's classification of *East Lynne* as a maternal melodrama. Pykett argues that 'the reader is repeatedly invited to identify with Isabel through the text's staging of the spectacle of her maternal suffering' (13). Cvetkovich also reads *East Lynne* as a maternal melodrama in *Mixed Feelings*, interrogating the social function of such a narrative: 'Generating affect from the spectacle of the mother separated from her child, the maternal melodrama presumes that nothing is more natural and inevitable than a mother's love' (112).
4 For instance, in 1966, Vineta and Robert Colby argued that the 'crudely melodramatic plot almost totally obscure[s] the important issues of the book' (49); in 1975, Valentine Cunningham complained that the '"sensation" element ... constantly diverts attention from the chapel' (240); and in 1995 Elisabeth Jay echoed, '*Salem Chapel* suffers badly from the sensational plot' (5).
5 As I noted, Jones argues that the novel replaces sensual passion with maternal passion via Mrs Vincent. Tromp examines Oliphant's representation of marital violence and Rachel Hilyard as a victimised female figure in *The Private Rod*. Heller focuses on the ways that Susan 'reflects Victorian anxieties about both women's sexuality and their speech' (96).
6 Broughton, too, makes the connection between Shakespeare and sensationalism explicit by using a line from *Othello* as a title for her novel *Not Wisely, but Too Well*.
7 Henry James confessed in a letter, 'what a pity she was almost of the pre-photographic age – I would give so much for a veracious portrait of her *then* face' (qtd in Jacobson 300).
8 Along similar lines, Laurence Talairach-Vielmas argues that Gwilt is a writer who 'anticipates the extent to which her own life is a fiction' (81), and Deborah Wynne notes that she is 'a skilful manipulator of plots, secrets, and suspense' (154).

4

Crowds and Bodily Sympathy in Wood and Clive

In 1862, a riot formed outside of the Religious Tract Society in London, with 'protesters storming . . . Paternoster Row and threatening to put the windows out' (Arnold 148).[1] The rioters were pro-unionists, and they formed not as the result of some political agitation or legislation but in protest of a sensation novel, Ellen Wood's *A Life's Secret*. The novel was serialised anonymously that year in *The Leisure Hour*, a periodical published by the Religious Tract Society. *A Life's Secret* depicts an attempted strike and lockout, and it is pointedly critical of trade unions and the impact of strikes on workers' families. As Wood herself put it in the preface to the 1867 edition of the novel, 'The appearance of the story in 1862 did not please everybody, and angry remonstrances came down on the managers of "The Leisure Hour"' (vi). This is a rare instance in which a novel that expressed a fear of a working-class mob actually provoked one.

I will return to the specific example of Wood's novel, but my broader focus in this chapter is the way in which sensation authors depicted crowd and mob behaviour and how such depictions of the transmission of affect are related to the narrator's directive sympathy. The mob, which might be understood as the crowd with intention, is a deeply affective entity, in which people can experience a loss of inhibition and act spontaneously and even violently. In his 1895 study of the crowd, French psychologist Gustave LeBon argues that a crowd exhibits intense affects and lower intellectual functioning than separated individuals. In a crowd, the individual 'is no longer himself, but has become an automaton who has ceased to be guided by his will' (32). In this chapter, I explore the notion of the crowd as a space for heightened affects and wilful abandon. The crowd demonstrates what Stephen Ahern calls the most central insight of affect theory, that 'no embodied being is independent, but rather is affected by and affects other bodies, profoundly and perpetually as a condition of being in the world' ('Introduction' 4). The crowd and the related phenomenon of the mob are important subjects for sensation fiction, so invested as the genre is in wilful, affective bodies. This chapter thus offers another way of understanding public feelings and, like the last chapter, relates the crowd to a group of readers, swayed by certain narratives more than others.

Representations of mobs were certainly not restricted to sensation novels in the mid-Victorian period, as 'mutiny novels' that depicted the Sepoy Rebellion demonstrate. The Rebellion more often figures as a backdrop in sensation fiction, however, and a very conflicted or even critical one. For example, *Lady Audley's Secret* registers the trauma of British soldiers returning from India; the villain in Felicia Skene's *Hidden Depths* (1866) was a British 'hero' in the Rebellion; and in *The Moonstone*, the British Herncastle is the villain while the Indians are victims of imperial violence (Tomaiuolo 116).[2] *The Moonstone* is set much earlier, but its prologue occurs during the 1799 siege of Seringapatam, the victory that positioned the British with their stronghold in the country. It would likely have called to mind the events of 1857 for readers (Nayder, 'The Empire' 446).[3] The sensation novel's investment in contemporary and local settings, as well as class politics, means that mobs in these novels are more often related to working-class conflicts. Yet even when descriptions of mobs concern white Englishmen, the language employed to describe them is frequently racialised and steeped in colonial ideology, as I explain.

In this way, sensation fiction draws from Condition of England novels like Charlotte Brontë's *Shirley* (1849) and Gaskell's *North and South* (1855), which depict working-class mobs and the reactions of the factory-owning protagonists. In *North and South*, a mob forms in protest to Thornton's decision to replace his workers with Irishmen: 'As soon as they saw Mr Thornton, they set up a yell, – to call it not human is nothing, – it was as the demoniac desire of some terrible wild beast for the food that is withheld from his ravening' (176). The 'demoniac' men are working-class men whose behaviour is related to us via the perspective of the observing middle-class protagonists. Dickens, too, was interested in the mechanics of crowd behaviour even before his depiction of the French Revolution in *A Tale of Two Cities* (1859). In *Barnaby Rudge* (1841), set during the Gordon Riots of 1780, he portrays the mob as all affect: 'The great mass never reasoned or thought at all, but were stimulated by their own headlong passions' (438). I am not proposing that sensation novels necessarily betrayed a deeper investment in crowd dynamics than these novels. However, since depictions of intense affect and mechanised behaviour were an aspect of the very form, crowds, mobs and riots were key mechanisms by which sensation authors not only explored class or racial conflict but also presented theories about affect and its transmission – namely, how affects come into meaning when placed in the context of such conflict. If we consider sensation novelists to be early affect theorists, then it is worth asking what kinds of theories they developed about crowd behaviour and sympathetic contagion.

While I discuss Caroline Clive's proto-sensation novel *Paul Ferroll* (1855) and, briefly, Dickens's *A Tale of Two Cities*, Ellen Wood's fiction is the primary focus of this chapter because of her attention to both class politics and the politics of feeling. Deborah Wynne, for instance, notes that the major theme Wood pursued throughout her career was 'class conflict, her favoured plots depicting a righteous bourgeoisie asserting their values over an enfeebled, yet corrupt, aristocracy and infantilized, occasionally troublesome, working class' (62). In addition, Wood was particularly invested in shared feeling, both between fictional characters and between characters and readers. In terms of the latter, this frequently takes the form of encouraging the reader to feel for, or even with, her flawed heroines. Wood's narrative voice bears similarities to what Robyn Warhol has called the 'engaging narrator', a narrator who frequently employs the second person in order to appeal to readers and encourage them to 'identify with the "you" in the texts' ('Toward a Theory' 812). Wood additionally uses free indirect discourse and detailed descriptions of her heroine's bodily affects to encourage readerly feeling for her beleaguered heroines. Yet the idea of feeling with others – so central to sensation novels – clearly becomes complicated in the context of a mob and especially a male, working-class mob.

In what follows, I first explore the ways in which late Victorian crowd psychologists and nineteenth-century authors conceptualised ideas of affective contagion and crowd behaviour. As I explained in the introduction, many Victorian writers used the term 'sympathy' to refer to the transmission of affect. In this chapter, I consider how sympathy informs ideas of crowd affects across a range of writing. While theorists from the late nineteenth century, twentieth century and early twenty-first century all imply that the crowd erases social differences, Victorian writers tend to invoke the crowd in order to make social differences visible. The two ways in which mid-Victorians understood sympathy – as embodied as well as cognitive – inform my readings of Wood's *A Life's Secret* and Clive's *Paul Ferroll*. *A Life's Secret*, in addition to depicting a working-class mob, explores the limits of feeling for and with others, especially working-class others. What Wood stresses in this novel is that the mindless, emotional mob is led by a single leader, an argument that has important implications for both class politics and her own narrative strategies. The chapter then analyses Clive's *Paul Ferroll*, a proto-sensation novel that features a mob scene and centres around the protagonist's inability to empathise with others. In both novels, the mob is an affective tool, allowing Wood and Clive to theorise the moral murkiness of shared feelings: Wood's novel betrays an interest in how sympathy can be directed or manipulated – both via the character Sam Shuck, a union leader, and her narrator – while Clive's explores what happens when characters and readers cannot feel along with others. Through an emphasis on Paul's affectless body and an avoidance of free indirect discourse, Clive's narrative directs readers away from feeling with him, his inscrutability rendering him a figure of both horror and fascination.

Collective sympathy, or the crowd

As I outlined in the introduction, for Victorian writers like Henry George Atkinson, Charles Darwin and Alexander Bain, 'sympathy' referred to a drifting of affect, an involuntary exchange of sensations from one body to another or between various bodies – hence the association between sympathy and crowd dynamics. Sympathy, for Bain, is 'the surrender of self to others', an apt description for crowd dynamics and collective affects (180). Bain is quite idealistic about sympathy, arguing that the 'disposition to take on the states of others, irrespective of the warm attachments and likings of our nature is ... the real source of our vicarious impulses, and of our generous, humane, and social sentiments; it is the disinterested element of the moral sense' (179). And this disinterested element is rooted in our perceiving bodies. This connection between bodily sympathy and generosity is striking, especially in an emergent industrial and imperial age in which mimicry and imitation were starting to seem unsettlingly mechanistic. While Bain offers an optimistic portrayal of sympathy, the mob presents a potentially frightening instance of individual identity and affect being 'softened down into uniformity' (182). For many Victorians, the mob most clearly called to mind working-class protest, from the 1819 Peterloo Massacre to the nationwide Chartist assemblies of the late 1830s. As Wood notes in her preface to *A Life's Secret*, 'strikes, as we all know, have been latterly growing in notoriety' (v). For their Romantic predecessors, however, the mob was most readily associated with the French Revolution. Literary critic Mary Fairclough has in fact linked crowd dynamics to sympathy in the Romantic era, arguing that in this period, sympathy can account for group behaviour since it was seen as 'a medium for the transmission of energies, ideas and emotions within a collective', a notion of sympathy that was still at work in the Victorian period (3). Fairclough focuses in particular on ways in which the sympathetic transmission of feeling acquired new political significance following the French Revolution. Collective sympathy became more pointedly read as a threat or 'a disruptive social phenomenon which functioned to spread disorder and unrest between individuals and even across nations like a "contagion"' (1). She argues that the association between sympathy and 'unruly collective action' became more consistent by the end of the eighteenth century (6). Again, by the time we move into the Victorian period, we can see 'sympathy' beginning to shift into our more contemporary sense, in which it is aligned with pity and compassion, but this notion of contagious, collective sympathy remains, as does the idea that collective sympathy 'disrupts understandings of autonomous, unitary selfhood' (5).

While the term 'sympathy' largely ceases to be associated with unruly crowds by the end of the nineteenth century, concepts of shared feeling remained vital to classical crowd psychology. In Gustave LeBon's 1895 account of crowd behaviour, he characterises the crowd as a collection of human automatons, not guided by their own conscious will. While his study has been subject to critique for its essentialist claims – namely, the notion that all people and all crowds will react similarly, regardless of historical or cultural differences – his emphasis on contagious affects has affinities with both contemporary affect theory and Victorian collective sympathy, but also allows their differences to come into focus. LeBon emphasises the overwhelming nature of the crowd, to such an extent that an individual will sacrifice his 'personal interest to the collective interest' and function much like he is hypnotised (30). An individual within a crowd is 'transformed' as it 'puts them in possession of a sort of collective mind which makes them feel, think, and act in a manner quite different from that in which each individual of them would feel, think, and act were he in a state of isolation' (27). Yet LeBon understands this collective mind – which might better be understood as a collective body – as intellectually inferior to the single individual, noting that in a crowd, 'man descends several rungs in the ladder of civilization. Isolated, he may be a cultivated individual; in a crowd, he is a barbarian . . . a creature acting by instinct' (32). This statement echoes Dickens's description of the mob as abandoning reason for passion. It further betrays the fact that evolutionary thinking was crucial to how emotions were understood after Darwin. Indeed, as Sara Ahmed claims, emotions still 'get narrated as a sign of "our" pre-history, and as a sign of how the primitive persists in the present' (*Cultural Politics* 3). LeBon's assertions further recall Gaskell's characterisation of the working-class crowd as a 'wild beast' and betray his reliance on the racist late Victorian principles of degeneration and recidivism.

How we talk about crowds thus tells us which emotions and bodies we value. In the twentieth century, Elias Canetti's *Crowds and Power* (1960) has similarly, and fairly, been criticised by critics for his essentialism.[4] In contrast to LeBon, though, he describes the potentially freeing nature of the collective. Echoing Teresa Brennan's notion that the affects of one person can 'enter into' another, he writes: 'The man pressed up against him is the same as himself. He feels him as he feels himself. Suddenly it is as though everything were happening in me and the same body' (15–16). With his emphasis on the pressing of bodies, Canetti, like Collins in the opening of *The Woman in White*, emphasises the power of touch to initiate a process of bodily sympathy. He argues, in fact, that it is 'only in a crowd that man can become free of this fear of being touched' (15). Canetti's formulations betray affinities with contemporary affect theorists such as Ben Anderson, who characterises collective affects as 'atmospheres'. Anderson notes that our understanding of an atmosphere – existing in a society, city or collective, but generated by bodies – can approximate the concept of affect, 'where affect is taken to be the transpersonal ... intensities that emerge as bodies affect one another' (78). While Victorian authors often used the word 'atmosphere' to describe an environment or space, they just as often used it to describe feelings. In *The Woman in White*, Marian speaks of 'the humdrum atmosphere of Limmeridge House' and Gilmore confesses that he 'live[s] professionally in an atmosphere of disputation' with other lawyers (35, 119). Anderson claims that the notion of atmosphere upsets the distinction between affect and emotion (80). He associates affect with 'the impersonal and objective', and emotion with 'the personal and subjective'; yet 'atmospheres' do not fit neatly into either affect or emotion since they are impersonal, belong to a collective, and yet are felt as intensely personal (80).

Reading such work alongside Victorian literature can make crowd dynamics and atmospheres existing in Victorian texts more visible. That said, sensation authors depart from both essentialist writing on crowd psychology and the strain of affect theory that places affect as outside of social context in key ways. For instance, an important aspect of Canetti's notion of the crowd is that it releases social differences. He says that 'the discharge' is 'the moment when all who belong to the crowd get rid of their differences and feel equal' (17). Canetti's idea about 'the discharge' as being outside social signification bears some similarity to ideas of affective autonomy or the notion that '[y]ou cannot read affects, you can only experience them' (O'Sullivan 126). Assuming that the affective crowd trumps differences of class, race or gender diverges from the ways in which the Victorians wrote about crowd behaviour, especially within fiction. Indeed, for writers like Clive, Dickens and Wood, the crowd, and especially the mob, is a site in which social distinctions matter and often become visible. The Victorian crowd thus emerges not as a site in which difference is discharged but in which difference is charged. In descriptions of crowds, Victorian authors are attentive to the ways in which sympathy is transmitted between bodies, but they also show – implicitly or explicitly – the ideological baggage attached to specific bodies. Importantly, in most descriptions of crowds in Victorian fiction the perspective is from outside of the crowd. Thus, we typically do not receive a narration of the transmission of affect from within, but rather an observation of the mob from without, and, often, from the point of view of an alarmed, middle-class character.

When discussing the mob, I thus emphasise that it matters which bodies are described, what affects or emotions they betray and if the crowd is directed by a single figure. These points all relate because, most often in sensation fiction, 'the mob' implies a crowd that is working class, predominately male and visibly angry. Jonathan Loesberg has claimed that sensation novels are at their most sensational when they are narrating a loss of class identity. He relates this to 'a fear of a general loss of social identity as a result of the merging of the classes', an anxiety that was frequently expressed in debates over social and parliamentary reform in the 1860s (117). For Loesberg, this class fear isn't a fear of the lower classes, exactly, but rather its logic is that 'when one loses one's legal and class identity, one enters an anonymous world that operates by no rules one has ever learned before' (120). Loesberg's observation is striking when placed in the context of crowd affects. The mob is typically depicted as lower class and thus seems to represent a fear of the lower classes, specifically lower-class mobilisation. Additionally, however, the fear associated with the mob is that it has the potential to somehow infect or swallow up others that may lie in its path, even middle-class others or women. Loesberg's 'anonymous world' thus bears affinities to a crowd of bodies in which individual identities aren't erased, exactly, but blur. The fear of the Victorian crowd and especially the mob, then, is both a fear of working-class violence and a fear that working-class bodies may infect or permeate other bodies and identities. As is typical of sensation fiction, however, that fear is also mixed with a degree of fascination.

A Life's Secret and working-class sympathy

Ellen Wood was, and remains, one of the best-known sensation writers, along with Braddon and Collins. She published her first novel, *Dansbury House*, in 1857 after her husband was forced to retire early, thus beginning a period of high productivity and success which culminated in her editing her own magazine, *Argosy*. Her religious background and penchant for moralising distinguish her from many of her fellow sensationalists. Beth Palmer argues that Wood cultivated a 'staid and domestic reputation in order to distance herself from the more dangerous facets of sensationalism even while her fiction worked to elicit the most sensational effects on its readers' (83). Indeed, her work exhibits the sensational plotting and sensorial emphasis that I mark as typical and distinctive of the genre. Her demand that her readers feel for her sinning heroines is certainly the most radical aspect of her writing. As I have noted, she frequently employs the second person and addresses a feeling 'reader'. At various points in *East Lynne*, she pleads for the reader to feel for the adulterous Isabel Carlyle: 'Poor thing! Poor Lady Isabel!' (283). The narrator even anticipates a judgemental and affective reader who might protest that Isabel should never have returned to see her children, as I noted in the introduction. She confronts her, insisting, 'cool your anger . . . are you quite sure that you would not have done the same, under the facility and the temptation?' (591). In *A Life's Secret*, however, the narrator does not urge for the same degree of feeling for the wayward strikers; instead, she reserves her pity for the male owner of the building firm.

Given Wood's interest in the ways in which a reader might feel for and with her characters, it comes as no surprise that she is also interested in how a crowd may be swayed by strong feeling. In *East Lynne*, her narrator notes, 'An English mob, gentle or simple, never gets up its excitement by halves. Whether its demonstration be of a laudatory or a condemnatory nature, the steam is sure to be put on to bursting point' (575). Wood uses the term 'mob' in *East Lynne* to describe both the innocuous crowd watching the upper-class locals attend a concert, and the rowdy working-class mob that dunks Francis Levison in a local pond. Yet even the mob that dunks Levison is not frightening, since they act out the desires of a middle-class character, Miss Carlyle, sympathising with her disgust of Levison. When Squire Pinner learns that his labourers were responsible for the dunking, he says, 'This is glorious news. My labourers? I'll give 'em a crown a piece for drink to-night' (468). The labourers are thus paid for what is read as an act of service to the upper- and middle-class residents of West Lynne rather than an act of primitive or violent passion. In contrast, the mob (and the proposed strike) in *A Life's Secret* radically challenges class hierarchies and is depicted as threatening to middle- and upper-class stability.

A Life's Secret is perhaps the most political of Wood's novels, but it opens in a typically sensational manner. Wood focuses on the life of Austin Clay, who leaves his country home to seek his fortune in London. He finds work with a London building firm and although he has a managerial position, he rents a modest room from a builder's family, situated in an area called 'Daffodil's Delight', where the rest of the novel takes place and most of the builders live. The secret of the title concerns his employer, Mr Hunter, who believes that he has accidentally committed bigamy only to learn near the end of the novel that he has in fact been duped by his first wife's sister, an angry woman seeking revenge. Yet as the novel goes on, this sensational plot feels less central as the stories of the striking workers move into the foreground. Mr Hunter's workers and those of many other building firms around the city decide to strike in the hope of reducing their workday from ten hours to nine. The narrator writes:

> If any workmen had enjoyed of late years (it may be said) unlimited prosperity, they were those connected with the building trade. Therefore, being so flourishing, it struck some of their body, who in a degree gave laws to the rest, that the best thing they could do was to make themselves more flourishing still. As a preliminary, they began to agitate for an increase of wages: this was to be accomplished by reducing the hours of labour, the proposition being to work nine hours per day instead of ten. They said nothing about relinquishing the wages of the extra hour: they would be paid for ten hours and work nine. (vol. 1, 194–5)

The narrator attributes the decision to reduce their work hours not to a desire for more time with their families or for leisure, but to a greedy impulse 'to make themselves more flourishing'. This leads to a conflict between the workers and their employers, who pre-empt the strike by announcing a lockout. The masters 'resolved to employ only those men who would sign an agreement, or memorandum, affirming that they were not connected with any society which interfered with the arrangements of the master whose service they entered' (vol. 1, 295). The workers 'styled it "the odious document"' (vol. 1, 295).

Wood borrows all of these details from a widespread strike in the building industry in 1859–60, in which workers agitated for the reduction of hours from ten to nine, and employers locked out their workmen and refused to employ anyone who would not sign 'the document', the terms of which Wood cites verbatim. Wood's novel also borrows from the actual outcome, in which the workers came to a compromise and the nine-hour issue was simply dropped (Pelling 44–5). Historian Henry Pelling notes that the document and arguments against trade unionism received widespread support from the press and middle-class circles in general: exponents of economic theory held that wages were determined by the laws of supply and demand, and thus unions could not arbitrarily set demands; they also argued that if a group of workers received advances in wages through collective pressure, it would come at the expense of other workers (47). Wood's novel further implies, though, that striking workers were grasping and even lazy, and their attempts to set the terms of their own employment would upset the master–worker hierarchy. As one of the characters questions, 'is it in accordance with the fitness of things, that a master should be under the control of his men?' (vol. 1, 215). Yet she further suggests that the strike occurs not as a result of careful, deliberate contemplation but through the combined effect of a manipulative union leader, Sam Shuck, and the sympathetic contagion of the crowd.

Early in the novel, the narrator seems to praise the capacity for strong, shared feeling amongst the working classes. When word gets around that one of the inhabitants of Daffodil's Delight is dying, the narrator writes,

> Daffodil's Delight was in a state of commotion. It has often been remarked that there exists more real sympathy between the working classes, one for another, than amongst those of a higher grade; and experience generally seems to bear it out. From one end of Daffodil's Delight to the other, there ran just now a deep feeling of sorrow, of pity, of commiseration. (vol. 1, 144)

Wood here uses 'sympathy' as synonymous with pity, but the passage also relates the community's sympathy to a form of contagion. She records that men pass each other, repeating the same enquiries, while women gather at doorways asking, 'How is she? What does the doctor say?' (vol. 1, 144). Their expressions of sympathy are clearly gendered but also presented as a blurring of individual and group feeling: 'The neighbours came to help; to nurse; to shake up the bed and pillows; to prepare condiments over the fire; to condole; and, above all, to gossip: with tears in their eyes and lamentation in their tones, and ominous shakes of the head, and uplifted hands; but still, to gossip' (vol. 1, 145). Gossip here functions as an instance of both sympathy-as-pity and sympathy-as-imitation, since Wood stresses its repetitive nature and the bodily forms of imitation that it comprises: shared tears, head-shakes and outstretched hands.

While this sympathy results in the exchange of gossip, the narrator does not explicitly critique working-class collective affect until the builders gather to discuss the strike. Importantly, the scene moves from a mixed-gender community of neighbours to working-class men. The focus also shifts in terms of the object of feeling – from a dying woman to a seemingly unfair employer – and the shared feeling itself – from pity to anger. The narrator can attempt to appeal to readerly sympathy in the former case, but once the emotional register shifts to anger, the depiction of the working-class community changes. Wood includes a lengthy exchange between various workers about the reasons for and implications of striking. Sam Shuck, the key agitator, ends the debate 'by demanding, with fierce looks all round, whether they were men, or whether they were slaves, and the men answered, with a cheer and a shout, that Britons never should be slaves' (vol. 1, 222). The colonialist and racial implications of this chant are clear, as is the (somewhat ironic) appeal to the men's agency. Shuck draws from the patriotic song 'Rule, Britannia!' (1740), in particular the repeated, 'Britons never will be slaves'; it is an effective and affecting strategy. What Wood details in this scene is a transition from a contentious debate into a more unified social mind and body, brought together by Shuck as well as by the men's combined affects.

The debate culminates in the announcement of a strike, and soon afterwards the narrator offers a description of the men (and a few women) as forming a mob. As 'a fresh crowd came jostling down Daffodil's Delight', a working-class woman, Mrs Dunn, leaves her conversation with Austin Clay and 'rushe[s] up to the mob to follow in their wake' (vol. 1, 270). The men start to sing their own version of 'Rule, Britannia!' – one revised to announce and celebrate the strike:

> Shouting, singing, exulting, dancing; it seemed as if they had, for the nonce, gone mad. Sam Shuck, in his long-tailed coat, ornamented with its holes and its slits, was leading the van, his voice hoarse, his face red, his legs and arms executing a war-dance of exaltation. He it was who had got up the excitement and was keeping it up, shouting fiercely: 'Hurrah for the work of this day! Rule Britannia! Britons never shall be slaves! The Strike has begun, friends! H—o—o—o—o—r—rah! Three cheers for the Strike!' (vol. 1, 270–1)

Following this description, the narration only notes, 'Yes. The Strike had begun' (vol. 1, 271). Her dry assessment is in contrast to the 'mad' men in the mob, who appear to be overtaken by their affects. Wood focuses specifically on Shuck as the leader of the crowd, but even in his case, his body seems to have agency over his mind, with 'his legs and arms executing a war-dance of exaltation'.

Wood's depiction of Shuck leading the crowd with a dance recalls the Carmagnole scene from Dickens's *A Tale of Two Cities*, published three years prior. In both scenes, the affective crowd, which demonstrates feeling through dancing and shouting, results in an atmosphere of intensity and potential violence. Alan Palmer and Adam Steir note that Dickens had a particular interest in 'the mechanics and operations of crowd behaviour', an investment that is perhaps nowhere more evident than in *A Tale of Two Cities* (561).[5] Lucie Darnay watches the dancing crowd with fear:

> There could not be fewer than five hundred people, and they were dancing like five thousand demons. There was no other music than their own singing. They danced to the popular Revolution song, keeping a ferocious time that was like a gnashing of teeth in unison. Men and women danced together, women danced together, men danced together, as hazard had brought them together. At first, they were a mere storm of coarse red caps and coarse woollen rags; but, as they filled the place, and stopped to dance about Lucie, some ghastly apparition of a dance-figure gone raving mad arose among them. (288)

Dickens here relates how the group alters from a storm of caps and rags into a single 'ghastly apparition of a dance-figure gone raving mad'. The comparison of their movement to 'a gnashing of teeth' gestures to the bestial nature of the crowd, as well as its potential for violence. The fact that women are included in the mob only seems to make it appear more abject. As in *A Life's Secret*, the dancing mob is viewed from the outside: in Wood's novel, Mrs Dunn breaks her conversation with Austin to join, thus implicitly placing him as the observer. He is the protagonist of the novel, so much of the action is in fact narrated from his perspective, and he often functions as a mediator between the working-class and upper-class characters. In *Tale*, it is Lucie, both inside and outside of Parisian culture, who, 'frightened and bewildered', watches the mob's collective sympathy (289). Like Austin, Lucy's resistance to the crowd demonstrates her lack of shared values as well as an unwillingness to let their affects take hold of her. She is certainly affected by the crowd, but she cannot share in the same wild affects.

Nicholas Daly argues that Dickens's target in *A Tale of Two Cities* is not France of the 1790s, but rather England of the 1850s, a period in which 'fears of the masses had not gone away' (36). In fact, despite its historical setting, *Tale* is in many ways a typical sensation novel, employing a melodramatic plot, a self-reflexive narrator and affective language.[6] Dickens, Daly claims, presents the mob as 'something with a fierce group consciousness . . . and something mechanical with its own cyclical routines' (38). Note the similarities here to Bain's notion of sympathy as 'the surrender of self to others' (180) and LeBon's later notion of the collective mind. Daly's characterisation of the mob, both as possessing a group consciousness and as mechanical, is a compelling description for Wood's novel as well. Daly also draws parallels between *A Tale of Two Cities* and *The Woman in White*, arguing that it is possible to see Collins's novel as a revision of Dickens's (39). While he calls attention to the similar plots of spying, surveillance and secret societies, he contrasts Dickens's frightening mob with the French crowd that gathers to view Fosco in *The Woman in White*, arguing that 'what Dickens presents as the political mob out for blood appears to Collins as the crowd out for entertainment, an entity that comes to stand for Collins's understanding of his own readership' (40). This reading aligns with my claim, in the previous chapter, that Collins understood the 'public' to be a mass of readers.

If we also think of the mob in Wood's novel as a metafictional tool, we might not only consider to what extent readers and crowds are aligned but we might also question to what extent the devious union leader Sam Shuck and the narrator (or even Wood herself) are aligned, since both use their rhetorical and storytelling skills to elicit specific affective responses from their audiences. What Wood theorises about the working-class mob is that it is directed by one individual 'who had got up the excitement and was keeping it up' (vol. 1, 270). The mob's group consciousness is led by a single, persuasive consciousness. In her preface to the novel, Wood notes that Shuck, 'who filled a somewhat conspicuous part in [the novel's] pages, was particularly repudiated' (vi). Indeed, she continually casts blame on Shuck. Mr Hunter, when announcing the lockout to the men, insists, 'it is not with you that the chief blame lies. You have suffered evil persuaders to get access to your ears, and have been led away by their pernicious counsels' (vol. 1, 297–8). One of the neighbourhood women, Mrs Quale, similarly calls out Shuck's influence and the men's lack of agency: 'How you men can submit to be led by such a fellow as him, just because his tongue is capable of persuading you that black's white, is a marvel to me. Talk of women being soft!' (vol. 1, 275). She critiques the men's submission to Shuck as effeminate and also compares them to cows, 'a-flocking in a line after their leader, behind each other's tails' (vol. 1, 276). Shuck tries to overturn these gendered implications when he tells the crowd, 'we want to be regarded as MEN . . . Let us display manly courage and join the strike' (vol. 1, 283).

Shuck permits Wood not just to demonstrate the susceptibility and contagious sympathy of the working-class men but to question the authentic feelings behind the strike. As I noted earlier, the narrator records her distrust of the men's motives early on and implies that they are striking due to their greed. Similarly, Shuck is not depicted as a figure who cares deeply about the union or workers' rights, but rather is motivated by the money that the union pays him. His character thus questions the motivations of all the striking workers and implies that the mob is motivated by selfish impulses rather than a genuine sense of injustice. If the dancing mob is a frightening example of embodied sympathy, it is also moved by the wrong object and the wrong man.

Wood's narrator thus works as a force to oppose the arguments of Shuck. Again, while Wood's narrators often employ direct address to demand sympathy for her heroines, in *A Life's Secret*, the narrator uses the same device to demand sympathy for Mr Hunter, the employer who locks out his employees. When Hunter's daughter is concerned that the striking men's children are starving, he tells her, 'If a man sees his children starving before him, and will not work to feed them, he deserves to find them ill' (vol. 2, 79). The narrator then interjects to say,

> Do not judge of Mr Hunter's humanity by the words, or deem him an unfeeling man. He was far from that . . . . He considered, as did most of the other London masters, that to help the men or their families in any way, would but tend to prolong the dispute. And there was certainly reason in their argument – if the men wished to feed their children, why did they not work for them? (vol. 2, 79–80)

The narrator here repeats Hunter's own thoughts and the so-called reasonable thoughts of other masters, and she uses his daughter's questioning to anticipate any possible judgements on the part of the reader. Her use of 'reason' sets up a distinction between the rational middle classes and the unthinking – and greedy – working classes.

The novel includes not just narratorial interjections to guide readerly feeling, but also extradiegetic explanations from the editor of *The Leisure Hour* and Wood herself. The editor, James Macaulay, included a footnote in the February 20th issue, immediately following the chapter in which the men first meet to discuss the strike (117). It is reprinted in the 1867 novel edition at the end of the same chapter, 'A Meeting of the Workmen', and it serves as a fascinating interruption within the text. He writes defensively, 'It need scarcely be remarked, that Sam Shuck and his followers represent only the ignorant and unprincipled section of those who engage in strikes. Working men are perfectly right in combining to seek the best terms they can get, both as to wages and time; provided there be no interference with the liberty either of masters or fellow-workmen' (vol. 1, 220). While I cannot confirm the exact date of the riot, Macaulay's interjection is likely a response to the protest outside the offices of the Religious Tract Society. Wood's own response soon followed, but she was less measured in her comments. In May 1862 she wrote the following, also included as a footnote and reprinted in her 1867 preface:

> In writing this story the author's object has not been to deal with the vexing questions between masters and men, between capital and labour, about which there must always be conflicting opinions, so much as to depict the injurious social results which these quarrels produce, and the misery they leave behind them. It was written in the kindest, heartiest spirit towards the men, and in the truest sympathy with their suffering families. (Preface vii)

In the original printing, this occurs in the middle of the final chapter, directly following a speech by Mr Hunter in which he lectures to his men. He tells them, 'I, for my part, will always be ready to receive and consider any reasonable proposal from my men. If there is no attempt at intimidation, and no interference on the part of others, there ought to be little difficulty in discussing and settling matters, with the help of the "golden rule"' (no. 543,

24 May, 323). In following up Hunter's lecture with her own words, Wood consolidates her voice with his, both the fictional Hunter and the actual Wood serving as middle-class figures dispensing wisdom but also reprimanding working-class men.

In 1867, Wood states, 'Every word of this last note I would repeat now' (vii). Wood's 'truest sympathy' is aligned both with the supposedly well-intentioned masters and the families forced to suffer under their fathers' or husbands' decisions to strike. Indeed, the novel makes much of this by depicting the starving, even dying children, who bear the brunt of their fathers' choices. Again, her moral guidance is thus directly opposed to Shuck's. But her readers' own embodied, angry reactions suggest that his arguments were ultimately more compelling than hers or Mr Hunter's. Her novel suggests that the working-class mob must be directed by a single voice, but what the actual incident at Paternoster Row in 1862 shows is that the mob may actually have a mind of its own, an even less comforting concept for middle-class Victorians.

Paul Ferroll and the limits of sympathy

While Wood's novel offers a fascinating instance of an audience rejecting the narrator's directive sympathy, Caroline Clive's *Paul Ferroll* is striking for its utter lack of narrative guidance. *Paul Ferroll* was published as 'By the Author of IX Poems by V'. *IX Poems* was Clive's first collection of poetry, published in 1840 under the pseudonym V, and it was followed by four more poetry collections until she tried her hand at fiction at the age of fifty-four with *Paul Ferroll*. The novel, published in 1855, has been cited as a precursor to sensation fiction, largely due to its melodramatic plot. It was a bestseller, and Elizabeth Gaskell noted that it 'made a great sensation' in England (qtd in Gavin para. 8). Following its opening sentence – 'Nothing looks more peaceful and secure than a country house seen at early morning' – the novel proceeds to juxtapose the happy façade of the country home with a violent murder (1). The plot opens with the murder of Paul Ferroll's wife, then centres on his life with his second wife, Elinor, who had been his first love; only late in the novel does Clive reveal that Paul was himself the murderer. Anne-Marie Beller argues that the novel anticipates sensation fiction of the 1860s both through its murderous protagonist and by 'employing a detached, almost clinical narrative voice, which refuses to condemn either the murderer or his crime' ('Sensation Fiction' 13). While some sensation novelists did feature a narrator resistant to judgement, such as Reade's narrator in *Griffith Gaunt*, many, including Wood, actively guided their readers towards pity or sympathy. The clinical narrative voice is a key aspect of Clive's text and one that made it controversial at the time of publication. Even more unique, this detached voice is mirrored by the protagonist's own emotional limitations. Indeed, the entire novel is a meditation on the limits of sympathy and empathy, with a central scene focused on Paul's dramatic interaction with a working-class mob, an event that ends with him murdering a local man.

Paul's most prominent characteristic is his cold, unfeeling nature, what Adrienne Gavin, the only critic other than Beller to recently discuss the novel, calls his 'detached criminality, and dislocated, probably psychopathic, personality' (para. 52). While the narrator does not interject to condemn his actions, she does consistently record Paul's non-normative feelings, noting his tendency to mime or perform what he seems to deem appropriate affects and his perverse excitement in inappropriate contexts. Early on, for instance, Paul tells a local woman that he broke Elinor's heart when he left her to marry his first wife. She finds this 'shocking!' and Paul repeats that it is '"shocking indeed!" . . . (imitating her manner, but so that she did not perceive it)' (20). Paul's imitation seems to both betray his ridicule of this woman's surprise, as well as his own uncertainty about how to act in response to her comments. We might call this performative empathy, one that is reliant on Theory of Mind, since Paul knows that the woman expects him to be upset by his past actions. The narrator relates that Paul 'enjoyed life' and that no 'sensibility to the sufferings of another, disturbed him' (44). Often, he does not express outward feeling in contexts that would encourage it. For instance, when he is finally arrested for the murder of his first wife and appears in court, he is 'unmoved' (275). Elsewhere in the novel, Clive records his incongruous affects, clear warning signs for a reader of his immorality or psychopathy, even without an explicit intervention from the narrator herself. For these reasons, I should note, I would not classify him as an affect alien, as I did the female characters in Chapter 2, as it is not the case that he is simply out of step with social expectations for happiness, for instance, or that he feels alienated from others. That is, Paul's affects do not simply challenge social expectations but rather are marked as distinctly antisocial.

In addition to the use of third-person narration, the novel includes extracts from Paul and Elinor's shared journal, a narrative form that Beller notes anticipates Collins's fiction, and which works to further detail Paul's inappropriate affects. As with Lydia's journal in *Armadale*, the entries are a way of 'allowing the reader more intimate access to the psychology of these characters' (Beller, 'Sensation Fiction' 15). The entries are included with the abrupt introduction, 'Here the Author gives extracts from the Journal kept in common by Mr Ferroll and Elinor' (48). Early in his journals, Paul records his excitement when his town suffers from a cholera epidemic: 'the excitement of rushing about with a human spectacle everywhere, so kindled my spirits, that I stopped at the end of a by-way, and indulged in one quiet laugh' (52). He also laughs during his first murder trial. But even more than the eruption of laughter during the trial, his laughter while observing death and suffering reveals his lack of sympathy for others. He admits to finding a dying man 'the most absorbing and interesting spectacle that we can see' and confesses that 'the atmosphere of horrible smells gives me pleasure', the narrator never interjecting to comment on such behaviour (53, 66). The only human being that he seems to be able to feel for or with is Elinor. She notes in their shared journal – itself a symbol of their ability to sympathise with one another – that when he returns home, 'everything he has seen and done is reproduced for me, so that I and he become one as to the events and feelings of the day he has passed' (56). Lest their shared feelings emerge as Paul's one positive attribute, Clive also shows how his love for Elinor is possessive and fuelled by jealousy: when Elinor takes their daughter away briefly to care for her during an illness, Paul is wild with jealousy and even fantasises about catching cholera: 'Little Janet has nothing but measles; *I* want Elinor most. I will fall ill to get Elinor' (63).

Paul's inability to sympathise with anyone but his wife, and certainly not with the poor of his community, helps to set up what happens during the riot scene. The novel is less concerned with class politics than *A Life's Secret*; working-class concerns only occur in the background of the novel while the drama associated with Paul, a respected landowner, Lord-Lieutenant of the County and successful author, is central. Early in the novel, the narrator explains that in consequence of reduced wages, the 'poor population had become exceedingly riotous', destroying property and setting barns on fire (32). A 'season of considerable danger seemed impending' (32). The danger occurs later in the novel, after a breakfast with the local sheriff, attended by Paul and other prominent local men. A working-class man whom Paul helped during the cholera epidemic, James Skenfrith, warns him that when they return to town they will be met by a large crowd of angry men who are frustrated at their inability to survive on their small wages. The working-class men gather outside the prison and attempt to block the entrance of the sheriff and local landowners as they return from their meal. As Paul and the other men try to negotiate their way through the crowd, someone smashes the window of a local shop, and this works like a signal, transforming the crowd into a mob: 'The sound acted like contagion on the multitude; it was like the rush of galloping heard by a horse; all that were near houses seemed by the clatter that ensued to do as the first breaker had done. Shouts and huzzas followed, and all the multitude swayed to and fro with the impulse which ran through it' (101). Clive calls attention to the 'contagion' of this action on everyone and employs a description typical of Victorian mobs: the men act like animals and are driven by impulse.

As with my examples from Dickens and Wood, the mob scene is narrated from without, but this soon shifts as Paul, due to his perverse excitement in moments of distress, dives into the crowd. The other men try to reason with the mob, but Paul thinks that they should shoot the leader dead rather than attempt to persuade the 'maddened' men (103). Things escalate quickly when Paul enters the crowd: 'The mob yelled; James Skenfrith, with imprecations, waved his hand, clenching a bludgeon, and pressing with all his might to get before Mr Ferroll; that was his last effort. Mr Ferroll drew a pistol from his breast, cocked it, and shot him dead' (103). Paul leaves the murder scene and gallops home on his horse, incongruously 'happy in the past excitement, happy in the present exercise' (105). He is later charged and found guilty of murder, but his respected social position, and presumably his wealth, grants him a full pardon. While the legal and social implications of the pardon validate his actions, the novel implies that his murder of James was not necessary. Instead, when placed within the context of his past behaviour – ranging from his choleric excitement to his cold-blooded murder of his first wife – his actions in the mob emerge as more perverse than self-defensive. What is intriguing about this in terms of crowd dynamics is that it renders Paul's reasoned actions during the riot as out of place.

While Clive does emphasise, like Dickens and Wood, the contagious, animalistic and impulsive actions of the mob, she also suggests that this is typical human behaviour when in a crowd. The mob scene is thus most significant in this novel for what it can tell us about Paul. His resistance to the affective atmosphere – he feels with neither the angry rioters nor the frightened landowners – warns readers, and possibly other characters, that he does not value the lives of working-class men and that he is curiously resistant to embodied sympathy, whether that sympathy involves socially beneficial or harmful affects.

Following his murder of James, Paul rides home and pauses to view the pretty rural scene in front of him. The narrator records, 'If he had been in the habit of talking over his secrets to himself, it is probable he might have said something very much to the purpose of this story. However, he was not; so what he thought remains unrevealed' (106). This is a significant moment in this text, in which the narrator seems to acknowledge her own limitations. Why can't she access his thoughts? Paul's face is 'impassable to those with whom he talked' (215) and to the reader: 'no one knew whether or not there was any agitation within his breast' (217). There is a pragmatic reason for this, of course: Clive wants to keep his murder of Mrs Ferroll a secret and so sustain the reader's interest in the narrative. As I noted in the previous chapter, Braddon does something similar with Lucy Audley. Braddon, though, allows the reader a few brief moments of access to Lucy's mind (via third-person narration) and further reveals her emotion through embodied transparency. There is only one moment that comes close to embodied transparency in Clive's novel. Aware that the news of his first murder will likely be exposed, Paul leaves his family and sits outside alone. Yet the narrator still does not reveal precisely what he is feeling in this moment of vulnerability:

> The mind at times is so oppressed by its own burthen that it seems unable to take thought for its companion the body; it rather gives itself up to the mechanical impressions of the body, and like two whom fate has joined and inclination severed, they abide together, but neither does its office friendly, to the other. Thus he sat, certain that he was unseen; and released, therefore, from all necessity of acting a part – the dark spirit communing with itself, the listless body abandoning itself to all the painful impressions of cold and desolation. (219–20)

This passage anticipates sensation fiction in its focus on the 'mechanical impressions of the body' and in the 'necessity of acting a part' (219). While the narrator doesn't detail Paul's thoughts, this moment is revelatory for simply calling attention to the fact that Paul does perform a part and is capable of 'painful' feelings. Yet rather than signalling a key turning point for Paul, he shakes off this moment of the 'body abandoning itself' and returns home. By focusing largely on the exterior of Paul's body, Clive not only anticipates sensation fiction's attention to bodily affects but also its emphasis on the difficulty of reading those affects.

A striking narratological choice made by Clive is to further keep readers on the surface by avoiding free indirect discourse, even though she includes a few diary entries. She thus does attempt to direct readerly empathy, although in less explicit ways than Wood. Keen emphasises the use of free indirect discourse as a possible tool for narrative empathy, claiming that 'authorial (omniscient) narration that moves inside characters' minds . . . promotes character identification and readers' empathy' (219).[7] Without assuming that FID always invites empathy – and it is certainly debatable that it would for a murderous psychopath – Clive's avoidance of FID means that one possible route to narrative empathy is closed off and that readers are forced to focus attention on Paul's body. As Megan Ward notes, the paradox inherent in FID is that 'we cannot actually know a person in the way that we deem most realistic in fiction', but readers nonetheless value 'the interior that reads like pure information' in contrast to the slipperiness of bodily descriptions (110). And Paul's body is particularly slippery. When he writes a letter to Elinor, telling her that he is being arrested for his first wife's murder, what could be scripted as a moment of melodrama and emotional expressiveness instead focuses on Paul's horrifying unreadability: 'No trace of emotion appeared on his face; and those to whom this was a sudden and new horror could not reconcile their emotion about it' (270). Similarly, when he is in his prison cell, the narrator records: 'Whatever he might feel, it was easy for a man with such habits of self-command, perfectly to conceal it' (271). Just like the characters in the novel, readers must contend with Paul's inscrutable body; we cannot know 'Whatever he might feel', nor can we feel it ourselves (271). As Gavin notes, 'The narrative presents him as a strangely attractive yet repellent specimen for observation, but readers do not *feel* with him as an erring being who ultimately seeks redemption' (para. 54).[8]

For both Wood and Clive, then, the crowd allows them to theorise the transmission of affect. The appearance of the mob in Clive's novel is brief but significant. It shows readers not only that Paul is unaffected by the mob but that he is capable of murder. Even if Lucie and Austin in Dickens and Wood's fiction are not part of the embodied consciousness of the mob, they nonetheless are affected by the atmosphere: Austin is alarmed and Lucie is 'frightened and bewildered' (289). For Clive, as with Dickens and Wood, the mob works to establish an emotional hierarchy. Ahmed notes that the 'story of evolution is narrated not only as the story of the triumph of reason, but of the ability to control emotions, and to experience the "appropriate" emotions at different times and places' (3). For the Victorians, the mob was typically read as a descent into primitivism or inhuman behaviour. Wood's distinction between the reasoned factory owner and the wild working-class mob is a good example of this model in action. In Clive's novel, though, the mob is rendered human precisely because of its deep feeling. This is ultimately what makes Clive's novel more sensational than Wood's and such an important precursor to the genre: in her depictions of the mob and of Paul, Clive depicts a lack of affect as inhuman, rather than too much.

In focusing only on the exterior of Paul's body, Clive, in addition to discouraging readerly sympathy, paints his character as all surface in a manner that challenges Victorian realism's commitment to characterological interiority. Yet this challenge did not last long. Five years later, she published a prequel, *Why Paul Ferroll Killed his Wife* (1860), in an attempt to offer a psychological explanation for Paul's murder, utterly absent from the first novel. This prequel does develop Paul's interiority, but it still depicts him as a cruel and insensitive figure. He enjoys the 'pleasure of pretending to feelings, and, as it were, acting them' (11). The plot details how Paul is tricked by the devious Laura into marrying her, instead of Elinor. It is in his marriage to Laura that he seems to become most human, as he is overwhelmed by feelings of regret and depression. Fittingly, all he can do is read sensation fiction: 'The habits of his mind made him resort as necessarily to reading, as his bodily appetite to food; but the only subjects which could fix his attention were the stern expression of great passion, the details of strong purpose and of grand crimes' (213). Paul's identification with passion and crime is as good an example as any that Victorian bodily sympathy could be ethical and compassionate but also destructive and antisocial.

Earlier in the chapter, I argued that for Victorian writers, the crowd, and especially the mob, is a site in which social distinctions matter and become visible. In Wood's novel, sympathy can be given to the starving families of the striking workers but not to the workers themselves, whom she depicts as destructive and unsympathetic. In contrast, Paul's inability to see James as human marks him as inhuman. The distinction made visible by the mob in Clive's novel is thus not only class hierarchy but the capacity for shared feeling associated by Atkinson, Bain and Darwin with sensitivity and anti-individualism. The next chapter focuses even more on the positive elements of shared feeling, exploring bodily sympathy as compassionate and even healing.

Notes

1. Details of the riot are sparse. An obituary of Wood includes the following details: 'One of her stories, "A Life's Secret", dealt with the evil tendencies of strikes and trades unions, was published anonymously, and caused a riot in front of the premises of the Religious Tract Society, which brought it out' (641).
2. George tells Robert, '"Do you know, Bob," he said, "that when some of our fellows were wounded in India, they came home, bringing bullets inside them. They did not talk of them, and they were stout and hearty, and looked as well, perhaps, as you or I; but every change in the weather, however slight, every variation of the atmosphere, however trifling, brought back the old agony of their wounds as sharp as ever they had felt it on the battle-field"' (47).
3. It is worth noting, too, that *Armadale* begins with a prologue on the eve of the Emancipation Act of 1833; it was, however, serialised while the Morant Bay Rebellion in Jamaica occurred in 1865.
4. For instance, John Plotz notes that Canetti's *Crowds and Power* 'has unmistakable genius, but I can no more imagine arguing with it than I can arguing with De Quincey's vision of "the glory of motion". Canetti offers no proof for his essentialist claims . . .. It is possible to be moved by him (he moves me), but it is not possible to be educated' (5).
5. Dickens's responses to public hangings also demonstrate his interest in crowd dynamics. In his well-known letter published in *The Times* in November 1849 after he saw Maria and Frederick Manning hanged for murder, Dickens wrote, 'I believe that a sight so inconceivably awful as the wickedness and levity of the immense crowd collected

at that execution this morning could be imagined by no man, and could be presented in no heathen land under the sun' (*Letters* 200). Dickens's moral judgement is not just for the act of corporal punishment but for the inappropriate affects of the crowd. Public hangings continued until May 1868, when the Capital Punishment Act came into force, moving them into the spaces of the prison.

6 Doctor Manette's obsessive shoe-making demonstrates just one way in which Dickens explores bodies governing minds in the text.

7 It is also worth considering Clive's avoidance of FID in terms of the relationship between narrator and character that FID implies. As Rosemarie Bodenheimer notes, 'FID is often discussed as a personal relationship between narrator and character, as if they were two sentient entities' (706). It could thus be read as an exercise in empathy between the narrator and the character or a moment of shared affect between two entities. In this way, Clive protects herself, or her authorial persona, from feeling along with a murderer.

8 Despite the ways in which Clive discourages readers from feeling with Paul, reviewers predictably condemned the novel. Beller notes that the 'absence of authorial judgement troubled many critics, even those who praised the originality and power of the novel' ('Sensation Fiction' 14). She cites a reviewer, for instance, who complains that 'the interest and sympathy excited in favour of the murderer, proves how false is the morality, and how greatly abused has been the gift of authorship' (qtd in Beller 14).

5

Collins, Hardy and Reade's Sympathetic Doubles

I begin this chapter by returning to Anne and Walter's confrontation in *The Woman in White*. At the moment that Anne touches him, Walter is 'idly wondering ... what the Cumberland young ladies would look like' (20). Even before Walter and the reader come to learn that Anne and Laura are half-sisters and pawns in the hands of Count Fosco and Sir Percival Glyde, the women are aligned in the same bewildering moment, as Anne's touch and Walter's imagined image of Laura arrest his senses at once. The next evening, when Walter tries to fall asleep in Limmeridge House, he asks, 'What shall I see in my dreams to-night ... the woman in white? or the unknown inhabitants of this Cumberland mansion?' (30). As Cvetkovich observes, the 'memory of Anne is mingled with his anticipation of the other women' (*Mixed Feelings* 82). Walter's role in the doubling plot of Anne and Laura is significant: he identifies their likeness and works to right the wrongs of the other men in the novel. A number of critics have suggested that this novel is as much a narrative of Walter's manhood gained as it is Laura's identity restored.[1] Yet to emphasise Walter's role in the novel is to risk missing the relationship developed between the women, specifically that between Laura and Anne, which has received less attention than the intense sisterly bond between Laura and Marian. In fact, Anne has another significant sensational confrontation in the novel when she finds Laura at the boathouse, and surprises her much as she surprised Walter. For Laura, looking at Anne is like looking at 'my own face in the glass after a long illness' (282).

In many ways, for Laura, confronting the illegitimate, 'dazed' Anne is a confrontation with her sensational self (282). Their relationship calls to mind anxieties associated with sensational

Sympathetic Doubles   157

and immersive reading practices. As I have noted in earlier chapters, reviewers articulated concerns that young women reading sensation novels would be unable to distinguish between fiction and reality, and between their own desires and those of sensational heroines. Implied in such anxieties about sensational reading was the exaggerated notion that women readers might somehow become the characters about whom they read. Oliphant remarked that in these novels an 'eagerness of physical sensation . . . is represented as the natural sentiment of English girls, and is offered to them . . . as the portrait of their own state of mind' ('Novels', 259). Oliphant articulates the way that a woman reader could locate her own sensations in the mind and body of the sensation heroine; she could read of others' experiences as though they were her own. These notions of affective reading were, for Victorian critics and reviewers, noticeably gendered. Implicit in such assessments was not just a fear of women acting badly, but also a fear about the collapse of discrete identity. The perceived tendency for women to somehow merge with other women was also detailed in the novels themselves and is the focus of this chapter.

In what follows, I explore the relationship between Anne and Laura, alongside other pairings, as examples of doubling. Many sensation novels crafted a vision of the double that differed from the paranoid constructions so frequently found in Victorian reviews and in gothic literature. While doubling is my focus, I see these plots as yet another example of sensational self-reflexivity: these plots and characters see sensation authors rewriting the concerns of conservative Victorian reviewers as well as conventional characterological tropes. In the gothic tradition, the appearance of one's double is typically a warning of death. Otto Rank, in 'The Double as Immortal Self', explains that though doubles were first symbols of man's immortal soul, they function in Western culture as a reminder of an individual's mortality, as 'the announcer of death itself' (76). Sigmund Freud also refers to the double as a 'harbinger of death' (142). Narratives of one's double murdering the original or stealing his or her life are common in gothic narratives of the eighteenth and nineteenth centuries, from James Hogg's *Private Memoirs and Confessions of a Justified Sinner* (1824) to Robert Louis Stevenson's *The Strange Case of Dr Jekyll and Mr Hyde* (1886). *Jane Eyre* depicts the gothic doubling of two women who bear the name Mrs Rochester. When Jane looks into her mirror only to see Bertha looking back at her, the double is represented as an uncanny collapse of identity. In line with the gothic tradition, Bertha's death enables Jane's marriage to Rochester and the novel's happy ending.

Stories about paranoid or competitive doubles can certainly be found in Victorian sensation fiction but many sensation novels, especially those by Wilkie Collins, challenge the notion that the doubling plot must always be fearful, oppositional and violent. My primary examples of female doubling are from *The Woman in White*, Charles Reade's *Griffith Gaunt* and Thomas Hardy's *Desperate Remedies*. In contrast to a paranoid gothic mode of interaction, these novels enact what I call sympathetic doubling: as one woman imagines herself in the other's place, she also is confronted with the contingency of human (and especially female) identity, and such a realisation prompts sympathetic bonds of suffering, rather than desires for the other's death. As in the last chapter, I am using 'sympathy', as the mid-Victorians did, to mean both the mental process of feeling for another and the transmission of shared affects, or bodily sympathy. In fact, the combination of these two understandings of sympathy works to blur notions of discrete and separate identities in these novels.[2]

More than simply suggesting that characters like Anne and Laura are doubles, I argue that they are counterfactual selves: Laura's recognition that Anne looks like a traumatised version of herself reveals that, despite their similarities, Anne's illegitimacy and social circumstances have led to her life of suffering. In order to make such an argument, I draw from Andrew Miller's work on the optative as well as Robyn Warhol's concept of shadow narratives. As I explain in more detail below, Miller's work on 'lives unled' in *The Burdens of Perfection* shows how counterfactual thinking, and, I would add, counterfactual feeling, are key features of the Victorian novel. Miller draws on Stuart Hampshire's notion of the 'optative', a mode of retrospection that 'understands one's past though an acknowledgement of what one has not done, what one has not been', to argue that the optative is a fundamental feature of nineteenth-century realistic representation (*Burdens* 193). Similarly, shadow narratives are narratives that the reader can construct based on instances in which a character or narrator details what might have happened in place of what actually did. In these novels, as characters confront possible future or past versions of themselves in the form of a double, one's counterfictional life becomes not only a theoretical concept or shadow narrative but a living, breathing being. Sensation fiction thus most clearly articulates the optative through melodramatic doubling plots. In *The Woman in White*, Anne is a future, traumatised version of Laura, and in Thomas Hardy's *Desperate Remedies*, Cytherea Aldclyffe is depicted as a future, heartbroken version of Cytherea Graye. Despite the suffering of these characters, a significant aspect of the doubling plot is the way in which these relationships are informed by a discourse of bodily responsiveness and sympathy. This chapter thus offers another way in which sensation authors theorised affect as transpersonal.

Later in the chapter, I question whether the same relationship can hold for male characters. My argument clearly has gendered implications, since the sympathetic bonds that I identify between the female characters are forged based on the perilous nature of women's social and legal identities. In Dickens's *A Tale of Two Cities*, however, Sydney Carton and Charles Darnay set up a sympathetic and sacrificial relationship also exhibited in Collins's sibling-doubles Ozias Midwinter and Allan Armadale in *Armadale* and Nugent and Oscar Dubourg in *Poor Miss Finch*. Collins draws sympathetic attachments between these male doubles, attachments forged despite economic and romantic competition. These narratives of male friendship expose as harmful the very competition that defines men as masculine; thus, rather than reading them as narratives of misogynistic male bonding, I read them as critiquing patriarchal structures. Further, the novels demonstrate how the blurring of identities and bodies characteristic of the doppelgänger plot can be exciting and even healing.

Counterfictions and shadow narratives

How did Victorian fiction imagine alternative lives? Miller locates counterfictional lives – lives that one is not living but could be – in the novels of Dickens, Eliot, Hardy and James, and I extend his observations to sensation novels. We notice the optative mode when characters say things like: how different I might have been but for this, or when Pip in *Great Expectations* tells Biddy, 'if I could have settled down and been but half as fond of the forge as I was when I was little, I know it would have been much better' (102). Characters can offer other characters the 'image of a viable alternative life', but Miller stresses that the optative also foregrounds and makes melodramatic the notion of the event, so that each decision, especially the decision of whom to marry, takes on great significance (*Burdens* 194). This proclivity to imagine counterfictional lives is used by Victorian writers to emphasise how, on the one hand, we are '*nailed* to ourselves', but also how, on the other hand, our present self is contingent (192). This way of thinking was popularised in the Victorian period due to a variety of factors but most explicitly because increased class mobility opened up the possibilities for one's professional and marital decisions. In a later article on *Great Expectations*, Miller argues that the fantasy of a life unled is especially significant in this novel, in which Pip struggles with both how to become a gentleman and the decision of whom to marry ('A Case of Metaphysics' 775). Miss Havisham, of course, presents an exaggerated example of the way in which one event can take on life-changing significance. And like Pip, she shows how the optative mode is linked to regret – or the attempt to forestall regret.

If Miller's work demonstrates how fascinated Victorian authors were with alternative lives, Warhol's notion of shadow narratives helps to show how this concept takes shape narratively. Shadow narratives or shadow worlds are related to Warhol's concept of 'narrative refusals'. This narrative device, in which a text details specific possibilities only to negate them, can create a shadow narrative or a 'vividly *present absence*' ('"What Might Have Been"' 231). Narrative refusals include both unnarration (narrators saying they cannot or will not tell what happened) and disnarration (telling something that did not happen in place of what did). Disnarration is especially relevant to counterfictional lives, since it more explicitly gestures to other narrative possibilities. Warhol says that narrative refusals 'open up alternative stories that do for narration what the "depth effect" (created by, for example, free indirect discourse or focalization) does for character' ('Narrative Refusals' 259). The concept of narrative refusals, akin to the unconscious of a text, allows Warhol to identify sentence-level instances that are enough to open up a shadow narrative and which may even challenge conventional plotlines and endings.[3]

Warhol's comparison of free indirect discourse and shadow narratives is intriguing, since shadow narratives create a sense of depth that supports a kind of realism: they imply that fictional characters, like real people, could have other possible lives beyond the page. Sensation novels certainly include narrative refusals, but also make the notion of the counterfictional embodied and sensational through the doubling of actual characters. Sensation novels thus tend to be not so much interested in shadow narratives as shadow selves, as characters model for other characters possible plots of which they could have been a part. Miller mentions that *East Lynne* 'reduces the juices of the optative to a pungent essence' ('A Case of Metaphysics' 786). Isabel is forced to look longingly at her family through blue-coloured glasses, 'a fantastic concatenation of events devised, it seems, solely to allow her to be an intimate spectator of the life she might still be living but is not' (786). Instead, she watches Barbara, the new Mrs Carlyle, living 'the life she cannot lead' (786). Miller uses this novel to argue that the bigamy plot shows counterfictionality in excess, but what is also significant is the way that Isabel physically interacts with this alternative life. She is not merely a spectator, watching from a distance, but engages affectively and tactilely with her children and former husband.[4] As her child lies dying, she 'leaned over him, laying her forehead upon his wasted arm' and 'burst into a flood of impassioned tears' (577). And later, when she is dying, Mr Carlyle 'pushed aside the hair from her brow with his gentle hand, his tears dropping on her face' (616). Discoveries are made and forgiveness is granted, but this occurs through the body, not merely through internal realisations.

While *East Lynne* certainly makes the counterfictional sensational and affective, the novel never provides us with a teary, sympathetic encounter between Isabel and Barbara. Isabel dies before Barbara learns the truth about her rival, which Archibald only conveys to his second wife in the final lines of the novel. While Isabel demands that Archibald, 'Think what it has been for me!' she never has a similar confrontation with the new Mrs Carlyle (615). In this respect, Wood's novel, like Brontë's *Jane Eyre*, differs from those that I discuss in this chapter. Collins, Hardy and Reade show their counterfictional doubles coming together in moments of shared sympathy – sympathy that is both cognitive and embodied, as they attempt to imagine what life has been for their double, and as they experience moments of bodily sympathy, initiated via touch.

The Woman in White and 'the twin-sisters of chance resemblance'

Before Walter meets Anne, he stands at a forked road, a scenario heavily laden with optative imagery. Miller notes that Hampshire's notion of the optative 'aims to evoke the discomfiting conjunction of two familiar impressions: the immediacy of one's experience and its thoroughgoing contingency' (774). This scene evokes both: this moment of intensity would not have occurred had Walter not turned down the road to London at this precise time (20). And while Walter chooses the road 'mechanically', he then consciously agrees to Anne's terms – to get her a fly and 'not to interfere with [her]' – and finds himself asking, 'What could I do?' (22). Yet even more than such moments of decision, the novel is obsessed with the counterfactuality of sex and class, the accident of our birth. Marian imagines, 'If poor Hartright had been the baronet, and the husband of her father's choice, how differently [Laura] would have behaved!' (186). Laura, too, tells Marian, 'I used to fancy what I might have been, if it had pleased God to bless me with poverty, and if I had been his wife. I used to see myself in my neat cheap gown, sitting at home and waiting for him, while he was earning our bread' (263). While Laura's fantasy may imply a naivety about the blessing of poverty, it is true that as a vulnerable, orphaned woman, her wealth only brings her unhappiness. Marian even imagines how different her life would be 'If [she] had been a man' (249). These are all sentence-level instances of the optative in which characters 'fancy what . . . might have been' by imagining other, specific possibilities (263).

In addition to these examples of dialogue, the counterfactuality of class and wealth forms the crux of the plot, specifically as it concerns Anne and Laura. While *The Woman in White* is likely well known to readers of this book, it is worth briefly recounting the relationship between Anne and Laura, since their shared roles in the plot are mediated through other characters. Neither woman narrates her own section of the patchwork narrative, although their letters are included by others. As a child, Anne lived for a time in Cumberland and was devoted to Laura's mother; we later learn that Anne is the illegitimate child of Laura's father. Despite their class disparity and personality differences – characterised by Anne as 'clever Miss Fairlie, and poor dazed Anne Catherick' – their physical similarity made Laura's unknowing mother attached to the young Anne (282). As women, however, their likeness is exploited by the villains of the novel. When Laura is engaged, Anne sends her a letter trying to warn her against Glyde and Fosco, who are responsible for placing Anne in the asylum in the first place; but Laura marries him anyway, only later realising that they desire access to her marriage settlement of £20,000. Anne reappears, promising to reveal to Laura a secret that will ruin Glyde. Instead, Laura is tricked into travelling to London, where Glyde swaps her with Anne: while Anne dies of a heart condition and is buried in Cumberland as Laura, Laura is drugged and placed in an asylum as Anne. Eventually, Marian and Walter rescue Laura and the rest of the novel narrates their attempt to restore her identity.

Walter is, of course, initially the vehicle by which the adult Anne and Laura are brought together in the text, and his descriptions of Anne and Laura are also descriptions of his own intense and perplexing sensations. This emphasis makes clear the important role that each woman plays in the narrative, but it also risks displacing their characters with Walter's impressions of their characters. When he first tries to depict Laura, for instance, he admits that his current feelings for her cloud his early memories: 'How can I separate her from my own sensations, and from all that has happened in the later time?' (48). She overwhelms Walter because of their present/future relationship, but also because she reminds him uncannily of Anne. Mingling with Walter's charming impressions of Laura is 'another impression, which, in a shadowy way, suggested to me the idea of something wanting' (51). Later, Walter hears the story of Anne Catherick from Marian at the very moment in which Laura passes through his frame of vision. Marian reads from a letter of her mother's, which notes the likeness between the two girls, and then Walter sees it for himself and experiences 'the same feeling which ran through me when the touch was laid upon my shoulder on the lonely high-road' (60). He perceives that Laura, dressed in white and standing in the moonlight, is 'the living image, at that distance, and under those circumstances, of the woman in white! . . . That 'something wanting' was my own recognition of the ominous likeness between the fugitive from the asylum and my pupil at Limmeridge House' (61). Janice Allan explains that Anne 'possesses the something "extra" that allows her to "complete" Laura's identity' (103). This is indeed how Walter frames it, but it's worth noting that the 'something wanting' is not merely Anne but Walter's own inability to puzzle out the relationship between the women. In other words, Walter frames Anne as merely an aspect of Laura's identity, but if we look outside of his framing, it is possible to understand Anne, and her connection to Laura, in richer ways.

Walter quickly realises that not only do the women look alike, but Anne stands as an ominous warning of Laura's possible future. Walter realises that if 'ever sorrow and suffering set their profaning marks on the youth and beauty of Miss Fairlie's face, then, and then only, Anne Catherick and she would be the twin-sisters of chance resemblance, the living reflexions of one another' (97). Yet their likeness is not due to 'chance', since they share the same father. Counterfactuality thus comes into play due to their social circumstances – What if Anne had been legitimate? What if Laura had not? – but also because Anne comes to symbolise Laura's future suffering. When Laura is placed in the asylum, she, wearing Anne's clothing and marked with Anne's name, finally embodies this future. The nurse tells her: 'Look at your own name on your own clothes, and don't worry us all any more about being Lady Glyde. She's dead and buried' (436). Although Anne has died, Anne and Laura now seem to meld into a single body: Walter finds that the 'outward changes wrought by the suffering and the terror of the past had fearfully, almost hopelessly, strengthened the fatal resemblance' between them (442). While Laura's experience in the asylum is terrifying, Anne's falsified death is a similarly violent act by the novel's male characters. Tamar Heller argues that Anne 'embodies the social invisibility that renders women blank pages to be inscribed by men' (112). Indeed, Anne becomes simply a placeholder for Laura's identity as her name is covered by Laura's even in the moment of her death. Though the novel devotes more attention to the recovery of Laura's identity, it also reveals how the social and psychological identities of these two women are both so fragile that they seem to merge into one being.

Much of what I have discussed so far fits easily into a paranoid, gothic reading of the novel and of these female doubles. Attending to the encounters between the women and moving outside of Walter's narration, however, opens up another way of understanding their relationship. While Laura is a largely passive figure in the novel, Anne is a surprisingly active character, as she attempts to circumvent male power and offer Laura a degree of agency. Anne's first warning comes not with their physical meeting, but with an anonymous letter that she sends to Laura, detailing a dream she had of Laura's wedding to Glyde. Anne explains that she sees Laura coming down a church aisle with a man:

You looked so pretty and innocent in your beautiful white silk dress, and your long white lace veil, that my heart felt for you, and the tears came into my eyes.

They were tears of pity, young lady, that heaven blesses and instead of falling from my eyes like the everyday tears that we all of us shed, they turned into two rays of light which slanted nearer and nearer to the man standing at the altar with you, till they touched his breast. The two rays sprang in arches like two rainbows between me and him. I looked along them, and I saw down into his inmost heart . . . . It was black as night, and on it were written, in the red flaming letters which are the handwriting of the fallen angel, 'Without pity and without remorse. He has strewn with misery the paths of others, and he will live to strew with misery the path of this woman by his side.' (78–9)

Anne's dream articulates an embodied and a spiritual understanding of sympathy as her pity-fuelled tears turn into rays of light. Her dream links her past and Laura's future, as they are both victims of Glyde and Fosco's cruelty and are symbolic of the precarious state of Victorian women more generally. She writes to Laura because, she explains, 'I have an interest in your well-being . . . . Your mother's daughter has a tender place in my heart – for your mother was my first, my best, my only friend' (79). The sympathetic bonds of friendship thus extend from the deceased Mrs Fairlie to Anne to Laura.

The letter positions Anne as a disturbed but clairvoyant figure with knowledge about Glyde's darkness and Laura's goodness. She begins the letter by asking Laura, 'See what Scripture says about dreams and their fulfilment', and her references to biblical narratives depart from the legal language of many of the other first-person narratives in the novel and gesture to other forms of knowledge (78). Their exchanges show Anne attempting, with mixed success, to warn, assist and prepare Laura for her difficult future. As Heller argues, 'Anne is more than simply the victim she initially appears to be. With her cry . . . – "I have been cruelly used and cruelly wronged" (19) – she also embodies the radically feminist version of the female Gothic plot' (114). Indeed, she provides Laura, as well as Marian and Walter, clues with which to understand the plots they are trying to uncover. She never gets her own entry in Walter's patchwork narrative, but this letter shows her desire to narrate and make sense of her own experiences and past. While Heller is right to suggest that *The Woman in White* contains elements of the female gothic plot – according to the gothic tradition, both women may not continue living – the sympathetic bond between the women is also a key way in which Collins develops and shifts the gothic plot into a sensational plot.

The scene in which Anne touches Walter is so pivotal that it is easy to overlook the important, if less sensational, encounter between Anne and Laura that occurs later in the novel. This later scene is also structured around touch and confused affects, but rather than an uneasy encounter between a man and a woman, it is a moment about the bonds of womanhood. Laura goes to the boathouse on the property to find a brooch that she had lost and is surprised to discover Anne there. While the two women meet, Marian, who narrates the section, is back at Blackwater Park, experiencing a prophetic dream that Walter is in danger.[5] She is eventually awakened by Laura's touch: 'I was aroused by a hand laid on my shoulder. It was Laura's' (279). Laura then begins to tell her story of Anne's arrival, but Marian finds that she needs to touch Laura to steady herself and understand what she is hearing. She feels Laura's brooch since there 'was something real in the touching of it ... which seemed to steady the whirl and confusion in my thoughts, and to help me compose myself' (280). This touch works to comfort them both. Laura then relates that when she saw Anne, 'it came over my mind suddenly that we were like each other! Her face was pale and thin and weary – but the sight of it startled me, as if it had been the sight of my own face in the glass after a long illness' (282). Just as Walter had done, Laura sees Anne as her future, suffering image. Recognising this physical similarity doesn't instantly lead to an understanding between the women, as Laura is initially startled by Anne's nervous affects. In fact, their meeting begins with some tension: Anne holds out the brooch that Laura has dropped and asks Laura if she can pin it back on for her. Laura recoils, finding the request made with 'extraordinary eagerness' (282). Anne reproaches her by saying, 'your mother would have let me pin on the brooch', and this causes Laura to take Anne's hand and place it 'gently on the bosom of [her] dress' (282). This touch seems to enable a sympathetic connection between the women, even as Laura remains somewhat uneasy.

The fact that their touch happens through the brooch suggests it figures as a symbol of female friendship and trust, since Marian gave it as a gift to Laura the night before her wedding. Heller has suggested that 'the novel's most central symbolic site is the grave of Laura and Marian's mother, which functions as an image for women's lack of identity' (113). Yet the brooch seems to figure differently, as a sign of the women's interconnectivity, which is tied not to death but to the body. Soon after this moment (and a few false starts in which they continue to misread one another), Anne confesses that she has come 'to make atonement' to Laura for not working harder to prevent her marriage to Glyde (283). Anne is filled with counterfactual regret, not for her own life but for Laura's. She exclaims, 'I ought to have warned you and saved you before it was too late. Why did I only have courage enough to write you that letter?' (284). These feelings of remorse propel her to 'want to undo all I can of the harm I once did' (284). Anne takes on a lot of responsibility for Laura's choices, perhaps too much. She explains that she will help Laura gain power over 'her wicked husband': 'I once threatened him with the Secret, and frightened him. You shall threaten him with the Secret, and frighten him, too' (285). This doesn't go according to plan, since they are interrupted before Anne can make a full confession, and she does not know the details of his illegitimacy in any case. Nevertheless, Anne constructs a scenario in which Laura must repeat and rectify Anne's sensational plot. As Laura is being abducted later in the novel she asks the housekeeper, Mrs Michelson, who sees her off at the train station, 'Do you believe in dreams?' (397–8). Kelly Marsh notes, 'That she echoes Anne's letter is just one of the signs that [Laura] has begun to understand Anne's message', and, I would add, to enact what Anne has predicted for her (103).

In a passage added in the novel proof, Walter concludes Anne's narrative in this way: 'So the ghostly figure which has haunted these pages, as it haunted my life, goes down into the impenetrable Gloom. Like a Shadow she first came to me in the loneliness of the night. Like a Shadow she passes away in the loneliness of the dead' (569). In many ways, Anne, appearing at night dressed in white, communicating through scripture and consistently talking of her own death, is a 'ghostly figure'. Critics typically describe her in this way. Jenny Bourne Taylor notes that she is 'Laura's ghost ... she is the trace, the shadow, and the mirror of the social and subjective transformation which Laura undergoes' (101). While this is how Walter characterises Anne, Collins is also at pains to show us that this woman is deeply embodied as she touches Walter and Laura and transmits her anxious affects. Cvetkovich points out that 'because Anne is illegitimate she is destined for the life that makes her body bear the marks of suffering' (*Mixed Feelings* 89). This is certainly true, but it's important to recall that her covering her body in white is a testament to her love for Mrs Fairlie. While it might make her appear spectral, it is an act of defiance: she uses her garments to pledge loyalty to a woman who was kind to her, in contrast to her own cruel mother. Her white dress, like the brooch touched by Anne, Laura, Marian and, imaginatively, by Mrs Fairlie, suggests a networked relationship among the vulnerable women in the novel. Marsh argues, in fact, that Anne's primary role is to encourage Laura to move her allegiances from her undeserving father to her caring mother (99).

In these ways, I read Anne as one of the most wilful bodies in the novel. Lillian Nayder makes the provocative point that Anne's demand that Walter 'promise not to interfere with me, and to let me leave you, when and how I please' raises a question that is central to the novel: 'what right, if any, do men have to control women?' (Collins 22, Nayder 77). What Anne desires from Walter in that opening scene is both his assistance and also that he respect her autonomy (Nayder 77). And her supposed helplessness – the fact that she needs him to call a fly for her – could also be read as her cannily using Walter's male body to perform an action that society would deem suspicious in a woman. If the sensational body is a body that involuntarily betrays and transmits its affects, then Anne is certainly a sensational body, one whose nervousness and 'madness' is apparent to others (283). Yet her story is also about resisting the restrictions of the body, as she escapes from the asylum, writes out her dreams and covertly meets with Laura. Anne's rebellious energies resonate in Laura's plot as Anne stands boldly as a visual reminder of what Laura could become and nearly does. While her death seems to permit Laura's eventual second life as Mrs Hartright, she too gets her wish, to be buried beside Mrs Fairlie. While it is a melancholy wish, it has been hers all along: she tells Laura that she is there to 'make atonement to you, before I meet your mother in the world beyond the grave' (283). Heller is right that the grave marks these women's invisibility, but it too figures as a symbol of their affective network.

Desperate Remedies and sympathetic touches

In Thomas Hardy's *Desperate Remedies*, we see a similar confrontation between a woman and her possible future self, one also characterised by both suffering and sympathetic bonds. Printed anonymously by the Tinsley Brothers in 1871, *Desperate Remedies* was Hardy's first published novel.[6] He later seemed embarrassed about his sensational foray into fiction: in the 1889 preface to the novel, he writes, 'The following story, the first published by the author, was written nineteen years ago, at a time when he was feeling his way to a method. The principles observed in its composition are, no doubt, too exclusively those in which mystery, entanglement, surprise, and moral obliquity are depended on for exciting interest' (Appendix 2). Yet he notes that 'some of the scenes, and at least one of the characters [presumably Miss Aldclyffe], have been deemed not unworthy of a little longer preservation' (Appendix 2). In fact, Hardy did preserve it, including the novel in Macmillan's 1912 Wessex Edition of his works and categorising it as one of his 'Novels of Ingenuity' alongside *The Hand of Ethelberta* (1876) and *A Laodicean* (1881). While it was largely left out of studies of Hardy's fiction in the twentieth century, Richard Nemesvari notes that the idea that the novel is 'a strange, somewhat embarrassing anomaly is losing ground' (*Thomas Hardy* 27). Nemesvari, in *Thomas Hardy, Sensationalism, and the Melodramatic Mode* (2011), argues compellingly that Victorian melodrama and 'the kinds of sensation fiction that grew out of and fed back into nineteenth-century dramaturgy' were central to Hardy's work (2). Indeed, Hardy's novels are filled with melodramatic plots, expressions of female sexual desire and descriptions of the surfaces and sensations of characters' bodies in ways that align with sensationalism.

Suzy Anger and Megan Ward have recently emphasised the ways in which Hardy's characters function as 'material networks of sensation' (Ward 99). Ward argues that in Hardy's fiction characterological intimacy is not achieved through psychological depth, but rather through 'an accumulation of superficial impressions', such that 'character is created through others' observations' (103, 104). The idea that the observation and felt affects of other bodies are linked to a deeper understanding of character in Hardy's fiction is another way in which his work can be understood as sensational. Both Ward and Anger mention

Hardy's avoidance of free indirect discourse at a time when many novelists were adopting this technique. Instead, Ward remarks, 'Hardy stresses the extent to which consciousness may be comprised of automated sensations beyond our own understanding' (115). Similarly, Anger encourages scholars to think of 'the many descriptions of characters who act "mechanically", "automatically", and "unconsciously" in Hardy's fiction' (498). She also notes that Hardy read and responded to the work of Alexander Bain, whose ideas about emotion and the will are aligned with sensation fiction.[7] Ward and Anger describe this interest in mechanical behaviour as typical of Hardy, but, as I have argued, it is also typical of sensation fiction. Thus, rather than finding characters that function as networked sensations or that act automatically as characteristic of Hardy's work specifically, I argue that Hardy develops such modes of writing from sensation fiction, the form in which he began his novelistic career.

While much of Hardy's work thus resonates with sensationalism, *Desperate Remedies* is certainly the most typically sensational of his novels. Additionally, like many of the novels that I have discussed, it is a self-conscious and parodic adoption of the form. While it differs from *The Woman in White* in that there is only one omniscient narrator, the novel similarly records the events of the narrative in precise detail, with chapter titles like 'The Events of One Day' or 'The Events of Eighteen Days', which are then broken up into hours, such as '*September the twentieth. Three to four, p.m.*'. The narrator explains that the 'object of this narration' is to 'present in a regular series the several episodes and incidents which directly helped forward the end' (69). This method of recording is typical of sensationalism, though it also betrays the novel's interest in fate and free will. Characters explicitly discuss causality and coincidence, with Cytherea noting that when multiple events 'coincide without any reason for the coincidence, it seems as if there must be invisible means at work' (146). This emphasis on determinism is a feature of both Hardy's later work and the sensation genre: Robert Audley, for instance, suggests that his actions are guided by the 'hand which is stronger than my own' (Braddon 148). The novel's interest in fate is furthermore related to its focus on counterfactual possibilities. Andrew Miller says of Hardy that 'his books make us see that the things that do happen, and those that do not are complementary parts of the narrative machinery, paired cogs with interlocking teeth' ('A Case of Metaphysics' 779).

Sympathetic Doubles 171

While I will focus on the most prominent female doubling plot in the novel, it is worth noting that the novel sets up various doppelgängers. Aeneas Manston and Edward Springrove can be regarded as doubles, as they are both architects and love interests of the young Cytherea. A physical brawl between them near the end of the novel results in them rolling on the floor, 'locked in each other's grasp as tightly as if they had been one organic being at war with itself' (360). Furthermore, Aeneas tries to hide the murder of his first wife, Eunice, by bringing in an actress to play her. As with Anne and Laura, both women are dehumanised by this action, with one woman's death rendering her invisible and the other functioning merely as a body. Yet the two women named Cytherea are doubled in explicitly counterfactual ways.

Cytherea Graye is left orphaned and vulnerable after the death of her father. Her poverty and the fact that her injured brother cannot support her mean that she is forced to find work as a lady's maid. This is how she encounters her double, the older Cytherea Aldclyffe (whom I call Miss Aldclyffe, as Hardy does). Miss Aldclyffe responds to Cytherea's advertisement, and they meet in a scene filled with images of doubling. First Cytherea, waiting in an adjacent room, 'had just laid her hand on the knob, when it slipped round within her fingers, and the door was pulled open from the other side' (54). On the other side is Miss Aldclyffe 'with the door in her hand' (54). Each woman confronts her double through the threshold of the door; they then move into the light of the window, which has the effect of making Cytherea mature and Miss Aldclyffe look younger:

> The warm tint added to Cytherea's face a voluptuousness which youth and a simple life had not yet allowed to express itself there ordinarily; whilst in the elder lady's face it reduced the customary expression, which might have been called sternness, if not harshness, to grandeur, and warmed her decaying complexion with much of the youthful richness it plainly had once possessed. (54)

This description recalls the moonlight that shines on Laura's face, making her look like Anne in *The Woman in White*. Hardy's heavy-handed imagery – the turning doors, the age-collapsing light – serve to set up the younger Cytherea as a counterfactual example for the older woman.

The orientation of the optative in this novel functions a bit differently from that in *The Woman in White*. In Collins's novel, Anne helps Laura to circumvent a possible future. Anne's regret is not only about her own misused life but her inability to save Laura from Glyde. In contrast, Hardy's novel largely focuses on Miss Aldclyffe's realisation that Cytherea is living the life that she could have led, and she must come to terms with her jealousy for this beautiful young woman. Nonetheless, we can parallel Anne and Miss Aldclyffe in that they are both filled with the regret of the optative, if for different reasons. Both are suffering women who will die while their beautiful double eventually lives out a happier life (though only after enduring suffering herself). In Hardy's novel, Cytherea and Miss Aldclyffe are both jilted by a lover, but Cytherea gets to relive and rework Miss Aldclyffe's plot. These women are more than doubled versions of one another, however, as Cytherea is literally the daughter Miss Aldclyffe could have had. Cytherea begins to realise that 'a strange confluence of circumstances ... had brought herself into contact with the one woman in the world whose history was so romantically intertwined with her own' (77). When Miss Aldclyffe was seventeen, she 'was cruelly betrayed by her cousin, a wild officer of six and twenty' (372). She became pregnant and was forced to give up the child for adoption; her cousin died while abroad. Fifteen months later she met Cytherea's father and they immediately fell in love, but she assumed that if he 'knew her secret he would have cast her out', and so she forced herself to say no to his proposal (373). She longed for him and her child for the rest of her life, and Mr Graye, unaware of the reason for her refusal, continued to love her to such an extent that he named his child, with another woman, after her. Cytherea, then, is both the child that Miss Aldclyffe could have had and also the innocent young woman she could have been, but for a misstep in sexual propriety. We might recall here Miller's notion that the optative makes melodramatic the idea of the event; in this case Miss Aldclyffe's affair is the event that irrevocably changes her life. Her story also demonstrates the gendered implications of the optative, namely the fact that Victorian women's choices have even greater impact than those made by their male counterparts.

Despite the parallels that I am drawing between the suffering Anne and Miss Aldclyffe, Cytherea is also like Anne in that her body is the most sensational body in the text. In the opening

Sympathetic Doubles 173

pages of the novel, Cytherea enters the Town Hall when a reading from Shakespeare is about to take place. Yet the townspeople, trained in body reading, are less interested in the play and more attentive to 'the entrance of the new-comers – silently criticising their dress – questioning the genuineness of their teeth and hair – estimating their private means' (11). While Cytherea's appearance is an 'interesting subject of study for several neighbouring eyes', what most attracts observers is her movement (11). The narrator explains, 'motion was her speciality . . .. The carriage of her head – motion within motion – a glide upon a glide – was as delicate as that of a magnetic needle' (11–12). Hardy's simile, that Cytherea moves her head as delicately as a magnetic needle on a compass, is an intriguingly mechanical way to describe her movements. Yet the narrator is also at pains to describe her movements as natural, insisting that this 'flexibility and elasticity had never been taught her by rule' (12). Like Anne, she is a sensational body whose presence shifts the atmosphere of the Town Hall or road.

In a passage that is hard not to read as Hardy poking fun at sensation fiction, the narrator then doubles down on this colourful description, providing a list of Cytherea's most remarkable affects. Displaying his own Theory of Mind at work, he explains that

> among the many winning phases of her aspect, these were particularly striking: –
> 1. During pleasant doubt, when her eyes brightened stealthily and smiled (as eyes will smile) as distinctly as her lips, and in the space of a single instant expressed clearly the whole round of degrees of expectancy which lie over the wide expanse between Yea and Nay.
> 2. During the telling of a secret, which was involuntarily accompanied by a sudden minute start, and ecstatic pressure of the listener's arm, side, or neck, as the position and degree of intimacy dictated.
> 3. When anxiously regarding one who possessed her affections. (12–13)

This quasi-medical list reads as a humorous way of detailing the expression of affect. These affects – her animated eyes and 'ecstatic' touch – are automatic and repeated when she is in doubt, telling a secret or looking at someone she loves. The opening passages emphasise that Cytherea is an object of study to the townspeople and even to the narrator, recalling Ward's notion that 'Hardy's subjects are most illuminated when they are objects to be read' (104). Miss Aldclyffe is also not immune to Cytherea's movements and agrees to employ her without any references because of the girl's effect on her. She imagines that it will be worthwhile having 'a creature who could glide round my luxurious indolent body in that manner, and look at me that way – I warrant how light her fingers are upon one's head and neck' (56).

Miss Aldclyffe's suggestive language implies early on that the women will be 'romantically intertwined' in more than one way, with Cytherea positioned as Miss Aldclyffe's counterfactual daughter, but also, because of her likeness to her father, as a figure of romantic attraction for her (77). As with Anne and Laura, the two women are connected by bonds of sympathy, a term Hardy uses frequently to describe their feelings for one another. For instance, reflecting on Miss Aldclyffe's temper, Cytherea checks the woman's 'weakness by sympathising reflections on the hidden troubles which must have thronged the past years of the solitary lady' (77). In this clear description of cognitive sympathy, Cytherea's frustration at Miss Aldclyffe's anger is softened by her attempt to imagine what the woman's life must have been. As they come to knowledge of their shared history, the two women become more and more fascinated with one another: 'In bed and in the dark, Miss Aldclyffe haunted [Cytherea's] mind more persistently than ever. Instead of sleeping, she called up staring visions of the possible past of this queenly lady, her mother's rival' (77). As the narrative continues, the 'possible past' of Miss Aldclyffe becomes intertwined with the possible future of Cytherea.

Miss Aldclyffe and Cytherea's relationship comes to be defined by intense physical intimacy, as well as by a slippage between the categories of mother, lover and alternate self. Miss Aldclyffe initiates this intimacy as she intrudes into Cytherea's physical space, initially making her uncertain and uncomfortable. Sometime between '*One to two o'clock, a.m.*', she comes down to Cytherea's room and whispers through her keyhole: 'Let me come in, darling' (79). This moment recalls William Cohen's observation that in Dickens's fiction the keyhole figures as a vivid manifestation of interior and exterior and can also symbolise 'certain openings in the body' (31). Most keyhole scenes in Dickens's fiction, Cohen notes, are followed by doors opening and bodies moving through them: 'Making tangible the speech, breath, and other matter that passes through the keyhole, rather than limiting the hole to a one-way channel of observation, Dickens transforms the device: not simply a mechanism that shields one character in the social hierarchy from another, more powerful one (or that temporarily reverses such power relations), the keyhole becomes a virtual bodily orifice' (31). This idea of the permeability and sensuality of the keyhole resonates in this scene. All social hierarchy collapses as Miss Aldclyffe whispers through the keyhole: 'It was now mistress and maid no longer; woman and woman only' (79). The women are no longer defined by their social roles but simply by their bodies. Miss Aldclyffe enters the room in her nightgown and asks if she can climb into Cytherea's bed. After flinging her arms around the younger woman, she 'pressed her gently to her heart' and commands Cytherea to kiss her, a request that takes Cytherea by surprise but which she performs (79).

Yet what might be read as a scene of affection is complicated by Miss Aldclyffe's potent regret. Miss Aldclyffe initially lets down her stern demeanour and admits to Cytherea that she longs to be 'artless and innocent, like you' (80). Yet when she learns that Cytherea has a lover, her jealousy takes hold and she insists, 'Cytherea, try to love me more than you love him ... don't let any man stand between us' (82). While it would be tempting to read this language as an expression of female solidarity, it is in fact a potent mixture of Miss Aldclyffe's feelings of shame and disappointment, as she rails against Cytherea for her supposed duplicity: 'I thought I had at least found an artless woman who had not been sullied by a man's lips' (82). Rather than yearning for Cytherea's future happiness in the manner of Anne, her own bitter suffering makes her warn Cytherea of – or even predict – a future like her own past as she tells Cytherea that Edward will eventually reject and cease to love her. In this way, she recalls Dickens's Miss Havisham, whose regret for her past mistreatment leads her to mistreat young Estella. Miss Aldclyffe experiences a range of heightened emotions and roles in the next few pages: the narrator notes that she was 'as jealous as any man' (84), but she also tells Cytherea, 'Put your hair round your mamma's neck and give me one good long kiss' (85). This scene, notorious as an erotic encounter, ends with them lying together with the 'twinning tresses of [Cytherea's] long, rich hair over Miss Aldclyffe's shoulders' (85), much like the image of the sisters in Christina Rossetti's 'Goblin Market' (1862).[8]

In fact, 'Goblin Market' and Miss Havisham's story are both, at least in part, about the worth of a woman on the Victorian marriage market, specifically the way in which a rejection or sexual indiscretion may mark her for life. Miss Aldclyffe's tortured language gestures to the ways in which this system not only devalues women who misstep but constructs all women as rivals: in order to feel sympathy for Cytherea, Miss Aldclyffe must overcome such patriarchal ways of thinking. Anne and Laura, too, must overcome this, since Walter notes his attraction to Anne: 'Remember that I was young; remember that the hand which touched me was a woman's' (23). Additionally, Laura and Marian are also counterfactual selves to some extent, being half-sisters with wildly different social and financial possibilities. They too must reject any sense of jealousy.

In another link to Collins's novel, Hardy shows that the women's growing sympathetic connection is established through their dreams and the deciphering of them. The keyhole-bedroom scene occurs between one and two a.m., and the next section takes place between two and five a.m. After the women have fallen asleep together, Cytherea hears a disturbing noise, 'a very soft gurgle or rattle', and throws her arms around Miss Aldclyffe (87). At 'the maiden's touch', Miss Aldclyffe awakens from a nightmare that was disturbing her (88). She tells the young woman, 'Oh such a terrible dream! . . . and your touch was the end of it' (88). In her dream, she sees 'Time, with his wings, hour-glass, and scythe, coming nearer and nearer to me – grinning and mocking: then he seized me, took a piece of me only' (88). While this dream can certainly be read as an expression of Miss Aldclyffe's anxieties about ageing, the 'piece of [her]', we soon learn, is her father. In the very moment that she has this dream, her father, in the room directly below, dies; this is the strange sound that Cytherea hears. It is his death and the recognition of their shared vulnerability that ultimately unites the women. As Miss Aldclyffe tells Cytherea the sad news, she asks, 'Is it a Providence who sent you here at this juncture that I might not be left entirely alone?' (95). Cytherea considers 'the strange likeness which Miss Aldclyffe's bereavement bore to her own: it had the appearance of being still another call to her not to forsake this woman so linked to her life' (95). The women then embrace and 'get more and more into one groove' (95). Despite this moment of cognitive and bodily sympathy, Miss Aldclyffe's associations with Miss Havisham do not entirely fade as she plots to end Cytherea and Edward's relationship and instead have Cytherea marry the son that she abandoned, Aeneas. He is the sensational villain of the novel, and it ends with him taking his own life and Cytherea later marrying Edward.

Immediately following Aeneas's death, however, is Miss Aldclyffe's own. Cytherea receives a letter warning her of Miss Aldclyffe's decline, and their final scenes together emphasise the women's affective bonds. When Cytherea returns to visit the dying woman, she enters the house quietly but 'the preternaturally keen intelligence of the suffering woman' catches the sound of her step (371). 'In the room', the narrator writes, 'everything was so still, and sensation was as it were so rarefied by solicitude, that thinking seemed acting' (371). While the women have achieved a nearly telepathic communication that makes 'thinking [seem] acting', they nonetheless do communicate: Miss Aldclyffe begs for Cytherea's forgiveness and Cytherea grants it. Miss Aldclyffe tells the story of her tortured past and her real relationship to Manston, in a scene filled with bodily sympathy: 'Tears streamed from Miss Aldclyffe's eyes, and mingled with those of her young companion, who could not restrain hers for sympathy' (372). Miss Aldclyffe melodramatically exclaims, 'To die unloved is more than I can bear! I loved your father, and I love him now' (373). 'This', the narrator states, 'was the burden of Cytherea Aldclyffe' (373). Yet their counterfactual plot suggests that Cytherea lifts that burden from the older woman as the 'sympathising and astonished girl' feels with and for her double. Indeed, their preternatural communication extends to the moment of Miss Aldclyffe's death, when her ghostly form appears at the foot of Cytherea's bed: 'No motion was perceptible in her; but longing – earnest longing – was written in every feature' (374). Miss Aldclyffe's longing is for Cytherea's love but also for a life unled. Early in the novel, Hardy notes that the 'maiden's mere touch seemed to discharge the pent-up regret of the lady as if she had been a jar of electricity' (72). Cytherea's touch forces Miss Aldclyffe to reconsider the life she could have had, but the young woman's sympathetic touch at her deathbed, when she 'clasped the lady's weak hand', suggests that she does not die unloved after all (371).

Both *The Woman in White* and *Desperate Remedies* show the ways in which cognitive and bodily sympathy take shape and coexist in sensational narratives. Cytherea thoughtfully imagines Miss Aldclyffe's suffering but also cries along with her. Cytherea is perhaps correct when she states in the novel that 'Nobody can enter into another's nature truly', but both novels posit the attempt to do so – via electric touch, dream visions, physical resemblances, shared histories and possible futures – as worthwhile (273).

Hardy once wrote of himself, 'It was his habit, or *strange* power of putting himself in the place of those who endured sufferings from which he himself had been in the main free, or subject to but at brief times' (291–2). Collins and Hardy represent the attempt to both imagine and feel another's suffering as a useful exercise, one that can eventually temper regret or pain and lead to new narratives to be written or enacted. These relationships between the women imply that sharing stories about women's victimisation can create sympathetic bonds and disrupt cycles of cruelty. Again, this reorients the arguments of reviewers who were concerned about Victorian women readers becoming only enamoured by romantic plots; instead, engagement with another's narrative leads to growth and understanding.

Reade's sympathetic bigamy plot

Despite my optimistic readings, traces of the gothic doubling plot do remain in these novels since Anne and Miss Aldclyffe die, seemingly sacrificing themselves for the happiness of Laura and Cytherea. Before turning to examples of male counterfictional doubling, I briefly offer an example of a sensation novel in which the sympathetic female doubles both remain living: Charles Reade's *Griffith Gaunt, or Jealousy*. Reade's novel details the life of its jealous protagonist, Griffith, who, believing that his wife Kate is having an affair with her priest, runs off and bigamously marries the innocent young Mercy Vint and has a child with her. Kate is left behind not only to raise their daughter on her own but, later, when the town believes (incorrectly) that Griffith has been murdered, to defend herself at the sensational trial. She is shocked when the young woman who arrives to offer testimony that will acquit her of the charge is Mercy herself. Kate, aware that Mercy is her husband's illegitimate wife, initially greets her with 'icy civility' (446). Yet Kate is relieved when Mercy insists, 'I hate you not' and explains that she feels guided by God to help (447). Reade's narrator insists at various points in the novel that women are better at reading minds and bodies than men, and Kate's ability to see Mercy's true nature is consistent with this idea. Nonetheless, the two women have huge conflicts to overcome: they are married, legally or not, to the same man and have children with him. Mercy even brings her child along with her. Yet rather than construct themselves as enemies, they recognise their shared vulnerability and suffering. Mercy admits, 'I'll not deny I did hate you for a time, when first I learned the man I had married had a wife, and you were she' (447). But, she explains, 'I have worn out my hate . . .. For 'twas the man betrayed me; *you* never wronged me, nor I you' (447).

Their bonds are cemented not only through their language but through their embodied sympathy. When Kate realises that Mercy can help her, 'tears of joy streamed down her face, and then Mercy's flowed too' (448). Kate even extends her love to Mercy's baby, resulting in a scene that Dickens notoriously found inappropriate: the women 'kissed his limbs and extremities after the manner of their sex, and comprehending at last that to have been both of them wronged by one man was a bond of sympathy, not hate, the two wives of Griffith Gaunt laid his child across their two laps, and wept over him together' (450).[9] What is remarkable about this scene is that they use the child – the very symbol of Griffith's betrayal – to cement their 'bond of sympathy'. As Richard Fantina says, the prominence of the child suggests Griffith's centrality but also 'highlights his irrelevance' (135). Indeed, the women even seem to stage their own marriage, as Mercy tells Kate that they are 'both one flesh and blood' and requests 'the one thing I pine for – a little of *your* love' (451). Much like Miss Aldclyffe, 'Mrs Gaunt caught her impetuously round the neck with both hands . . . and kissed her eagerly. They kissed one another again and again, and wept over one another' (451). They then spend the night together: 'They slept in one bed, and held each other by the hand all night, and talked to one another, and in the morning knew each the other's story' (452). Both cognitive and embodied sympathy are at work through their shared stories and affects.

This example is remarkable not only because of the women's rejection of rivalry but because Mercy saves Kate from dying. Kate articulates this at the trial: 'I am her rival after a manner; yet out of the goodness and greatness of her noble heart, she came all that way to save me from an unjust death' (461). Reade radically challenges not only Victorian morality, in insisting on Mercy's innocence, but also the gothic doubling plot. Mercy and Griffith's illegitimate child eventually dies, but Mercy is permitted some happiness when she later marries a kind gentleman, Sir George Neville. Kate and Griffith also reconcile. While the narrator notes that the two couples avoid one another at social events, the women remain in contact and work together 'in saving young women, who had been betrayed, from sinking deeper' (488). The narrator explains, 'Living a good many miles apart, Lady Neville could send her stray sheep to service near Mrs Gaunt; and *vice versa*; and so, merciful, but discriminating, they saved many a poor girl who had been weak, not wicked' (488). This novel, even more than Collins and Hardy's novels, sees sensational doubling breaking cycles of male cruelty, as the women's compassionate and affectionate bonds extend beyond them to other vulnerable young women.

Male doubles in Collins

By way of conclusion, I explore the ways in which Collins depicted male counterfictional selves in his later sensation novels. In *Armadale* and *Poor Miss Finch*, Collins's sympathetic male doubles similarly develop attachments despite the fact that their identities must be formed as a result of economic and romantic competition with other men. While the men don't experience the social vulnerability of female characters like Anne or Miss Aldclyffe, Collins does imply that masculinity itself, so reliant on rivalry and aggression, is damaging and in need of reform. Like Collins and Hardy's female pairings, Collins's male doubles are comprised of one man who struggles with Victorian domesticity and conventionality, and another who achieves a happy romantic ending. The fact that one man's happiness must be sacrificed seems to simultaneously confirm and critique the notion that Victorian masculinity is built and maintained through competition with other men. As with the female characters, however, competition is replaced with sympathy, even as this sympathy is paired with suffering.

Collins's sympathetic male doubles are clearly influenced by Dickens (and we might say vice versa). Collins's play *The Frozen Deep* (staged in 1856 and published in 1866), which Dickens edited and performed in, and Dickens's *A Tale of Two Cities* both contain narratives in which a man saves the life of his rival. Dickens notes in the preface to the first volume edition of *A Tale of Two Cities*: 'When I was acting, with my children and friends, in Mr Wilkie Collins's drama of The Frozen Deep, I first conceived the main idea of this story' (Appendix II, 397). Richard Wardour in Collins's Arctic adventure anticipates the character of Sydney Carton in *Tale*. Wardour, who wanted to murder his rival Frank Aldersley because of his love for Clara Burnham, ends the play by saving Frank's life and sacrificing himself. In *Tale*, Carton despises Charles Darnay, the exiled Frenchman who also loves Lucie Manette. Carton is an alcoholic lawyer who admits that he does not deserve Lucie, but he still wrestles with his dislike of Darnay. Looking in the mirror, Carton asks himself,

> why should you particularly like a man who resembles you? ... A good reason for taking to a man, that he shows you what you have fallen away from and what you might have been! Change places with him, and would you have been looked at by those blue eyes as he was, and commiserated by that agitated face as he was? Come on, and have it out in plain words! You hate the fellow (89).

Yet Carton eventually comes to terms with his counterfactual regret: he develops 'a strange sympathy' for Lucie and Charles's children and notoriously gives up his own life for Darnay's, suffering himself to be executed on the guillotine (219). The novel concludes with his own words and redemption, like *The Frozen Deep*: 'It is a far, far better thing that I do, than I have ever done; it is a far, far better rest that I go to, than I have ever known' (390). The acts of Carton and Wardour can be interpreted as acts of love for the women that they might have married 'If it had been otherwise' (366); each man's actions also permit the happiness of his rival.

While the moments of forgiveness and sacrifice in *Armadale* and *Poor Miss Finch* may not be quite as dramatic as Carton's execution, in these novels the love between the men at times challenges the heterosexual romance plots, such that the bonds between the men are not merely in the service of the woman's happiness but, rather, their own friendship. In *Armadale* and *Poor Miss Finch*, the men's relationships are formed through sympathetic touches. When cousins Allan Armadale and Ozias Midwinter (who, recall, was born Allan Armadale) meet, they immediately possess an intense attachment to one other, one that repairs their fathers' murderous rivalry. The two men bear no physical resemblance to one another; while Allan is a white Englishman, the 'tawny' Ozias is consistently racialised (67). His mother was of 'mixed blood of the European and the African race', and he possesses 'hot Creole blood' (23, 479). Despite their differences, their names and shared family history make them counterfactual figures. The men rarely articulate optative longing for one another's lives, and instead it is Lydia, an agent and antagonist in the plots of both generations of Allan Armadales, who most clearly articulates the optative. She imagines a life in which she 'had married Midwinter for love', not mercenary reasons, and one in which they had children who 'were sleeping quietly in their cribs' (513). She also goes so far as to wish that she 'had been born an animal. My beauty might have been of some use to me then' (594). If Allan and Ozias don't ponder 'what if' questions to such an extent, they do acknowledge that their futures are tied to the past of their fathers. Ozias's father, in his 'dying conviction', sets up the novel's refrain in articulating 'a Great Doubt – the doubt whether we are, or are not, the masters of our own destinies' (55). While he hopes that 'mortal freewill can conquer mortal fate', he nonetheless proclaims, 'Never let the two Allan Armadales meet in this world: never, never, never!' (55). The notion that 'our past possibilities live within us' is made potent by the presence of the other Allan (Miller, 'A Case of Metaphysics' 775).

Yet throughout the novel, their relationship is dictated by their care for one another, exemplified by the fact that when Ozias arrives, disordered and suffering from brain fever, Allan immediately pays for his stay at a local inn and his care by a doctor. As Allan says, 'Why can't the people who have got money to spare give it to the people who haven't got money to spare, and make things pleasant and comfortable all over the world in that way?' (71). Allan's generosity is easily matched by Ozias, who, as Carolyn Denver argues, 'chooses to fight fate with love' (117). Ozias begins to take a more prominent role in the narrative, and he functions, much like Anne in *The Woman in White*, as a catalyst for change. Like Anne, he responds to a prophetic dream about the men's shadowy future (although it is Allan's, not his own). Ozias's response to Allan's dream – with the 'Shadow of a Man' and 'Shadow of a Woman' clearly standing in for Ozias and Lydia – differs from the pragmatic medical doctor's response (171). As Tabitha Sparks puts it, 'the devastating logic of Mr Hawbury, a doctor, challenges Ozias Midwinter's dark presentiment that a dream foretells his destiny', yet Midwinter's intuition is ultimately proven correct (*The Doctor* 88). The dream, in fact, with its 'Man-Shadow' and 'Woman-Shadow', can be understood as an articulation of counterfactual possibilities, these shadow selves mapping out a future that Ozias tries to influence.

Even more than the content of Allan's dream, the way in which Midwinter stops Allan's dream epitomises their connection. As Midwinter catches Allan mid-nightmare, he questions, 'Was the murder of the father revealing itself to the son ... in the vision of a dream?' (164). Midwinter then touches Allan's forehead:

> Light as the touch was, there were mysterious sympathies in the dreaming man that answered it. His groaning ceased, and his hands dropped slowly. There was an instant of suspense and Midwinter looked closer. His breath just fluttered over the sleeper's face. Before the next breath had risen to his lips, Allan suddenly sprang up on his knees – sprang up, as if the call of a trumpet had rung on his ear, awake in an instant. (164)

The similarities to scenes in *The Woman in White* and Hardy's *Desperate Remedies* are striking: the touch of the double transmits 'mysterious sympathies', even while, or perhaps especially while, dreaming. Although Lydia's arrival complicates the men's relationship, her sacrificial death mimics Ozias's willingness to sacrifice himself for Allan. The novel ends by focusing not on Allan and his new wife, Neelie, but on the two reunited men, suggesting the centrality of their story. The play adaptation also ends with a tableau of the two men: '*As ALLAN bends over MIDWINTER and takes his hand the curtain falls*' (qtd in Denver 115). While this ending is not very generous to Lydia or Neelie, it, at the very least, opens up the possibility for new masculine models that are focused on healing rather than violence.

Poor Miss Finch, however, doesn't sacrifice the novel's plucky heroine in favour of its male doubles. This strange novel exemplifies the way in which sensation fiction explored a materialist understanding of the body in the world: the heroine, Lucilla Finch, is blind and has 'eyes in the tips of her fingers', and the hero, Oscar, has epilepsy, a medical example of the body governing the mind (142). Oscar is grateful to his twin brother, Nugent, for saving his life when he is falsely accused of murder. Yet Oscar's adoration is excessive in that he wants to actually be Nugent. He exclaims, 'Ah, what would I not give to have a heart like his and a mind like his! It's something – isn't it? – to have a face like him' (50–1). Nugent, too, returns his brother's love. At the news of Oscar's marriage to Lucilla, Nugent tells him, 'Your happiness is my happiness. I feel with you' (125). But Nugent feels too deeply. We soon learn that he in fact loves Lucilla so much that he attempts to steal his brother's fiancée. As with Allan and Ozias's shared attraction to Lydia, Collins still relies on the gothic trope in which the arrival of the double always signals competition with the other.

The novel's judgemental narrator, Madame Pratolungo, Lucilla's French companion, makes matters more complicated by setting the men in opposition to one another and introducing the language of the optative. She prefers the supposedly more manly and capable Nugent, noting that he is 'So utterly different in his manner from Oscar ... and yet so like Oscar in other respects, I can only describe him as his brother completed' (135), a comment that echoes the notion that Anne 'completes' Laura's identity in *The Woman in White*. Madame emphasises the counterfactual aspect of the plot when she tells Lucilla that if she had met Nugent first, she would have preferred him: 'It happens to have been Oscar. Turn it the other way – and Nugent might have been the man' (172). Lucilla, however, rejects this idea. Instead of emphasising the accident of their meeting, she underscores her own affects and her desire for Oscar: she can tell the twins apart by touching their hands, explaining, 'Something in me answers to one of them and not to the other ... It answers to Oscar. It doesn't answer to Nugent – that's all' (147). Lucilla's directness and lack of modesty – which Madam Pratolungo attributes to her blindness – finds her assisting in her own proposal with the shy Oscar.[10] Lucilla's love for and attraction to Oscar thus works to challenge counterfictional plotting as she emphasises not the accident of their bond but the force of her desire.

Yet as the novel's complicated love plot takes shape, Oscar must take a more active hold over his own narrative. When an experimental procedure briefly restores Lucilla's sight, Oscar, in a moment of panic, pretends to be his brother, forcing Nugent to play the part of the lover. He does this because the silver nitrate that he takes as a result of his epilepsy has turned his skin blue and Lucilla has a horrid fear of dark skin. (The novel's compassionate depiction of Lucilla's blindness is coupled with a tolerance for her ostensible racism.) In what follows, Oscar leaves, thinking that Lucilla would be much happier with his brother, and Nugent keeps up the ruse, attempting to trick Lucilla. With the help of Madame Pratolungo, Oscar eventually returns and wins back his former fiancée. The final scene with these four characters together is loaded with affective touches and attempts at sympathy. When the villainous Nugent enters the hotel room where they have all gathered, Madame watches Oscar. Collins avoids detailing Oscar's interiority, instead having another character read his body: 'His face expressed the struggle in him of some subtly-mingling influences of love and anguish, of sorrow and shame' (420). Like Midwinter, Oscar resolves his affective dissonance by choosing love. He 'laid his hand on his brother's arm', touch again initiating sympathy, and asks Nugent, 'Are you the same dear good brother who saved me from dying on the scaffold, and who cheered my hard life afterwards?' (420). He then continues by removing Nugent's hat and with a 'careful, caressing hand, he parted his brother's ruffled hair over the forehead' (420). With this touch, he says, the 'vile unbrotherly thoughts I have had of being revenged on you . . . are gone!' (420). Lucilla and Madame watch the melodramatic reconciliation, with Madame insisting, 'He will deserve our sympathy; he will win our pardon and our pity yet!' (420).

The novel ends with the brothers' reconciliation but it also repeats the plots of the earlier novels in which one double must endure suffering and forgo either his own life or, in the case of Midwinter, the life of his wife. After Oscar and Nugent reunite, Nugent throws his arm around his brother only to find the pistol Oscar has been hiding in his breast-pocket. Deflating the potential violence, Nugent asks, 'Was this for me? . . . My poor boy! you could never have done it, could you?' (422). He then kisses Oscar and pushes him away 'with a firm and gentle hand' (422). What is different about this form of doubling, as Catherine Peters has noted, is that the twins do not have 'a mysterious affinity with each other, nor access to each other's thoughts' (xx). Indeed, it is Lucilla who is 'literally "in touch" with her feelings' and can tell one brother from the other (when she is still blind) (xxi). Yet despite their lack of strange sympathies, the brothers still reach a state of fellow feeling, brought about by the very object of their antagonism. In this way, the novel bears similarities to *The Frozen Deep* and *A Tale of Two Cities*, since the men's bond is facilitated by their love for the same woman. *Poor Miss Finch* in fact explicitly recalls Collins's earlier play, since Nugent leaves England for an Arctic exploration trip. He is found frozen on the boat, two years after his death, holding a lock of Lucilla's hair. Oscar, however, happily marries.

Miller notes that marriage 'invites the optative in part simply because it rules out alternatives and does so forever' (785). Yet he also shows that in mid-century England this defining feature of marriage was in contention, evinced by the cultural fascination with Mormon polygamy and debates about the Divorce and

Matrimonial Causes Act of 1857. In a later article, Miller briefly links the optative mode to sensation fiction via its perversion of the marriage plot: 'The rage for sensation novels capitalized on this interest in the exclusivity of marriage, many of them featuring bigamy and rendering the experience of bigamy an experience of lives unled' (786). Indeed, all of these novels flirt with – and in the case of *Griffith Gaunt*, explicitly depict – bigamy plots, and they all present marriage as a sensational event, a key moment of counterfactuality: if only Laura hadn't married Glyde, if only Miss Aldclyffe had married Cytherea's father, if only Griffith hadn't married Mercy, if only Lydia had married Ozias for love, if only Oscar had married Lucilla right away. Yet these continually expressed 'what ifs', these articulations of the optative, are all paired with sympathetic doubles who help to enact and rectify new futures.

On the one hand, sensational narratives double down on the notion of the optative with characters like Isabel Carlyle, Miss Aldclyffe and Lydia Gwilt, characters who know that their unhappy lives might have been different. On the other hand, the notions of affective bodies and permeable identities that are such a feature of these narratives work to temper the optative. Miller considers, 'To the extent that I think of myself as having a fluid, permeable life, not fixed in one identity – or think of myself as having several lives at once – I am unlikely to experience the optative' (778). Once characters acknowledge their shared sensations and shared pain, the sensational double becomes not a frightening figure that destabilises one's sense of self but, rather, an extension of the self. The double, just like the affective potential of the sensational touch, disrupts notions of discrete bodies and identities, and allows these characters to imagine new ways of knowing and being.

Notes

1 For instance, Jenny Bourne Taylor writes, 'The tensions of *The Woman in White* hinge on the destruction and re-forming of Laura's identity, but the narrative devices by which it generates and resolves them make it also the story of Walter Hartright's social and psychological transformation – of his progress from marginalized lower-middle-class drawing master to the father of the heir of Limmeridge and revitalizer of the stagnant and incipiently morbid Fairlie family' (108).

2 Notably, I do not use the term 'empathy' in this chapter: many of the moments that I explore might now be understood as empathetic, but I am more invested in enhancing our understanding of the rich meaning of 'sympathy' as employed in these sensation novels and the Victorian period.

3 Similar concepts related to shadow narratives exist beyond those proposed by Warhol. For instance, Russell Reising locates shadow narratives primarily through endings that do not resolve the ideological tensions within texts (ix). These loose ends 'force us to return to the beginnings of the works we've just completed' by 'indirectly revealing shadow narratives that have been lying latent within the dominant thematics of the works from which they emerge' (12). In her recent book *The Submerged Plot and the Mother's Pleasure*, Kelly Marsh discusses submerged plots, which bear some similarity to shadow narratives. She reads novels of motherless daughters and finds that under 'the plot of maternal absence and filial disidentification [characteristic of these narratives], we can locate what I call a submerged plot of the daughter's search for the mother's story that surfaces at times and exerts consistent pressure on the surface plot' (6). The mother's story is not narrated in the text, and Marsh defines it as unnarratable because it is a story of her pleasure, but the daughter discovers and relives the mother's story.

4 Audrey Jaffe's *Scenes of Sympathy* includes a persuasive chapter on *East Lynne* and spectatorship, which she argues is key to the novel's understanding of sympathy: 'Eliciting readerly sympathy for Isabel is largely though the mechanism of spectatorship – requiring readers, as a condition of sympathy for her, to gaze both at and through the eyeglasses that mark her as spectator and spectacle – Wood ties readerly sympathy to a condition of spectatorship' (100). I find this reading compelling, though I also read Isabel's own spectatorship collapsing into moments of affect and touch.

5 This passage was added to the novel proof and is not in the serialised version of the novel.

6 *Desperate Remedies* is a revised version of his first completed novel, *The Poor Man and the Lady*. Notoriously, Hardy was advised by George Meredith to write a narrative with 'more plot' than his first attempt, and *Desperate Remedies* was the result (Ingham ix).

7 Suzy Anger explains that Hardy inserted in his literary notebooks a leaf of notes and diagrams entitled 'Diagrams Shewing Human Passions, Mind, & Character', which he completed in 1863. All but one of the diagrams depict ideas from Bain's *On the Study of*

Character (1861) (499). Anger argues that the notes and drawings suggest that 'Hardy is influenced strongly by that early reading of Bain, in his views on the relations between will, emotion (passion), and intellect in the representation of character, terms which recur in Hardy's work from first to last' (499).

8 Hardy evidently attempted to dissuade readers from reading too much into their relationship, with the narrator at one point stating, 'It was perceived by the servants of the House that some secret bond of connection existed between Miss Aldclyffe and her companion. But they were woman and woman, not woman and man, the facts were ethereal and refined, and so they could not be worked up into a taking story. Whether, as old critics disputed, a supernatural machinery be necessary to an epic or no, an ungodly machinery is decidedly necessary to a scandal' (111). This comment, as Patricia Ingham records in her notes to the novel, also might have the opposite effect.

9 Dickens admitted that, as author or editor, he would not have 'passed the passage where Kate and Mercy have the illegitimate child upon their laps and look over its little points together' (qtd in Fantina 29).

10 While I have focused on the many ways in which characters' blushes help to shape sensation plots as characters frequently (mis)read this most ambiguous and visible of affects, Lucilla is a fascinating anomaly. As Madame Pratolungo explains, 'modesty is essentially the growth of our own consciousness of the eyes of others judging us – and that blindness is never bashful, for the one simple reason that blindness cannot see' (59). While Lucilla doesn't blush, Oscar, in the early days of their courtship, 'start[s] violently ... his colour coming and going like the colour of a young girl' (37).

Coda: The Affective Pleasures of Reading and Not Reading

Throughout this book, I have discussed the ways in which sensational reading was sometimes seen as dangerous or unhealthy. But reading these novels was of course also pleasurable. It certainly has been for me. In this brief coda, I attend to the pleasurable affects associated with sensational reading, but also to the affects associated with not reading, or what Leah Price calls 'nonreading', by which I specifically refer to the pauses between serial reading or distracted reading.[1] I have identified a trope in these novels of characters picking up a novel and attempting to read it, only to be distracted by the more compelling events occurring in their lives. This differs from the immersive reading that I discussed in Chapter 1, but it presents a similar theory of narrative affect.

First, to attend to the pleasures of sensational reading. While I discussed serialisation in the introduction, I have not explored seriality at length in the book, instead focusing on narration, characterisation and the language of affect and emotion in these novels. My own experience as a reader has, with few exceptions, been with novels rather than with the original serial publications of these texts. Yet the serial reading of sensation fiction clearly had, and has, specific pleasures and affects. While Oliphant complained of the speed associated with serial reading, the enforced pauses between instalments are an important aspect of the form and the affects it can generate. Breaks between instalments can allow readers to emotionally engage with and gossip about characters. In fall 2018, I taught a class on sensation fiction in which students read *The Woman in White* serially. Our interaction with the text over such a long period of time (months rather than the weeks that we gave to other texts) made the students even more invested in this narrative. We used the spaces between instalments to discuss what might happen next and share our predictions together, an activity that now tends to be reserved for television shows.

As we did this, we formed our own affective community, with shared in-jokes and a shared language (if not always shared opinions). Robyn Warhol, in *Having a Good Cry*, explains that our experience was not unique:

> Though serial reading might place the solitary reader (then or now) literally in an isolated space, serial fiction creates virtual spaces both inside and outside the diegesis that are locations for connection and contact with others. Outside the text, serial fiction creates a community of readers ... who exchange books as gifts and loans, who meet one-on-one or in groups, in person or online ... to talk about their predictions for and reactions to the fiction. (87)

Indeed, part of the pleasure in reading this novel serially was the way in which we could form strong connections with characters, as well as fellow readers, over a long period of time. For instance, Marian quickly emerged as the universal favourite, and students fantasised about alternative endings for her.

While my students were engaged readers, I started to notice that readers within *The Woman in White* were not. The novel does not have many instances of novel reading, but those present suggest that the characters are not very diligent readers. Before Walter and Anne meet, he rouses himself 'from the book which [he] was dreaming over rather than reading' (6). Later, Marion writes in her journal, 'Reading is out of the question – I can't fix my attention on books' (200). Even the pious Mrs Michelson admits, '[I tried to] compose my mind with the volume of my husband's Sermons. For the first time in my life I found my attention wandering over those pious and cheering words' (398). Why fill a novel with descriptions of bad readers? Mrs Michelson provides a clue when she says that 'Lady Glyde's departure must have disturbed me far more seriously than I had myself supposed', and she puts her volume aside to take a walk instead (398). In all of these examples, the characters cannot read because they are distracted by real events occurring in their lives.

This trope occurs in fiction beyond Collins's novel. In Wood's *East Lynne*, Barbara is introduced 'listlessly turning over the leaves of a book' (21). Braddon, that most metafictional and intertextual of sensation writers, fills her novels with distracted readers. Alicia, bored with her life at Audley Court and desperate for her cousin Robert to notice her, is a particularly distracted reader. In one instance, Lady Audley asks her to join her on a walk, and Alicia agrees, admitting, 'I have been yawning over a stupid novel all the morning, and shall be very glad of a little fresh air' (288). Braddon's narrator says wryly, 'Heaven help the novelist whose fiction Miss Audley had been perusing, if he had no better critics than that young lady. She had read page after page without knowing what she had been reading; and had flung aside the volume half-a-dozen times to go to the window and watch for that visitor whom she had so confidently expected' (288). Braddon sets up a scenario in which Alicia is too impatient for Robert's arrival for her to pay attention to her reading. In this way, the 'stupid novel' figures as a barometer for Alicia's feelings, as well as a temporal and affective guide for readers. Like Alicia, we too should be attentive to Robert's arrival; she has laid down her book, but we need not. In a similar scene in Braddon's *Eleanor's Victory*, Eleanor impatiently waits for the return of her father, 'trying in vain to bury herself in the romance' she is reading (vol. 1, 114). She then starts to use the novel to measure time: 'she thought, "Before I turn over to the next page, papa will be home", or, "Before I can finish this chapter I shall hear his step upon the stairs"' (vol. 1, 114). These scenes of distracted reading are scenes of distracted affects: Eleanor feels too anxious about her father to focus on the fictional mystery in front of her. Again, this can help to orient the reader in that I too start to feel suspense and measure time via pages and chapters, though ideally with more attention to and interest in my fictional narrative.

These moments imply that 'good' reading is always affective and, ideally, immersive. If fiction creates virtual spaces 'inside ... the diegesis that are locations for connection and contact with others', these instances show us that these readers are too affectively engaged in their actual worlds to make the jump into the diegesis (Warhol 87). A final example, from Braddon's *John Marchmont's Legacy*, helps to demonstrate this point. The heartbroken Olivia Marchmont

> had a book in her hand, – some new and popular fiction, which all Lincolnshire was eager to read; but although her eyes were fixed upon the pages before her, and her hand mechanically turned over leaf after

leaf at regular intervals of time, the fashionable romance was only a weary repetition of phrases, a dull current of words, always intermingled with the images of Edward Arundel and Mary Marchmont, which arose out of every page to mock the hopeless reader. (190)

Olivia's 'mechanical' hand tells readers that she is not actively engaged, even before Braddon explains that she is picturing Edward and Mary. The narrative never coheres or comes alive for her: it is 'weary' and 'dull'. She finally flings 'the book away from her at last, with a smothered cry of rage' (190). It is perhaps this moment that the reviewer in the *Christian Remembrancer* is referencing when he complains that in sensation novels, 'the victim of feeling or passion sinks at once into the inspired or possessed animal, and is always supposed to be past articulate speech; and we have ... the *smothered cry of rage*' (109). Indeed, Olivia is a 'victim of feeling', but Braddon depicts this both via her 'smothered cry' and her inability to enter a fictional world. Her own jealousy and anger prevent her from cognitively and affectively engaging with – let alone caring about – fictional characters or plotlines. This differs from a representation of novel reading as escapist, as she is so grounded in her own affects that she cannot escape into the world of a novel.

These moments of distracted reading exemplify the claims that I have made throughout this book: that sensation novelists developed theories of bodily and narrative affects and playfully reflect on the reading experience in their fiction. Talia Schaffer has recently argued that 'sensation fiction can make a case for an alternative set of values – a warmly spontaneous, personal, intensely affective mode' ('Sensational Story' 59). While the sharing of affects is certainly not always ethical or generous in sensation fiction, these novels do work to formulate realistic theories of feeling in a world of difference and embodied experience. Sensation authors do not enforce the theory that reading fiction necessarily makes you a better or more caring person, but nor do they concur with Victorian reviewers who worried that reading of sensational worlds was inherently dangerous. Those reviewers who were concerned that reading sensation fiction would make young women unhappy with their domestic realities or marriage prospects unintentionally made significant observations about the lack of options available to young Victorian women and the ways in which sensational narratives could in fact offer lessons about both bodily autonomy and bodily interconnection. Indeed, these narratives, stretching across a range of genres and authors, are wilful, much like the bodies depicted within them. They play with readerly expectations, push at the boundaries of realistic representation and offer pleasures to willing readers.

Note

1 Price's *How to Do Things with Books in Victorian Britain* is a fascinating study on the materiality of the book, as represented in novels from the period. Many of her examples are even larger departures from the act of reading than I offer here: for instance, she discusses the act of holding a book instead of reading it, or using a book for some other valuable purpose than reading.

Works Cited

Ahern, Stephen. 'Introduction: A Feel for the Text'. *Affect Theory and Literary Critical Practice: A Feel for the Text*, edited by Ahern, Palgrave, 2019, pp. 1–21.
Ahmed, Sara. *The Cultural Politics of Emotion*. Routledge, 2004.
———. *The Promise of Happiness*. Duke University Press, 2010.
Alcott, Louisa May. *Behind a Mask*, edited by Madeleine Stern, Perennial, 2004.
———. *Little Women*. Vintage, 2008.
Allan, Janice M. 'The Contemporary Response to Sensation Fiction'. Mangham, pp. 85–98.
———. 'Dora Russell'. Gilbert, 2011, pp. 361–73.
———. 'Sensationalism Made Real: The Role of Realism in the Production of Sensational Affect'. *Victorian Literature and Culture*, vol. 43, 2015, pp. 97–112.
Anderson, Ben. 'Affective Atmospheres'. *Emotion, Space and Society*, vol. 2, no. 2, 2009, pp. 77–81.
Anger, Suzy. 'Naturalizing the Mind in the Victorian Novel: Consciousness in Wilkie Collins's *Poor Miss Finch* and Thomas Hardy's *Woodlanders*'. *The Oxford Handbook of the Victorian Novel*, edited by Lisa Rodensky, Oxford University Press, 2013, pp. 483–506.
Appletons' Annual Cyclopaedia and Register of Important Events of the Year 1887, vol. XII. New York, D. Appleton and Co, 1889.
Arnold, Catharine. *Necropolis: London and Its Dead*. Simon & Schuster, 2006.
Atkinson, Henry George, and Harriet Martineau. *Letters on the Laws of Man's Nature and Development*. Boston, Josiah P. Mendem, 1851.
Bachman, Maria K. 'Concealing Minds and the Case of *The Woman in White*'. *Victorian Secrecy: Economies of Knowledge and Concealment*,

edited by Albert Pionke and Denise Tischler Millstein, Ashgate, 2010, pp. 75–94.
Bailey, Amanda, and Mario DiGangi. 'Introduction'. *Affect Theory and Early Modern Texts: Politics, Ecologies, and Form*, edited by Bailey and DiGangi, Palgrave, 2017, pp. 1–23.
Bain, Alexander. *The Emotions and the Will*. 2nd ed., London, Longmans, Green and Co., 1865.
———. *Mind and Body: The Theories of their Relation*. New York, D. Appleton and Co., 1873.
———. *The Senses and the Intellect*. New York, D. Appleton and Co., 1855.
Beller, Anne-Marie. 'Amelia B. Edwards'. Gilbert, 2011, pp. 349–60.
———. 'Popularity and Proliferation: Shifting Modes of Authorship in Mary Elizabeth Braddon's *The Doctor's Wife* (1864) and *Vixen* (1879)'. *Women's Writing*, vol. 23, no. 2, 2016, pp. 245–61.
———. 'Sensation Fiction in the 1850s'. Mangham, pp. 7–20.
———. 'Sensational Bildung? Infantilization and Female Maturation in Braddon's 1860s Novels'. *New Perspectives on Mary Elizabeth Braddon*, edited by Jessica Cox, Brill, 2015, pp. 113–31.
Beller, Anne-Marie, and Tara MacDonald. 'Introduction'. *Beyond Braddon: Re-Assessing Female Sensationalists*, special issue of *Women's Writing*, edited by Beller and MacDonald, vol. 20, no. 2, May 2013, pp. 143–52.
Bernstein, Susan D. 'Ape Anxiety: Sensation Fiction, Evolution, and the Genre Question'. *Journal of Victorian Culture*, vol. 6, no. 2, 2001, pp. 250–70.
Blair, Kirstie. 'Poetry and Sensation'. Gilbert, 2011, pp. 107–19.
Boardman, Kay, and Shirley Jones. 'Introduction'. *Popular Victorian Women Writers*, edited by Boardman and Jones, Manchester University Press, 2004.
Bodenheimer, Rosemarie. 'Free Indirect Discourse'. *Victorian Literature and Culture*, vol. 46, nos 3–4, 2018, pp. 706–9.
Bourrier, Karen. '"The Spirit of a Man and the Limbs of a Cripple": Disability, Masculinity and Sentimentality in Charlotte Yonge's *The Heir of Redclyffe*'. *Victorian Review*, vol. 35, no. 2, 2009, pp. 117–31.
Braddon, Mary Elizabeth. *The Doctor's Wife*, edited by Lyn Pykett, Oxford University Press, 1998.
———. *Eleanor's Victory*. London, Tinsley Brothers, 1863. 3 vols.
———. *John Marchmont's Legacy*, edited by Toru Sasaki and Norman Page, Oxford University Press, 1999.

———. *Lady Audley's Secret*, edited by Lyn Pykett, Oxford University Press, 2012.
Brennan, Teresa. *The Transmission of Affect*. Cornell University Press, 2004.
Brontë, Charlotte. 'Biographical Notice of Ellis and Acton Bell'. *Wuthering Heights*, Penguin, 2003, pp. xlii–xlix.
———. *Jane Eyre*, edited by Margaret Smith, Oxford University Press, 2008.
———. *Villette*, edited by Margaret Smith and Herbert Rosengarten, Oxford University Press, 2008.
Broughton, Rhoda. *Cometh Up as a Flower*, edited by Pamela K. Gilbert, Broadview, 2010.
———. *Not Wisely, but Too Well*, edited by Tamar Heller, Victorian Secrets, 2013.
Canetti, Elias. *Crowds and Power*. Farrar Straus Giroux, 1988.
Charlotte Mary Yonge Website. Charlotte Mary Yonge Fellowship, 2000–2017. http://www.cmyf.org.uk/.
Clive, Caroline. *Paul Ferroll*. Forgotten Books, 2012.
———. *Why Paul Ferroll Killed His Wife*. New York, Carleton, 1862.
Cohen, William A. *Embodied: Victorian Literature and the Senses*. University of Minnesota Press, 2009.
Cohn, Elisha. *Still Life: Suspended Development in the Victorian Novel*. Oxford University Press, 2015.
Colby, Robert A., and Vineta Colby. *The Equivocal Virtue: Mrs Oliphant and the Victorian Literary Marketplace*. Archon Books, 1966.
Collins, Wilkie. *Armadale*, edited by Catherine Peters, Oxford University Press, 2008.
———. *The Frozen Deep*. Boston, William F. Gill and Company, 1875.
———. *The Law and the Lady*, edited by Jenny Bourne Taylor, Oxford University Press, 1992.
———. *The Letters of Wilkie Collins*, edited by William Baker and William M. Clarke, 2 vols, St Martin's Press, 1999.
———. *Poor Miss Finch*, edited by Catherine Peters, Oxford, 2008.
———. *The Moonstone*, edited by John Sutherland, Oxford, 2008.
———. 'The Unknown Public'. *My Miscellanies, The Works of Wilkie Collins*, vol. 20, New York, Peter Fenelon Collier, 1899, pp. 157–77.
———. *The Woman in White*, edited by John Sutherland, Oxford University Press, 1998.
Cunningham, Valentine. *Everywhere Spoken Against: Dissent in the Victorian Novel*. Clarendon Press, 1975.

Cvetkovich, Anne. *Mixed Feelings: Feminism, Mass Culture, and Victorian Sensationalism*. Rutgers University Press, 1992.
——. 'Public Feelings'. *South Atlantic Quarterly*, vol. 103, no. 13, 2007, pp. 459–68.
D'Albertis, Deirdre. *Dissembling Fictions: Elizabeth Gaskell and the Victorian Social Text*. Palgrave, 1997.
Daly, Nicholas. *Literature, Technology, and Modernity, 1860–2000*. Cambridge University Press, 2004.
——. *Sensation and Modernity in the 1860s*. Cambridge University Press, 2013.
Dames, Nicholas. '1825–1880: The Network of Nerves'. *Emergence of Mind: Representations of Consciousness in Narrative Discourse in English*, edited by David Herman, University of Nebraska Press, 2011, pp. 215–42.
——. *The Physiology of the Novel: Reading, Neural Science, and the Form of Victorian Fiction*. Oxford University Press, 2007.
Darwin, Charles. *The Expression of Emotions in Man and Animals*. Penguin, 2009.
——. *On the Origin of Species*. Penguin, 2009.
Denver, Carolyn. 'The Marriage Plot and Its Alternatives'. *The Cambridge Companion to Wilkie Collins*, edited by Jenny Bourne Taylor, Cambridge University Press, 2006, pp. 112–24.
Dickens, Charles. *Barnaby Rudge*, edited by Gordon Spence, Penguin, 2003.
——. *Bleak House*, edited by Nicola Bradbury, Penguin, 1996.
——. *David Copperfield*, edited by Jeremy Tambling, Penguin, 1996.
——. *Great Expectations*, edited by Edgar Rosenberg, Norton, 1999.
——. *Letters of Charles Dickens: 1833–1870*, edited by Georgina Hogarth and Mary Dickens, Cambridge University Press, 2011.
——. *A Tale of Two Cities*, edited by Richard Maxwell, Penguin, 2003.
Dickinson, Emily. 'I like a look of Agony'. *The Poems of Emily Dickinson*, edited by R. W. Franklin, Belknap Press, 1999.
Dixon, Thomas. *From Passions to Emotions: The Creation of a Secular Psychological Category*. Cambridge University Press, 2003.
Edwards, Amelia B. 'The Art of the Novelist'. *Contemporary Review*, August 1894, pp. 225–42.
——. *Barbara's History*. The Rubicon Press, 2000.
——. *Hand and Glove*. The Rubicon Press, 2000.
——. *Lord Brackenbury*. London, Hurst and Blackett, 1880.
——. *My Brother's Wife*. London, Hurst and Blackett, 1855.

Edwards, Annie. *Miss Forrester: A Novel*. London, Tinsley Brothers, 1868.
Eliot, George. *The George Eliot Letters*, edited by Gordon Sherman Haight, 9 vols, Yale University Press, 1954.
Fairclough, Mary. *The Romantic Crowd: Sympathy, Controversy and Print Culture*. Cambridge University Press, 2013.
Fantina, Richard. *Victorian Sensational Fiction: The Daring Work of Charles Reade*. Palgrave, 2010.
Fetterley, Judith. 'Impersonating "Little Women": The Radicalism of Alcott's *Behind a Mask*'. *Women's Studies*, vol. 1, 1983, pp. 1–14.
Flint, Kate. *The Woman Reader, 1837–1914*. Oxford University Press, 1993.
Freedgood, Elaine. *Worlds Enough: The Invention of Realism in the Victorian Novel*. Princeton University Press, 2019.
Freud, Sigmund. *The Uncanny*. Translated by David McLintock, Penguin, 2003.
Garrison, Laurie. 'The Seduction of Seeing in M. E. Braddon's *Eleanor's Victory*: Visual Technology, Sexuality, and the Evocative Publishing Content of *Once a Week*'. *Victorian Literature and Culture*, vol. 36, no. 1, 2008, pp. 111–30.
Gaskell, Elizabeth. *The Letters of Mrs Gaskell*, edited by J. A. V. Chapple and Arthur Pollard, Manchester University Press, 1966.
———. *The Life of Charlotte Brontë*, edited by Elisabeth Jay, Penguin, 1997.
———. *North and South*, edited by Angus Easson, Oxford, 1998.
Gavin, Adrienne. '"deepen[ing] the power and horror of the original": Caroline Clive's *Paul Ferroll* as Descendant of *Jane Eyre*'. *LISA e-journal*, vol. 7, no. 4, 2009. https://journals.openedition.org/lisa/839.
Gibbs, Anna. 'After Affect: Sympathy, Synchrony, and Mimetic Communication'. *The Affect Theory Reader*, edited by Melissa Gregg and Gregory J. Seigworth, Duke University Press, 2010, pp. 186–205.
Gilbert, Pamela K., editor. *A Companion to Sensation Fiction*. Wiley-Blackwell, 2011.
———. *Disease, Desire, and the Body in Victorian Women's Popular Novels*. Cambridge University Press, 1997.
———. 'Introduction'. *Cometh Up as a Flower*. Broadview, 2010, pp. 9–39.
———. *Victorian Skin: Surface, Self, History*. Cornell University Press, 2019.
Gilmore, Dehn. *The Victorian Novel and the Space of Art: Fictional Form on Display*. Cambridge University Press, 2013.

Glasgow Poisoning Case: Unabridged Report of the Evidence in this Extraordinary Trial, with all the Passionate Love Letters by the Prisoner to the Deceased, and Numerous Illustrations, including a Portrait of Madeleine Smith. London, George Vickers, 1857.
Golden, Catherine. *Images of the Woman Reader in Victorian British and American Fiction*. University Press of Florida, 2003.
Gore, Clare Walker. '"Setting Novels at Defiance": Novel Reading and Novelistic Form in Charlotte M. Yonge's *The Heir of Redclyffe*'. *Nineteenth-Century Gender Studies*, vol. 1, no. 1, 2014. http://www.ncgsjournal.com/issue101/gorearticle.htm.
Hardy, Thomas. *Desperate Remedies*, edited by Patricia Ingham, Oxford, 2003.
Hartman, Mary. *Victorian Murderesses: A True History of Thirteen Respectable French and English Women Accused of Unspeakable Crimes*. Dover Publications, 1977.
Heller, Tamar. *Dead Secrets: Wilkie Collins and the Female Gothic*. Yale University Press, 1992.
———. '"No Longer Innocent": Sensationalism, Sexuality, and the Allegory of the Woman Writer in Margaret Oliphant's *Salem Chapel*'. *Nineteenth Century Studies*, vol. 11, 1997, pp. 95–108.
Hemmings, Clare. 'Invoking Affect: Cultural Theory and the Ontological Turn'. *Cultural Studies*, vol. 19, no. 5, 2005, pp. 548–67.
Herbert, Christopher. *War of No Pity: The Indian Mutiny and Victorian Trauma*. Princeton University Press, 2007.
Hughes, Linda K. 'Alexander Smith and the Bisexual Poetics of *A Life-Drama*'. *Victorian Poetry*, vol. 42, no. 2, 2004, pp. 491–508.
Hughes, Winifred. *The Maniac in the Cellar: Sensation Novels of the 1860s*. Princeton University Press, 1980.
Hutton, Richard Holt. 'East Lynne'. *The Spectator*, 28 September 1861, pp. 1068–9.
Ingham, Patricia. 'Introduction'. *Desperate Remedies*. Oxford, 2009, pp. ix–xxvi.
Jacobson, Karin. 'Plain Faces, Weird Cases: Domesticating the Law in Collins's *The Law and the Lady* and the Trial of Madeleine Smith'. *Reality's Dark Light: The Sensational Wilkie Collins*, edited by Maria Bachman and Don Cox, University of Tennessee Press, 2003, pp. 283–312.
Jaffe, Audrey. *Scenes of Sympathy: Identity and Representation in Victorian Fiction*. Cornell University Press, 2000.
James, Henry. 'Miss Braddon'. *The Nation*, 9 November 1865, pp. 593–5.

Jameson, Frederic. *The Antinomies of Realism*. Verso, 2013.
Jay, Elisabeth. *Mrs Oliphant: 'A Fiction to Herself'*. Clarendon Press, 1995.
Jones, Anna Maria. *Problem Novels: Victorian Fiction Theorizes the Sensational Self*. Ohio State University Press, 2007.
Jones, Shirley. 'Motherhood and Melodrama: *Salem Chapel* and Sensation Fiction'. *Women's Writing*, vol. 6, no. 2, 1999, pp. 239–50.
Keen, Suzanne. *Empathy and the Novel*. Oxford University Press, 2007.
Ladino, Jennifer. *Memorials Matter: Emotion, Environment and Public Memory at American Historical Sites*. University of Nevada Press, 2019.
Langbauer, Laurie. *Novels of Everyday Life: The Series in English Fiction, 1850–1930*. Cornell University Press, 1999.
Lanser, Susan. 'Till Death Do Us Part: Embodying Narratology'. *Edinburgh Companion to Narrative Theories*, edited by Zara Dinnen and Robyn Warhol, Edinburgh University Press, 2018, pp. 117–31.
LeBon, Gustave, *The Crowd: A Study of the Popular Mind*. Viking Press, 1960.
Leighton, Mary Elizabeth, and Lisa Surridge. 'The Plot Thickens: Toward a Narratological Analysis of Illustrated Serial Fiction in the 1860s'. *Victorian Studies*, vol. 51, no. 1, 2008, pp. 65–101.
Levine, George. *The Realistic Imagination: English Fiction from Frankenstein to Lady Chatterley*. University of Chicago Press, 1981.
Leys, Ruth. 'The Turn to Affect: A Critique'. *Critical Inquiry*, vol. 37, no. 3, 2011, pp. 434–72.
Linton, Eliza Lynn. *Sowing the Wind: A Novel*. London, Tinsley Brothers, 1867.
'Literature: Miss Braddon's New Novel'. *Morning Post*, 14 October 1865, p. 2.
Loesberg, Jonathan. 'The Ideology of Narrative Form in Sensation Fiction'. *Representations*, vol. 13, no. 3, 1986, pp. 115–38.
MacDonald, Tara. 'Bodily Sympathy, Affect, and Victorian Sensation Fiction'. *Affect Theory and Literary Critical Practice: A Feel for the Text*, edited by Stephen Ahern, Palgrave, 2019, pp. 121–37.
———. '"I veer about between hope and despair": Utopian Visions in Victorian Sensation Fiction'. *Victorian Popular Fictions Journal*, vol. 4, no. 1, 2022, pp. 1–20.
———. *The New Man, Masculinity and Marriage in the Victorian Novel*. Routledge, 2015.
———. 'Sensation Fiction, Gender and Identity'. Mangham, pp. 127–40.

———. '"Vulgar Publicity" and Problems of Privacy in Margaret Oliphant's *Salem Chapel*'. *Other Sensations*, special issue of *Critical Survey*, edited by Janice Allan, vol. 23, no.1, 2011, pp. 25–41.

Mangham, Andrew, editor. *The Cambridge Companion to Sensation Fiction*. Cambridge University Press, 2013.

Mansel, Henry. 'Sensation Novels'. *Quarterly Review*, vol. 113, 1863, pp. 481–514.

Marsh, Kelly. *The Submerged Plot and the Mother's Pleasure from Jane Austen to Arundhati Roy*. Ohio State University Press, 2016.

Massumi, Brian, 'Notes on the Translation and Acknowledgements'. *A Thousand Plateaus: Capitalism and Schizophrenia* by Gilles Deleuze and Félix Guattari, University of Minnesota Press, 2005, pp. xvi–xix.

Maunder, Andrew, 'Mapping the Victorian Sensation Novel: Some Recent and Future Trends'. *Literature Compass*, vol. 2, no. 6, 2005, pp. 1–33.

———, editor. *Varieties of Women's Sensation Fiction: 1855–1890*, 6 vols, Pickering and Chatto, 2004.

McAleavey, Maia. *The Bigamy Plot: Sensation and Convention in the Victorian Novel*. Cambridge University Press, 2015.

Meadows, Elizabeth. *Morbid Strains in Victorian Literature from 1850 to the Fin de Siècle*. Dissertation, Vanderbilt University, 2010.

Mill, John Stuart. 'On Liberty'. *The Basic Writings of John Stuart Mill*. Modern Library, 2002, pp. 3–119.

Miller, Andrew. *The Burdens of Perfection: On Ethics and Reading in Nineteenth-Century British Literature*. Cornell University Press, 2008.

———. '"A Case of Metaphysics": Counterfactuals, Realism, *Great Expectations*'. *ELH*, vol. 79, no. 3, 2012, pp. 773–96.

Miller, D. A. 'Cage Aux Folles: Sensation and Gender in Wilkie Collins's *The Woman in White*'. *Representations*, vol. 14, 1986, pp. 107–36.

Moon, Brenda. *More Usefully Employed: Amelia B. Edwards, Writer, Traveller and Campaigner for Ancient Egypt*. Egypt Explorations Society, 2006.

Morgan, Benjamin. *The Outward Mind: Materialist Aesthetics in Victorian Science and Literature*. University of Chicago Press, 2017.

Morgan, Monique R. *Narrative Means, Lyric Ends: Temporality in the Nineteenth-Century British Long Poem*. Ohio State University Press, 2009.

Mozley, Anne. 'Clever Women'. *Blackwood's Magazine*, vol. 104, October 1868. Rpt. In *The Clever Woman of the Family*, Broadview, 2001, pp. 591–8.

Nayder, Lillian. 'The Empire and Sensation'. Gilbert, 2011, pp. 442–54.

———. *Wilkie Collins*. Twayne, 1997.
Nemesvari, Richard. *Thomas Hardy, Sensationalism, and the Melodramatic Mode*. Palgrave, 2011.
Ngai, Sianne. *Ugly Feelings*. Harvard University Press, 2007.
'Not a New "Sensation."' *All the Year Round*, vol. 9, 1863, pp. 517–20.
Odden, Karen M. '"Reading coolly" in *John Marchmont's Legacy*: Reconsidering M. E. Braddon's Legacy'. *Studies in the Novel*, vol. 36, no. 1, 2004, pp. 21–40.
Oliphant, Margaret. 'Novels'. *Blackwood's Edinburgh Magazine*, vol. 102, September 1867, pp. 257–80.
———. *Salem Chapel*. Virago Press, 1986.
———. 'Sensation Novels'. *Blackwood's Edinburgh Magazine*, vol. 91, May 1862, pp. 564–80.
Ortiz-Robles, Mario. 'Figure and Affect in Collins'. *Textual Practice*, vol. 24, no. 5, 2010, pp. 841–61.
'Our Female Sensation Novelists'. *The Christian Remembrancer*, vol. 46, July 1864, pp. 209–36.
Paget, Francis. *Lucretia; or, The Heroine of the Nineteenth Century*. London, Joseph Masters, 1868.
Palgrave, Francis. 'On Readers in 1760 and 1860'. *Macmillan's Magazine*, vol. 1, 1860, pp. 487–9.
Palmer, Alan. *Social Minds in the Novel*. Ohio State University Press, 2010.
Palmer, Alan, and Adam Steir. 'Crowds in Nineteenth-Century Fiction and Historical Writing'. *Poetics Today*, vol. 38, no. 3, 2017, pp. 549–68.
Palmer, Beth. *Women's Authorship and Editorship in Victorian Culture: Sensational Strategies*. Oxford University Press, 2011.
Pelling, Henry. *A History of British Trade Unionism*. Palgrave, 1992.
Peters, Catherine. *The King of Inventors: A Life of Wilkie Collins*. Princeton University Press, 1993.
Phegley, Jennifer. *Educating the Proper Woman Reader: Victorian Family Literary Magazines and the Cultural Health of the Nation*. Ohio State University Press, 2004.
Phegley, Jennifer, et al., editors. *Transatlantic Sensations*. Routledge, 2012.
Phelan, James. *Living to Tell about It: A Rhetoric and Ethics of Character Narration*. Cornell University Press, 2004.
Plotz, John. *The Crowd: British Literature and Public Politics*. University of California Press, 2000.

Price, Leah. *How to Do Things with Books in Victorian Britain*. Princeton University Press, 2012.
Prince, Gerald. *Dictionary of Narratology*. University of Nebraska Press, 1987.
Pykett, Lyn. *The 'Improper' Feminine: The Women's Sensation Novel and the New Woman Writing*. Routledge, 1992.
———. 'Mary Elizabeth Braddon'. Gilbert, 2011, pp. 123–33.
Rae, W. Fraser, 'Sensation Novelists: Miss Braddon', *North British Review*, vol. 43, 1865, pp. 92–105.
Rance, Nicholas. *Wilkie Collins and Other Sensation Novelists: Walking the Moral Hospital*. Fairleigh Dickinson University Press, 1991.
Rank, Otto. 'The Double as Immortal Self'. *Beyond Psychology*. Dover, 1941, pp. 62–101.
Reade, Charles. *Griffith Gaunt, or Jealousy*. New York, P. F. Collier & Son, n.d.
———. *Hard Cash*. New York, P. F. Collier & Son, n.d.
Reed, John. *Dickens's Hyperrealism*. Ohio State University Press, 2010.
Rees, Joan. *Amelia Edwards: Traveller, Novelist and Egyptologist*. Rubicon Press, 1998.
Reising, Russell. *Loose Ends: Closure and Crisis in the American Social Text*. Duke University Press, 1996.
Rev. of *Armadale*. *The Spectator*, vol. 39, 1866, pp. 638–40.
Rev. of *Barbara's History*. *The Athenaeum*, 2 January 1864, pp. 15–16.
Rev. of *Barbara's History*. *The Times*, 28 March 1864, p. 6.
Rev. of *Cometh Up as a Flower*. *The London Review*, 16 March 1867, pp. 324–5. Rpt in Broughton, *Cometh Up as a Flower*, Appendix B, p. 339.
Rev. of *Cometh Up as a Flower*. *The Spectator*, 19 October 1867, pp. 1172–4. Rpt in Broughton, *Cometh Up as a Flower*, Appendix B, pp. 342–4.
Rev. of *Half a Million of Money*. *The Standard*, 4 April 1866, p. 6.
Rev. of *Nigel Bartram's Ideal*. *Saturday Review*, vol. 27, 1869, pp. 59–60.
Rev of *No Name*. *Reader*, 3 January 1863, pp. 14–15.
Rev. of *Salem Chapel*. *The Spectator*, vol. 1807, February 1863, p. 1639.
Rev. of *Salem Chapel*. *The National Review*, vol. 32, April 1863, p. 350–62.
Rev. of *The Woman in White*. *The Saturday Review*, no. 252, vol. 10, 1860, pp. 249–51.
Richardson, Alan. *The Neural Sublime: Cognitive Theories and Romantic Texts*. Johns Hopkins University Press, 2010.

Rosenwein, Barbara H. 'Problems and Methods in the History of Emotions'. *Passions in Context*, vol. 1, 2010, pp. 1–32.

Rudy, Jason R. *Electric Meters: Victorian Physiological Poetics*. Ohio University Press, 2009.

Russell, Dora. *The Drift of Fate*. Literary Press, n.d.

Rylance, Rick. *Victorian Psychology and British Culture: 1850–1880*. Oxford University Press, 2000.

Sala, George Augustus. 'The Cant of Modern Criticism'. *Belgravia: A London Magazine*, vol. 4, 1867, pp. 45–55.

———. 'On the "Sensational" in Literature and Art'. *Belgravia: A London Magazine*, vol. 4, February 1868, pp. 449–58.

Schaffer, Talia. *Romance's Rival: Familiar Marriage in Victorian Fiction*. Oxford University Press, 2016.

———. 'The Sensational Story of West Lynne: The Problem with Professionalism'. *Women's Writing*, vol. 23, no. 2, 2016, pp. 227–44.

Shouse, Eric. 'Feeling, Emotion, Affect'. *M/C Journal*, vol. 8, no. 6, 2005. http://journal.media-culture.org.au/0512/03-shouse.php.

Showalter, Elaine. *A Literature of Their Own: British Women Novelists from Brontë to Lessing*. Princeton University Press, 1977.

Shuman, Amy, and Katharine Young. 'The Body as Medium: A Phenomenological Approach to the Production of Affect in Narrative'. *Edinburgh Companion to Narrative Theories*, edited by Zara Dinnen and Robyn Warhol, Edinburgh University Press, 2018, pp. 399–416.

Smiles, Samuel. *Self-Help*. London, John Murray, 1859.

Smith, Alexander. *A Life-Drama and Other Poems*. Boston, Ticknor and Fields, 1859.

Smith, Tiffany Watt. *On Flinching: Theatricality and Scientific Looking from Darwin to Shell Shock*. Oxford University Press, 2014.

Sparks, Tabitha. *The Doctor in the Victorian Novel: Family Practices*. Ashgate, 2009.

———. 'Fiction Becomes Her: Representations of Female Character in Mary Braddon's *The Doctor's Wife*'. *Beyond Sensation: Mary Elizabeth Braddon in Context*, edited by Marlene Tromp et al., State University of New York Press, 2000, pp. 197–209.

———. 'Sensation Intervention: M. C. Houston's *Recommended to Mercy* (1862) and the Novel of Experience'. *Beyond Braddon: Re-Assessing Female Sensationalists*, special issue of *Women's Writing*, edited by Beller and MacDonald, vol. 20, no. 2, May 2013, pp. 153–67.

———. *Victorian Metafiction*. University of Virginia Press, 2022.

Spencer, Herbert. 'The Physiology of Laughter'. *Macmillan's Magazine*, March 1860, pp. 395–402.
Stern, Rebecca. 'Moving Parts and Speaking Parts: Situating Victorian Antitheatricality'. *ELH*, vol. 65, no. 2, 1998, pp. 423–49.
Sturrock, June. 'Murder, Gender, and Popular Fiction by Women in the 1860s: Braddon, Oliphant, Yonge'. *Victorian Crime, Madness and Sensation*, edited by Andrew Maunder and Grace Moore, Ashgate, 2004, pp. 73–88.
Talairach-Veilmas, Laurence. 'The Substance and the Shadow: Invisibility and Immateriality in *Armadale*'. *Armadale: Wilkie Collins and the Dark Threads of Life*, edited by Mariaconcetta Costantini, Aracne, 2009, pp. 69–92.
Taylor, Jenny Bourne. *In the Secret Theatre of Home: Wilkie Collins, Sensation Narrative, and Nineteenth-Century Psychology*. Routledge, 1988.
Tennyson, Alfred. *Maud: A Definitive Edition*, edited by Susan Shatto, University of Oklahoma Press, 1986.
Terada, Rei. *Feeling in Theory: Emotion after the 'Death of the Subject'*. Harvard University Press, 2001.
The Bible. Authorized King James Version, Oxford University Press, 1998.
Tomaiuolo, Saverio. 'Sensation Fiction, Empire and the Indian Mutiny'. Mangham, pp. 113–26.
Tondre, Michael. '"The Interval of Expectation": Delay, Delusion, and the Psychology of Suspense in *Armadale*'. *ELH*, vol. 78, no. 3, 2011, pp. 585–608.
Trodd, Anthea. *Domestic Crime in the Victorian Novel*. Macmillan Press, 1989.
Trollope, Anthony. *An Autobiography*, edited by Michael Sadleir and Frederick Page, Oxford University Press, 1980.
Tromp, Marlene. *The Private Rod: Marital Violence, Sensation, and the Law in Victorian Britain*. University of Virginia Press, 2000.
———. 'Sensation Fiction'. *Victorian Literature and Culture*, vol. 46, no. 3/4, 2018, pp. 858–61.
Valdez, Jessica. *Plotting the News in the Victorian Novel*. Edinburgh University Press, 2020.
Vermeule, Blakey. *Why Do We Care About Literary Characters?* Johns Hopkins University Press, 2010.
'The Vice of Reading'. *Temple Bar*, vol. 42, 1874, pp. 252–4.
Vicinus, Martha. *Intimate Friends: Women Who Loved Women, 1778–1928*. University of Chicago Press, 2004.

Wagner, Tamara. 'Led Astray to be Newly Framed: Redeeming Sensational Fraud in Charlotte Yonge's Epistolary Experiments'. *Women's Writing*, vol. 14, no. 2, 2010, pp. 305–23.
Walters, Alisha. '"The tears I could not repress, rolling down my brown cheeks": Mary Seacole, Feeling, and the Imperial Body'. *Nineteenth-Century Gender Studies*, vol. 16, no. 1, 2020. http://ncgsjournal.com/issue161/walters.html.
Walther, LuAnn, 'The Invention of Childhood in Victorian Autobiography'. *Approaches to Victorian Autobiography*, edited by George P. Landow, Ohio University Press, 1979, pp. 64–83.
Ward, Megan. *Seeming Human: Artificial Intelligence and Victorian Realist Character*. Ohio State University Press, 2018.
Warhol, Robyn. *Having a Good Cry: Effeminate Feelings and Pop-Culture Forms*. Ohio State University Press, 2003.
———. 'Narrative Refusals and Generic Transformation in Austen and James: What Doesn't Happen in *Northanger Abbey* and *Spoils of Poynton*'. *Henry James Review*, vol. 28, no. 3, 2007, pp. 259–68.
———. 'Toward a Theory of the Engaging Narrator: Earnest Interventions in Gaskell, Stowe, and Eliot'. *PMLA*, vol. 101, 1986, pp. 811–18.
———. '"What Might Have Been Is Not What Is": Dickens's Narrative Refusals'. *Counterfactual Thinking/Counterfactual Writing*, edited by Dorothee Birke et al., De Gruyter, 2011, pp. 227–39.
Wilford, Florence. *Nigel Bartram's Ideal*. London, Wells Gardner, Darton & Co., n.d.
Wise, John Richard de Capel. 'Belles Lettres'. *Westminster Review*, vol. 30, 1866, pp. 268–80.
Wood, Ellen. *East Lynne*, edited by Elisabeth Jay, Oxford, 2005.
———. *A Life's Secret*. London: C. W. Wood, 1867.
———. 'A Life's Secret'. *The Leisure Hour*, 2 January – 24 May 1862.
Wynne, Deborah. *The Sensation Novel and the Victorian Family Magazine*. Palgrave, 2001.
Yonge, Charlotte Mary. *The Clever Woman of the Family*, edited by Clare A. Simmons, Broadview, 2001.
———. *Letters of Charlotte Mary Yonge*, edited by Charlotte Mitchell, Ellen Jordan and Helen Schinske. https://c21ch.newcastle.edu.au/yonge/.
Zerilli, Linda. 'The Turn to Affect and the Problem of Judgment'. *New Literary History*, vol. 46, no. 2, 2015, pp. 261–86.
Zunshine, Lisa. *Getting Inside Your Head: What Cognitive Science Can Tell Us about Popular Culture*. Johns Hopkins University Press, 2012.

———. 'Theory of Mind and Fictions of Embodied Transparency'. *Narrative*, vol. 16, no. 1, January 2009, pp. 65–92.
———. *Why We Read Fiction: Theory of Mind and the Novel*. Ohio State University Press, 2006.

Index

addiction, 87
affect
  alien, 8, 74, 84, 87–94
  narrating, 28–32
  narrative, 2
  theory, 20–8
affective
  communities, 97, 190
  disorientation, 68–9n
  dissonance, 68n, 91
  language, 58
  pleasures of reading and not reading, 189–93
  reader, 139
  return, 3, 20–8
  transmission, 3, 5, 21, 24–7, 153
affects
  bodily, 133, 152
  contagious, 135–6
  expression of, 173–4
  Victorian, 1–39
  wild, 143–4, 153
agency, 59, 67–8
  somatic, 15–16, 18, 19
Ahern, Stephen, 27, 132
  Affect Theory and Literary Critical Practice, 38n
Ahmed, Sara, 7, 16, 74, 84, 91, 136, 153
  The Cultural Politics of Emotion, 36n
Alcott, Louisa May
  Behind a Mask: or, A Woman's Power, 85, 93–4
  Little Women, 75, 85–7
All the Year Round, 'Not a New "Sensation"', 112–13
Allan, Janice, 2, 12
Anderson, Ben, 136–7
Anger, Suzy, 169–70, 187–8n
'anonymous world', 138
antipathy, 25
Argosy, 138
Aristotle, 68n
Athenaeum, 49, 53, 69n
Atkinson, Henry George, *Letters on the Laws of Man's Naure and Development*, 22
atmospheres, 136–7, 153
Audley, Robert, 170
Austen, Jane, 30
  Northanger Abbey, 52, 81
  Pride and Prejudice, 78–9
authorship
  female, 72–3
  knowledge model of, 71–2
  mechanical, 71, 93
  as performative activity, 93
  sensational, 71–95

Index   209

automatic movements, 1–2, 38n

Bachman, Maria K., 31
Bain, Alexander, 37n, 46, 134–5, 144, 170, 187–8n
  The Emotions and the Will, 15–16, 23–6
  Mind and Body: The Theories of their Relation, 16
  The Senses and the Intellect, 37n
Belgravia: A London Magazine, 72
Beller, Anne-Marie, 28, 37n, 68n, 69n, 72, 147–9, 155n
Bentley and Son, 57
Berlant, Lauren, 42
Bible, 58, 65, 66
bigamy plot, 36n, 49–56, 161, 186
  near-bigamy story, 57–8
  sympathetic, 178–80
Bildungsroman, 68n
  aborted, 57
  English, 42
Blackwood's, 90
  'Novels', 10–11
  'Sensation Novels', 10–11
Blair, Kristie, 60, 64
blushes, 5, 18, 46–7, 56–7, 78, 86, 123, 188n
Bodenheimer, Rosemarie, 155n
bodies
  misreading, 30–1, 78
  nervous, 18
bodily
  affects, 133, 152
  autonomy, 192–3
  description, 6, 54, 63
  interconnection, 192–3
  materiality, 58–9
  movements, 32
  sympathy, 24, 131–55
  touch, 136

body
  dying, 56–68
  giving away feelings, 96–7
  and mind, 15–16, 22, 26
  traumatised, 106–7
body language, 77–8, 106
  unguarded, 107–8
body reading, 75–82, 110–11, 173–4
Bourrier, Karen, 95n
Braddon, Mary Elizabeth, 13–14, 37n, 43, 68n, 71–2, 82
  The Doctor's Wife, 7, 14, 72
  Eleanor's Victory, 37n, 67, 191
  John Marchmont's Legacy, 43, 191–2
  Lady Audley's Secret, 9–10, 12–13, 93, 122–3, 190–1
  Vixen, 37n
Brennan, Teresa, 3, 20–1, 136
Brontë, Anne, 84
Brontë, Charlotte, 83–4, 95n
  Jane Eyre, 49–50, 53–8, 67, 69n, 157–8
  Villette, 49–50, 69n, 95n
Broughton, Rhoda, 130n
  Cometh Up as a Flower, 42–3, 56–68, 70n
  Not Wisely, but Too Well, 57, 70n
Burgess, Thomas, *Physiology or Mechanism of Blushing*, 46

Canetti, Elias, *Crowds and Power*, 136–7, 154n
characterological interiority, 153
Christian Remembrancer, 4–5, 192
class
  conflict, 133
  fear, 138
  middle-class women, 19–20
  mobs as working-class protest, 135, 138

class (*cont.*)
    working-class, 132–3, 138–47, 149–51, 153
Clive, Caroline, 131–55, 155n
    Paul Ferroll, 133, 134, 147–54
    Why Paul Ferroll Killed his Wife, 153
Cohen, William, 174–5
    Embodied: Victorian Literature and the Senses, 18
Cohn, Elisha, 62–3
Colby, Vineta and Robert, 130n
collective mind, 136, 144
collective sympathy, 134–8
Collins, Wilkie, 13, 30–1, 71, 156–88
    Armadale, 96–130, 154n, 159, 180–6
    The Frozen Deep, 180–1, 185
    The Law and the Lady, 120, 124
    male doubles in, 180–6
    The Moonstone, 132
    No Name, 31, 47
    'The Poisoned Meal', 120
    Poor Miss Finch, 18, 159, 180–6, 188n
    'The Unknown Public', 113–14
    The Woman in White, 1–2, 4, 7, 11, 18, 31, 37n, 128, 136–7, 144, 156, 159, 161–8, 171–2, 176, 177–8, 183, 186n, 189–90
colonialism, 142
coloninal ideology, 15, 16–17
communal surveillance, 97
Condition of England novels, 132–3
contagion, sympathetic, 141–3, 145, 150–1
contagious affects, 135–6
cosmetics, 123–4
counterfactual feeling, 158
    male selves, 180–6
    selves, 158–9, 171–2, 176–7
    thinking, 158
counterfactuality, and social circumstances, 162–4
counterfictions, 159–61
courtship and reading, 47–8
criminal trials, 114–15, 120–1, 126, 129n
criminals
    beautiful woman as, 121–4
    female, 119–29
critics, 100–1
    sexist nineteenth-century reviews, 5–6
crowds, 131–55
    bestial nature of, 143–4
    and social distinctions, 137
Cunningham, Valentine, 130n
Cvetkovich, Ann, 4, 9, 97, 98, 122, 130n, 156, 168
    Mixed Feelings: Feminism, Mass Culture, and Victorian Sensationalism, 19–20

D'Albertis, Deirdre, 83
Daly, Nicholas, 10, 11, 144
Dames, Nicholas, 38n
    The Physiology of the Novel: Reading, Neural Science, and the Form of Victorian Fiction, 18–19
Darwin, Charles, 14–15, 23, 46, 123, 136
    The Expression of the Emotions in Man and Animals, 27
    On the Origin of Species, 15–16, 37n
death, and desire, 65
decaying bodies, 65
Denver, Carolyn, 182
desire
    and death, 65
    for scandal, 110–11

Index 211

desiring bodies, 56–68
detachment, 109–10
　narrator, 147–8
detailism, 6–7, 12
determinism, 170
diary entries, 66, 125, 127–9
Dickens, Charles, 31, 35–6n, 46, 136, 154–5n, 174–5, 179, 188n
　All the Year Round, 112–13
　Barnaby Rudge, 133
　David Copperfield, 49–50, 69n
　Great Expectations, 11, 160, 175–6
　A Tale of Two Cities, 38n, 132–3, 143–4, 155n, 159, 180–1
Dickinson, Emily, 98–9
digitisation, 9
'discharge', 137
discrete identity, fear of collapse of, 157
disease and contamination, 74, 83
'disenchantment' plot, 42
Dixon, Thomas, 14
Dobell, Sydney, 61
domestic isolation, 111–12
domestic life and domestic body, 111–12
doubles, 161–168
　male, 159, 171, 180–6
　sympathetic, 156–8
doubling, gothic, 178
Dublin University Magazine, 57, 70n
Dutch paintings, 6
dying bodies, 56–68

eavesdropping, 105
Edwards, Amelia, 69n
　Barbara's History, 28–9, 42–3, 45, 49–56, 70n
　Half a Million of Money, 45, 49
　Hand and Glove, 44–9
　Lord Brackenbury, 45, 69–70n
　My Brother's Wife, 45
Edwards, Annie, *Miss Forrester*, 6–7
effeminacy, 41, 58, 74, 94–5n
Eliot, George, 21–2
　Adam Bede, 6
embodied sympathy, 145, 179
embodied transparency, 78–80, 98–9, 107–8, 117–20, 122–5
embodiment, 2, 14–20
'emotion word', 83
emotion-affect divide, 8, 22
emotional limitations, 148–54
emotions, 27, 136
　narrative, 29–30
empathy, 29–30, 38n, 187n
　performative, 148
emplotment, 41–2, 68n
　sensational, 40–70
'erotic sensationalism', 56–68, 70n
escapist fantasy, 45, 69–70n

factory-owning protagonists, 132–3
Fairclough, Mary, 135
Fantina, Richard, 179
'fascination', 46, 51, 69n
feeling
　counterfactual, 158
　history of, 4–5
　shared, 133
feeling fiction, 44–9
feelings, 36n
　mixed, 43
　of reading, 7–8
　what a woman should feel, 74
female authors, 72–3
female criminals, 119–29
female gothic plot, 165–6
feminine ideal, 90–1
feminine revolt, 57–8

Fetterley, Judith, 85
Flaubert, Gustave, *Madame Bovary*, 14
flinching, 37n
Flint, Kate, 43, 59
flushes, 123, 125–6
Foucault, Michel, 19
'found document' trope, 12
free indirect discourse (FID), 152, 155n, 160–1
  avoidance of, 170
free online access of texts, 9
free will, 14–20, 37n
Freedgood, Elaine, 13
'Free-will controversy', 14–17
French novels, 47–8, 76
French Revolution, 133, 135
Freud, Sigmund, 157

Gaskell, Elizabeth, 136, 147
  Life of Charlotte Bronte, 83–4, 95n
  North and South, 132
Gavin, Adrienne, 148, 152
gendered performance, 112–19
Genette, Gerard, 29
ghostly figure, 167–8
Gilbert, Pamela, 9, 36n, 61, 70n, 74, 86–7, 123
  Disease, Desire, and the Body in Victorian Women's Popular Novels, 19
  Victorian Skin, 4, 38n, 46–7
Gilmore, Dehn, 11, 35n
Glasgow Poisoning Case..., 121–2
Gordon Riots, 133
Gosling Society, 75
gossip, 51, 96–8, 108–12, 141–2
gothic doubling, 178
gothic literature, 9–10, 157
gothic plot, female, 165–6

Hampshire, Stuart, 158, 161–2
Hardy, Thomas, 156–88, 187–8n
  Desperate Remedies, 159, 169–78, 183, 187n, 188n
  melodramatic plots, 169
  'Novels of Ingenuity', 169
Heller, Tamar, 61, 101, 107, 130n, 165–8
Hemmings, Clare, 26
Herbert, Christopher, 17
Herman, David, 41–2
home
  as vulnerable, 105–6
  and vulnerable body, 96–130
Hughes, Winifred, 11
humour, 53–4, 58–9
hyperrealism, 1–39, 35–6n, 36n, 54, 103
  definition of, 9–14
hysterical woman, 122

immorality, 71–2
Indian Uprising, 16–17, 132, 154n
industrialisation, 11, 18, 64, 88
ingestion, 87
Ingham, Patricia, 188n
interconnectivity
  bodily, 192–3
  brooch as sign of, 166–7
intertextuality, 43, 54
invalidism, 108–12

Jacobson, Karin, 121–2
Jaffe, Audrey, *Scenes of Sympathy*, 21–2, 187n
James, Henry, 71, 130n
Jameson, Frederic, *The Antinomes of Realism*, 4, 63
Jay, Elisabeth, 110–11, 130n
jealousy, 26–7
Jewsbury, Geraldine, 57
Jones, Anna Maria, 56
Jones, Shirley, 104, 105, 130n
journals, 149
judgemental reader, 139
justice, 67–8

Keen, Suzanne, 24, 29–30, 38n
keyhole scenes, 174–5
knitting, 110–11
knowledge model of authorship, 71–2

Ladino, Jennifer, 68n, 91
Langbauer, Laurie, 103
Lanser, Susan S., 28
LeBon, Gustave, 131, 135–6, 144
letters, 127–9
Levine, George, 36n, 42
Lewes, George Henry, 37n
Leys, Ruth, 26
Linton, Elizabeth Lynn, *Sowing the Wind*, 94–5n
literary borrowing, 14
'lives unled', 158
Loesberg, Jonathan, 138
London Review, 57
losing control, 10
'low culture', 5–6
Lowe, Lisa, 15
lyric mode, 62–3

McAleavey, Maia, 36n, 50
  The Bigamy Plot, 35n
Macaulay, James, 146
MacDonald, Tara, 28
  '"I veer about between hope and despair": Utopian Visions in Victorian Sensation Fiction', 36n
Macmillan's Magazine, 32
male counterfactual selves, 180–6
male doubles, 159, 171, 180–6
Mansel, Henry, 10, 60–1, 69n, 71, 104
marriage, institution of, 9
marriage market, 66, 175–6
marriage plot, 185–6
Marsh, Kelly, 168
  The Submerged Plot and the Mother's Pleasure, 187n

Martineau, Harriet, 22
Massumi, Brian, 25
'material networks of sensation', 169–70
material rather than spectral, 9–10
materiality, 1, 4, 7, 9, 19, 22–3, 27, 37n, 58, 183, 193n
  bodily, 58–9
maternal melodrama, 107, 130n
maternal passion, 100, 130n
Maunder, Andrew, *Varieties of Women's Sensation Fiction* series, 70n
Maxwell, John, 72
Meadows, Elizabeth, 95n
mechanical
  authorship, 71, 93
  behaviour, 17–19, 88, 192
melodrama, dangers of, 105
melodramatic heroine, 52, 81
metafiction, 7, 12–14, 36n, 37n, 63–5, 87
metalepsis, 29
middle-class women, 19–20
Mill, John Stuart, 37n, 46
  On Liberty, 15, 18, 88
  Systems of Logic, 37n
Miller, Andrew, 158, 159–62, 170, 185–6
  The Burdens of Perfection, 158
Miller, D. A., 35n
mind, passive, 1–2
mind and body, 15–16, 22, 26
mind reading, 30–2, 77–80
misogyny, 5–6
misreading bodies, 30–1, 78
'mixed feelings', 43
mobs, 131–2, 139
  with single leader, 134, 144–5
  as working-class protest, 135, 138
'modern' genre, 10
modernity, 13

The Monthy Packet, 75
moral message, 58
morality, 69n
morbidity, 71–95, 94–5n
Morgan, Benjamin, 18
  The Outward Mind: Materialist Aesthetics in Victorian Science and Literature, 19
Morgan, Monique, 62–3
Morning Post, 54
Mozley, Anne, 'Clever Women', 90
'mutiny novels', 132
mystery woman, 97, 102–3

narrating affect, 28–32
narrative
  affect, 2
  emotions, 29–30
  guidance, 145–7
  impulse, 63
  refusals, 160
  theory, 28–32, 68n
narrators, 6–7, 13, 28–32, 36n, 91, 139, 145–6, 170, 184
  detached, 147–8
  engaging, 133
  limitations of, 151–2
National Review, 101
Nayder, Lillian, 168
Nemesvari, Richard, *Thomas Hardy, Sensationalism, and the Melodramatic Mode*, 169
nervous
  bodies, 18
  excitement, 10–11
  system, 10, 20–1
new technologies, 10
New Women fiction, 75, 91–2
new words, 14
newspapers, 97–9, 101–2, 108
Ngai, Sianne, 68–9n
not reading, 189–93

Odden, Karen M., 43
O'Farrell, Mary Ann, 5, 78
  Telling Complexions, 18
Oliphant, Margaret, 4, 13, 35n, 41, 55, 56, 71, 84, 157, 189
  The Chronicles of Carlingford, 100
  'Novels', 10–11, 40
  Salem Chapel, 96–130, 130n
  'Sensation Novels', 10–11, 40
optative, 158–62, 172, 182, 185–6
'outward effect', 119–29

Paget, Francis, 40
paintings, 70n
Palgrave, Francis, 118
Palmer, Alan, 143
  Social Minds, 30–1
Palmer, Beth, 37n, 93, 138
parodic commentaries, 7
Pelling, Henry, 140–1
performance, 37n, 50–1, 122–4, 129n, 152
  authorship as, 93
  gendered, 112–19
performative empathy, 148
periodical publications, 68n
periodical writer, 103–4
personhood, 21, 90
Peters, Catherine, 185
Phegley, Jennifer, 5–6
Phelan, James, 7, 28
physiological novel theory, 19
'pleasurable excitement', 54
Plotz, John, 154n
poetry, 58–62, 64–5
popularity, 40
Pre-Raphaelite paintings, 12–13, 64
Price, Leah, 189
  How to Do Things with Books in Victorian Britain, 193n
Prince, Gerald, 64
printed texts in stories, 99–100

privacy, 96–130
private lives, and fictional
    characters, 72–3
proximity, 10
public
    exposure and anxiety, 102
    hangings, 154–5n
    as mass of readers, 144
    scandal, 114–17
    'teeth', 115
'public feeling', 96–130, 130n
'Public Feelings' project, 98
Pykett, Lyn, 6, 37n, 130n
    The 'Improper' Feminine, 87

quotation, 59–62, 65, 66

racism, 25, 142
Rae, W. Fraser, 82
railways, 10
Rance, Nicholas, *Wilkie Collins and Other Sensation Novelists*, 82
Rank, Otto, 'The Double as Immortal Self', 157
Reade, Charles, 156–88
    Griffith Gaunt, or Jealousy, 26–7, 178–80, 186, 188n
    Hard Cash, 36n
readerly
    feeling, 29–30
    sympathy, 187n
readers
    becoming characters they are reading, 157
    distracted, 190–2
    judgemental and affective, 139
    physical sensations, 4
    'public' as mass of, 144
    townspeople as, 104–5
    within novels, 190–2
    young female, 40–1, 157, 192–3
reading
    affective pleasures of, 189–93

courtship and, 47–8
and crying, 39n
discipline of, 56
as eating, 86–7
family, 40
feelings of, 7–8
'good' reading as affective, 191–2
and gossip, 118
immersive, 40–70
interactions over texts, 189–90
not reading, 189–93
poetry, 59–62
public, 96–130
women's, 68n
realism, 4
as nonnarratable, 56
and spectacle, 13
and symbolism, 12
rebellion, 17
'rebellious', 14
Reed, John R., *Dickens's Hyperrealism*, 35–6n
Rees, Joan, 47–8
Reising, Russell, 187n
Religious Tract Society, 131, 146, 154n
The Leisure Hour, 131
repetition, 37n
Richardson, Alan, 30, 77–8
Ricoeur, Paul, *Time and Narrative*, 68n
rioters, 131
Romantic era, 135
romantic hero, 46, 51
Rose, Natalie, 46
Rosenwein, Barbara, 27, 83
Rossetti, Christina, 'Goblin Market', 175–6
Royal Literary Fund, 94
Russell, Dora, *The Drift of Fate*, 94n
Rylance, Rick, 15, 37n

Sala, George Augustus, 55
    'On the "Sensational" in Literature and Art', 113
Sand, George, 47–8
Saturday Review, 89
scene of 'still life', 62–3
Schaffer, Talia, 59, 192
self-censorship, 88–9
self-conscious use of fiction, 70n
self-critical reflection, 95n
self-determination, 15–16, 48
self-possession, 122
self-reflexivity, 2, 5, 7, 13–14, 35n, 37n, 43, 72, 89, 101–2, 157
sensation, definition of, 9–14
sensational
    authorship, 71–95
    emplotment, 40–70
    heroine, 84, 93
    heroine and pragamatic heroine, 43
    scripts, 100–8
sensationalism, 1–3
    detestable to Victorian reviewers, 4–5
    and domestic realism, 100
    limitations of, 7
    shared consumption of, 112–19
'sensory onrush', 10–12
sentiment, 38n
sentimental fiction, 39n
Sepoy Rebellion, 16–17, 132, 154n
serials, 40, 189–90
    periodical publications, 68n
    weekly publication, 10–11
sexual
    candour, 59
    denial, 81–2
    desires, 41, 124–5
    excitement, 62
shadow narratives, 158–61, 187n
Shakespeare, 58, 63–4, 113, 130n
shared feeling, 133

Shelley, Mary, *Frankenstein*, 106–7
Shouse, Eric, 25
Showalter, Elain, 45
skin, 1–2
Smiles, Samuel, *Self-Help*, 15
Smith, Adam, *Theory of Moral Sentiments*, 21–2
Smith, Alexander, 63–4
    A Life-Drama, 61–2
Smith, Madeleine, 98, 114–15, 119–29, 129n
Smith, Tiffany Watt, 37n
somatic agency, 15–16, 18, 19
Sparks, Tabitha, 36n, 182
    Victorian Metafiction, 70n
spasmodic poetry, 60–1, 64, 71
Spectator, 58, 64, 100–1, 123
spectatorship, 187n
speed, 10, 13, 36n, 40, 189
Spencer, Herbert, 37n
    'The Physiology of Laughter', 32
'spouse in the house' plot, 50
Standard, 49
Steir, Adam, 143
Stern, Madeline, 85
Stern, Rebecca, 18, 88, 90
strikes, 131, 135, 140–7
Sturrock, June, 89
suffering women, 20
sympathetic
    bigamy plot, 178–80
    contagion, 141–3
    doubles, 156–88
    touches, 169–78, 181–3
sympathetic contagion, 141–3, 145, 150–1
sympathy, 21–4, 38n, 77, 134, 141–2, 144, 180–6
    bodily, 24, 131–55
    collective, 134–8
    embodied, 145, 179
    limits of, 147–54
    working-class, 138–47

Talairach-Vielmas, Laurence, 130n
Taylor, Jenny Bourne, 13, 167, 186n
tears, 41
Tennyson, Alfred, Lord, 59–60
  Maud, 60
Terada, Rei, 8
Theory of Mind (ToM), 30–2, 47, 77–80, 93, 148, 173–4
threat of exposure, 97
threat to family, 110
The Times, 54, 69n, 154–5n
Tomaiulo, Saverio, 17
Tondre, Michael, 127
touch, 1–2, 31, 35n, 156, 166–8, 177, 182–3
  and bodily sympathy, 136
  sympathetic, 169–78, 181–3
trade unions, 131, 141
trains, 10
transmission of affect, 3, 5, 24–7, 153
The Trial of Madeleine Smith, 122
Tromp, Marlene, 20
  The Private Rod, 130n

unconscious selfhood, 90
'unnarrated', 64
unreadability, 152

Valdez, Jessica, 101, 114
Vermeule, Blakey, *Why Do We Care about Literary Characters?* 118
'The Vice of Reading', 41
Vicinus, Martha, *Intimate Friends*, 95n
voyeuristic pleasure, 97
voyeuristic witnessing, 107, 128
vulnerable bodies, 100–8
  and home, 96–130

Wagner, Tamara, 89, 95n, 100
Walker Gore, Clare, 89

Ward, Megan, 152, 169–70, 173–4
Warhol, Robyn, 7, 39n, 41, 43, 58, 64, 133, 158, 160–1
  Having a Good Cry: Effeminate Feelings and Pop-Culture Forms, 29, 190
'wife's secret' plot, 73
wild affects, 143–4, 153
Wilford, Florence, 94
  Nigel Bartram's Ideal, 72–83, 87–94
'the woman question', 87
womanhood, limited ideal of, 87
women's gifts for imposture, 123–4
Women's Writing, 28
Wood, Ellen, 14, 131–55
  Dansbury House, 138
  East Lynne, 5, 24, 29, 39n, 49–50, 70n, 74, 77, 130n, 139, 161, 187n, 190
  A Life's Secret, 131, 134, 135, 138–47
Wordsworth, William, 'Intimations of Immortality', 65
working-class, 138–47
  mobs, 132–3, 149–51, 153
  sympathy, 138–47
writers, periodical, 103–4
writing, 6–7, 56–68, 75–82, 127–8
Wynne, Deborah, 128, 130n, 133

Yonge, Charlotte Mary, 75–6, 94, 95n
  The Clever Woman of the Family, 75, 76, 89–90
  The Heir of Redclyffe, 95n

Zerilli, Linda, 26
Zunshine, Lisa, 30, 78–9, 99, 122

EU representative:
Easy Access System Europe
Mustamäe tee 50, 10621 Tallinn, Estonia
Gpsr.requests@easproject.com